UNHCR and International Refugee Law

This book considers the United Nations High Commissioner for Refugees' (UNHCR) contribution to international refugee law since the establishment of the UNHCR by the United Nations General Assembly in 1951. The book explores the historical and statutory foundations that create an indelible link between the UNHCR and international refugee law. This book charts the significant evolution that has occurred in the organization's role throughout the last 60 years, looking at both the formal means by which the UNHCR's mandate may be modified, and the techniques the UNHCR has used to facilitate the changes in its role, thereby revealing a significant evolution in the organization's role since the onset of the crisis in refugee protection in the 1980's. The UNHCR itself has demonstrated its organizational autonomy as the primary agent for the adaptation of its responsibilities and work related to international refugee law. The author does suggest, however, that the UNHCR needs to continue to extend and strengthen its role related to international refugee law if it is to ensure a stronger legal framework for the protection of refugees as well as a fuller respect for refugees' rights in practice.

UNHCR and International Refugee Law will be of particular interest to refugee lawyers as well as academics and students of refugee law and international law and anyone concerned with the important role that UNHCR plays in the protection of refugees today.

Corinne Lewis has drawn on her decade of experience as a legal officer with UNHCR, and her human rights and refugee law research to explore UNHCR's contribution to the development and effectiveness of international refugee law. She has taught courses on human rights, refugee law, and international organizations law, as well as the United Nations, and brings these areas together in this book.

Routledge Research in International Law

Available:

International Law and the Third World
Reshaping justice
Richard Falk, Balakrishnan Rajagopal and Jacqueline Stevens (eds)

International Legal Theory
Essays and engagements, 1966–2006
Nicholas Onuf

The Problem of Enforcement in International Law
Countermeasures, the non-injured state and the idea of
international community
Elena Katselli Proukaki

International Economic Actors and Human Rights
Adam McBeth

The Law of Consular Access
A documentary guide
John Quigley, William J. Aceves and Adele Shank

State Accountability Under International Law
Holding states accountable for a breach of jus cogens norms
Lisa Yarwood

International Organisations and the Idea of Autonomy
Institutional independence in the international legal order
Richard Collins and Nigel D. White (eds)

Self-Determination in the Post-9/11 Era
Elizabeth Chadwick

Participants in the International Legal System
Multiple perspectives on non-state actors in international law
Jean d'Aspremont

Sovereignty and Jurisdiction in the Airspace and Outer Space
Legal criteria for spatial delimitation
Gbenga Oduntan

International Law in a Multipolar World
Matthew Happold (ed.)

The Law on the Use of Force
A feminist analysis
Gina Heathcote

The ICJ and the Development of International Law
The lasting impact of the Corfu channel case
Karine Bannelier, Théodore Christakis and Sarah Heathcote (eds)

UNHCR and International Refugee Law
From treaties to innovation
Corinne Lewis

Forthcoming titles in this series include:

International Law, Regulation and Resistance
Critical spaces
Zoe Pearson

The Right to Self-determination Under International Law
"Selfistans," secession, and the great powers' rule
Milena Sterio

The Cuban Embargo under International Law
El bloqueo
Nigel D. White

Threats of Force
International law and strategy
Francis Grimal

Asian Approaches to International Law and the Legacy of Colonialism and Imperialism
The law of the sea, territorial disputes and international dispute settlement
Jin-Hyun Paik, Seok-Woo Lee, Kevin Y L Tan (eds)

UNHCR and International Refugee Law

From treaties to innovation

Corinne Lewis

Routledge
Taylor & Francis Group

LONDON AND NEW YORK

First published 2012
by Routledge
2 Park Square, Milton Park, Abingdon, Oxon OX14 4RN

Simultaneously published in the USA and Canada
by Routledge
711 Third Avenue, New York, NY 10017

Routledge is an imprint of the Taylor & Francis Group, an informa business

First issued in paperback 2014

British Library Cataloguing in Publication Data
A catalogue record for this book is available from the British Library

Library of Congress Cataloguing-in-Publication Data
Lewis, Corinne.
  UNHCR and international refugee law : from treaties to innovation /
Corinne Lewis.
  p. cm.
Includes bibliographical references.
  ISBN 978-0-415-52442-1 (hardback) – ISBN 978-0-203-11556-5 (e-book)
1. Office of the United Nations High Commissioner for Refugees.
2. Refugees–Legal status, laws, etc. 3. Refugees–International
cooperation. I. Title.
K3230.R45L49 2012
341.4'86–dc23

                                                                2011049088

ISBN 978-0-415-52442-1 (hbk)
ISBN 978-1-138-01687-3 (pbk)
ISBN 978-0-203-11556-5 (ebk)

Typeset in Times New Roman
by Cenveo Publisher Services

To my father Harlan Lewis
In memory of my mother, Lois Eddie, and my grandmother,
Louise Eddie
And, above all, to my husband Bruce Dresbach

Contents

Acknowledgements

I am grateful to Judge Christopher Greenwood at the International Court of Justice, who, in his prior role as a professor at the London School of Economics and Political Science, recognized that I was writing my thesis as a book and so, in fact, gave me the initial confidence to do so. Similarly, Professor Guy Goodwin-Gill at Oxford has provided support and encouragement throughout the process and I am appreciative to him for this. I also would like to thank Jean François Durieux and Louise Arimatsu, who in their role as examiners for my PhD thesis at LSE, helped me more clearly see the book as a whole.

My discussions and work with many admired and respected colleagues at UNHCR have helped shape the content of this book and, as they are too numerous to thank individually, I thank them collectively. I would, however, like to acknowledge my appreciation to Milton Moreno and Carl Söderbergh for their extensive comments on the text as well as to Maria Stavropoulou and Johannes vanderKlaauw for their valuable feedback. Also, my sincere thanks go to Frances Nicholson and George Okoth-Obbo, at UNHCR, for their assistance in ferreting out bits of information that otherwise I would not have been able to locate.

If it had not been for the appearance in this world of Tristan, Julien, and Sebastien, I never would have undertaken this work. They have served as both a distraction from, and a stimulus for, this book. Most importantly, my husband, Bruce, has provided unflagging support throughout the entire process of the research and writing of this book, and so my heartfelt thanks go to him.

Table of cases

xiv   *Table of cases*

Table of instruments

List of abbreviations

1936 Provisional Arrangement	1936 Provisional Arrangement Concerning the Status of Refugees Coming From Germany
1938 Convention	1938 Convention Concerning the Status of Refugees Coming From Germany
1951 Refugee Convention	1951 Convention Relating to the Status of Refugees
1965 Convention on the Elimination of Racial Discrimination	1965 International Convention on the Elimination of All Forms of Racial Discrimination
1967 Protocol	1967 Protocol Relating to the Status of Refugees
1969 OAU Refugee Convention	1969 OAU Convention Governing the Specific Aspects of Refugee Problems in Africa
1979 Convention on Elimination of Discrimination Against Women	1979 Convention on the Elimination of All Forms of Discrimination Against Women
1984 Cartagena Declaration	1984 Cartagena Declaration on Refugees
1984 Convention Against Torture	1984 Convention Against Torture and Other Cruel, Inhuman or Degrading Treatment or Punishment
1989 CRC	1989 Convention on the Rights of the Child
1990 Convention on the Protection of Migrant Workers	1990 International Convention on the Protection of the Rights of All Migrant Workers and Members of their Families
Dublin Convention	Convention Determining the State Responsible for Examining Applications for Asylum Lodged in One of the Member States of the European Communities

ECOSOC	United Nations Economic and Social Council
EU	European Union
EXCOM	Executive Committee of the High Commissioner's Programme
Final Act	Final Act of the 1951 United Nations Conference of Plenipotentiaries on the Status of Refugees and Stateless Persons
Handbook	Handbook on Procedures and Criteria for Determining Refugee Status
ICCPR	1966 International Covenant on Civil and Political Rights
ICJ	International Court of Justice
IGCR	Intergovernmental Committee on Refugees
ILC	International Law Commission
ILO	International Labour Organization
IMO	International Maritime Organization
IRO	International Refugee Organization
London Agreement on Travel Documents	1946 Agreement Relating to the Issue of a Travel Document to Refugees who are the Concern of the Inter-governmental Committee on Refugees
Nansen Office	Nansen International Office for Refugees
Rome Statute	Rome Statute of the International Criminal Court
Sub-Committee	Sub-Committee of the Whole on International Protection
UNESCO	United Nations Educational, Scientific and Cultural Organization
UNHCR	United Nations High Commissioner for Refugees
UNHCR Statute	Statute of the Office of the United Nations High Commissioner for Refugees
UNRRA	United Nations Relief and Rehabilitation Administration
WHO	World Health Organization

Introduction

In theory, if not always in practice, the international protection of refugees is undergirded today through the bias of two key components. The first of these is an international law framework with the 1951 Convention Relating to the Status of Refugees at its core. The second is an international organization,[1] the United Nations High Commissioner for Refugees, with primary responsibility for refugees.[2]

The 1951 Refugee Convention has been supplemented by very few international agreements specifically formulated to protect refugees. The 1957 Agreement Relating to Refugee Seamen, with its 1973 Protocol, expanded the protections for refugee seamen. The 1967 Protocol Relating to the Status of Refugees removed geographic and temporal restrictions in the 1951 Refugee Convention, and thereby broadened the notion of who was eligible to receive protection as a refugee under the 1951 Refugee Convention. However, apart from these agreements, and despite new flows of refugees around the world, the emergence of new issues, and the continued expansion of the international human rights law framework, no new international refugee law treaty has been created to update the collection of protections in the 1951 Refugee Convention.

Yet, refugee law has changed and adapted to new situations that have given rise to novel issues. A mere reference to concepts such as the rights of refugee children, temporary protection, and non-State agents of persecution, which cannot be found in the 1951 Convention but are familiar to most persons concerned with refugees today, demonstrates this point. UNHCR, the unique

---

1 The term 'international organizations' is subject to a number of definitions, but a broad one set forth by Philippe Sands and Pierre Klein is used herein: the international organization i) has a membership that is composed of States; ii) is established by treaty 'or other instrument governed by international law, such as a resolution adopted in an international conference'; iii) has 'an autonomous will distinct from that of its members and be vested with legal personality'; and iv) 'must be capable of adopting norms (in the broadest sense) addressed to its members'. *Bowett's Law of International Institutions* 15–6 (Philippe Sands & Pierre Klein, eds, 6th ed., 2009).

2 However, it should not be forgotten that the United Nations Relief and Works Agency, which was established in 1949, and thus, prior to the UNHCR, has a special responsibility for Palestinian refugees.

international organization responsible for refugees, has played a central, but often undervalued role in this evolution.

Moreover, UNHCR is clearly recognized within the international community for the critical role it plays in ensuring that international refugee law serves to protect refugees, which means that international refugee law is effective in assuring respect for their rights and human dignity. UNHCR's role in this area is neither straightforward nor free from criticism. States often resent UNHCR's intrusiveness, while refugee advocates and refugees themselves object that UNHCR does not do enough to ensure the adequate protection of refugees. Yet, UNHCR remains the most visible actor and uniquely situated as it attempts to foster refugee protection by States.

This book focuses on answering four major questions. First, what are the foundations for UNHCR's role related to the development and effectiveness of international refugee law? Second, what are the formal and informal means that have facilitated the adaptation of UNHCR's role? Third, how has UNHCR influenced the development of international refugee law and, finally, how has UNHCR enhanced the effectiveness of international refugee law?

UNHCR's role related to international refugee law did not emerge out of a void, but has a historical background derived from prior organizations concerned with the protection of refugees. The responsibilities and work of the refugee organizations that preceded UNHCR had a significant influence on the responsibilities UNHCR would be assigned in relation to international refugee law. The foundations for UNHCR's role related to international refugee law are contained in UNHCR's Statute. Therefore, Chapter 1 provides an overview of both the historical and statutory foundations that create an indelible link between UNHCR and international refugee law.

Under UNHCR's statutory mandate, UNHCR is assigned responsibilities in two key areas: the development of international refugee law and ensuring the effectiveness of such law. UNHCR has established general parameters and essential content to these responsibilities through the various activities it has carried out in order to fulfil its mandated responsibilities. Chapter 2 therefore examines the specific statutory responsibilities of UNHCR related to the areas of the development and effectiveness of international refugee law as well as the work the organization has carried out in order to fulfil these responsibilities.

UNHCR's international refugee law responsibilities are not static, but can vary and be adapted so as to permit UNHCR to address refugee problems and issues arising out of new circumstances, whether due to new flows of refugees, changes in the willingness of States of asylum to receive refugees, or other factors. Chapter 3 considers both the formal means by which UNHCR's mandate can be modified and the techniques used by UNHCR to facilitate the evolution in its role related to international refugee law.

As a crisis in international refugee law and refugee protection unfolded in the 1980s, the weaknesses in the legal framework and in the means for ensuring the effectiveness of international refugee law were brought to the fore. The origins of this crisis and the problems with refugee law and its effectiveness, which became more evident as a result of this crisis, are covered in Chapter 4. This crisis in international refugee law and protection then necessitated that UNHCR adopt new measures in order to redress the weaknesses in the framework and to ensure that refugee law was more effective. Chapter 5 covers the measures utilized by UNHCR to expand the treaty framework and address the weaknesses in the framework. Chapter 6 addresses steps taken by UNHCR to bolster the effectiveness of international refugee law, in the areas of States' ratification, implementation and application of refugee law.

Chapter 7 concludes the book with its two sections. The initial section weaves together the key points from the preceding six chapters in order to provide an overview of UNHCR's interaction with international refugee law. The second section then looks toward the future, with the goal of furthering UNHCR's contribution to the development and effectiveness of international refugee law, and therefore proposes suggestions for a more stable, constructive and refined role related to international refugee law for UNHCR.

The book is written with the intention of furthering the understanding of UNHCR's role related to the development and the effectiveness of international refugee law in order to illuminate the potential of UNHCR to strengthen and expand its role within the political context in which the organization operates. Therefore, the perspective within this publication is an international legal one and the political background and influences on UNHCR's work, other than with respect to the crisis in refugee protection, have not been explored in detail. In addition, as international law for the protection of refugees is the central concern herein, other groups of persons who are receiving protection from UNHCR, including returnees, internally displaced persons, persons who flee due to civil conflict or violence within their countries, and stateless persons, are only incidentally considered herein. I recognize, however, that their protection merits greater attention and further research.

Finally, it should be noted that the content is based on law and resources that existed as of October 2011.

1 Foundations for UNHCR's international refugee law role

1.1 Introduction

The United Nations High Commissioner for Refugees was not the first international organization with responsibilities for refugees. Following the establishment of the League of Nations, there was a succession of refugee organizations created to deal with groups of refugees. These organizations are presented as the precursors to UNHCR in refugee law texts, treatises on refugee law, and UNHCR's training manual on international protection.[1] The agreements for the protection of refugees that existed prior to the 1951 Convention on the Status of Refugees[2] are also presented. However, the narratives generally do not include how these organizations related to, and were involved with, refugee law. Such organizations and refugee law did not just coexist; refugee law was the centrepiece for the work of nearly all UNHCR's predecessors.

The mandates and work of UNHCR's predecessors significantly influenced the formulation of UNHCR's responsibilities, including those related to international refugee law, which are the focus of this book. This chapter, therefore, serves as a complement to the traditional background of UNHCR through its presentation of the responsibilities and work related to international refugee law of the refugee organizations created prior to UNHCR. In so doing, this chapter grounds the unique and enduring role of UNHCR, related to international refugee law, in the historical foundations of the refugee organizations that preceded UNHCR before it situates UNHCR's responsibilities related to international refugee law within the overall context of international protection and links those responsibilities to

---

1 See, for example, the textbook by David A. Martin, T. Alexander Aleinikoff, Hiroshi Motomura, and Maryellen Fullerton, *Forced Migration: Law and Policy* 34–38 (2007); the refugee law treatise of Guy Goodwin-Gill and Jane McAdam, *The Refugee in International Law* 15–20 (3rd edn, 2007); and Chapters 1 and 2 of the UNHCR protection training manual, *UNHCR, Self-Study Module 1: An Introduction to International Protection: Protecting Persons of Concern to UNHCR* (1 August 2005). Available at http://www.unhcr.org/refworld/docid/ 4214cb4f2.html (accessed 27 October 2011).

2 Convention Relating to the Status of Refugees, 28 July 1951, 189 U.N.T.S. 150 (hereinafter 1951 Refugee Convention).

the fundamental refugee law instrument, the 1951 Convention Relating to the Status of Refugees.

1.2 Historical foundations

The plight of people fleeing their homeland to seek protection in other lands is as old as persecution itself. Originally, when a person left his/her country and sought asylum in another country, it was up to the authorities in the country of asylum to decide whether the individual would receive protection and not be expelled. Since the sovereign was generally the source of law, s/he was the ultimate arbiter of how the individual would be treated and what rights would be accorded.

Collective action by States to confront the problem of forced migration did not occur until the formation of the League of Nations in 1919 following the end of the First World War. The League served as an international forum in which States could pursue co-operation not only in the political sphere to prevent wars and ensure peace, but also in the areas of social and economic matters.[3]

1.2.1 Refugee organizations created by the League of Nations

The displacement of about 1.5 million Russians, as a consequence of the 1917 Bolshevik Revolution, civil war, and the 1921 Russian famine,[4] served as the catalyst for collective State interest in the creation of the first international office for refugees. The lack of clarity as to which State was responsible for these people, many of whom required material assistance and lacked a recognized identity document, and their movement among countries, in some cases as a result of their expulsion by a country, created tensions among European States.[5]

Therefore, in 1921, the League of Nations created the office of the High Commissioner for Russian Refugees and appointed Dr Fridtjof Nansen as the first

3 The League of Nations created a number of committees to facilitate co-operation among countries, including a Committee for Intellectual Cooperation, which eventually became the United Nations Organization for Educational, Scientific and Cultural Organization, an Advisory Committee on Traffic in Opium and Other Dangerous Drugs, and an Advisory Committee on Traffic in Women and Children. The League also created a Permanent Health Organization in 1923, which was the precursor to the World Health Organization. John Knudson, *A History of the League of Nations*, 273, 246, 251, 265 (1938).

4 Tommie Sjöberg, *The Powers and the Persecuted: The Refugee Problem and the Intergovernmental Committee on Refugees (IGCR), 1938–1947*, 24–25 (1991). See also John Hope Simpson, *The Refugee Problem: Report of a Survey* 62 (1939) and Michael Marrus, *The Unwanted: European Refugees in the 20th century* 53–61 (1985).

5 See Sjöberg, *supra* note 4, at 26. See also Gil Loescher, *The UNHCR and World Politics: A Perilous Path* 24 (2001). Sjöberg also does not discount the importance of sympathy for the Russian refugees as a contributing factor to the initiative by the League to create the first refugee organization. See Sjöberg, *supra* note 4, at 27.

High Commissioner.[6] Initially, his responsibilities concerning the Russian refugees included defining their legal status, organizing their repatriation or allocation to various countries that might be able to receive them, assisting them with finding work, and with the assistance of aid groups, providing relief to them.[7] In 1924, his mandate was extended to include Armenian refugees who had fled Turkey and in 1928, to include Assyrian and Assyro-Chaldean and Turkish refugees.[8] He then carried out the same responsibilities for these two groups and the word 'Russian' was deleted from his title.

Following the death of the High Commissioner in 1930, the League of Nations created the Nansen International Office for Refugees to carry out the humanitarian assistance work for refugees previously handled by Nansen.[9] The secretariat of the League of Nations assumed responsibility for the legal and protection work handled by Nansen, but in practice, it was the Nansen Office that would carry out both the humanitarian and legal and protection aspects.[10]

In response to the exodus of persons from Germany, the League of Nations created a special organization in 1933, the Office of the High Commissioner for Refugees coming from Germany,[11] which initially was not part of the League of Nations system due to the membership of Germany in the League at the time. The office was to assist refugees from Germany in the same manner as the High Commissioner for Refugees and the Nansen Office, with the secretariat of the League, had supported other groups of refugees. In 1938, the Office of the High Commissioner for Refugees coming from Germany also became responsible for refugees fleeing Austria,[12] but this office was liquidated, along with the

---

6 The initiative for the creation of an office of a Commissioner for the Russian refugees originated with the International Red Cross, which noted the situation of 800,000 Russian refugees in Europe who lacked legal protection. Letter from The President of the Comité International de la Croix-Rouge of 20 Feb. 1921, 2 O.J.L.N. 227 (1921) and Memorandum from the Comité International de la Croix-Rouge at Geneva to the Council of the League of Nations of 20 February 1921, 2 O.J.L.N. 228-9 (1921). A request by the Secretary-General of the League of Nations to governments for their suggestions on the resolution of this problem, a report by Mr. Hanotaux, and discussions in the Council of the League of Nations then followed. See Report by M. Hanotaux adopted on 27 June 1921, 2 O.J.L.N.755-8 (1921) and Circular Letter by the Secretary-General to All States concerned in the Question of 7 July 1921, 2 O.J.L.N. 485-6 (1921). The Council adopted a resolution on 27 June 1921 in which it agreed to appoint a High Commissioner and on 20 August 1921 appointed Dr Fridjtof Nansen to the position. Paul Weis, 'The International Protection of Refugees', 48 *Am. J. Int'l. L.* 193, 208 (1954).
7 These responsibilities were proposed by the Secretary-General to the Council of the League. See Memorandum by the Secretary-General of 16 March 1921, 2 O.J.L.N. 225–226 (1921).
8 Weis, *supra* note 6, at 209 (1954).
9 Ibid.
10 See Work of the Inter-Governmental Advisory Commission for Refugees during its Eighth Session, 17 O.J.L.N. 140 (1936). The Statutes of the Nansen International Office for Refugees can be found at 12 O.J.L.N. 309–311 (1931).
11 Council of League of Nations, International Assistance to Refugees, 17 O.J.L.N. 126–129 (1936).
12 See Council of League of Nations, International Assistance to Refugees, 19 O.J.L.N. 367–368 (1938). Initially, the Office of the High Commissioner for Refugees Coming From Germany

Nansen Office, at the end of 1938, and replaced by a High Commissioner of the League of Nations for Refugees. Consequently, this new High Commissioner assumed responsibility for the refugees aided by the Nansen Office and the High Commissioner for Refugees coming from Germany.[13]

The organizations created by States through the League of Nations were the first international attempts by States to co-ordinate efforts related to refugees. However, each of the organizations mentioned earlier, like other entities created by the League to deal with specific refugee situations,[14] was only given responsibility for certain nationalities of refugees. States were not yet ready to deal with refugees as an international phenomenon, but instead considered them to be discrete localized problems. The refugees' nationality and the fact that they had crossed an international border were the defining characteristics of the groups of refugees.

1.2.1.1 *Responsibilities related to international refugee law*

When the League of Nations appointed Nansen as the first High Commissioner in 1921, international refugee law was non-existent.[15] However, Nansen's mandate included refugee law-related responsibilities. Specifically, he was to define the legal status of refugees, although his mandate did not establish how he was to do this. The problems encountered by the refugees would serve as the catalyst for Nansen's significant role in the development of international refugee law.

The practical difficulties faced by the de-nationalized Russian refugees, who lacked identity or travel documents, spurred the Council to call a conference of representatives of interested governments, which met in August 1921. A second conference was convened in September 1921, over which Dr Nansen presided, to further discuss the problem. Dr Nansen then consulted with the International Labour Office, legal authorities among the refugees, and a conference of private organizations, and prepared specific proposals on identity papers for the refugees

reported to its own governing body rather than to the Council of the League of Nations. Simpson, *supra* note 4, at 215–216.

13 The mandate of the High Commissioner of the League of Nations for Refugees is contained in the Report of the Council Committee Appointed to Draw Up a Plan for International Assistance to Refugees, 19 O.J.L.N. 365–366 (1938).

14 For example, the Greek Refugee Settlement Commission was established in 1923 to assist Greek refugees, a High Commissioner was created in 1926 for Bulgarian refugees and in 1933 a sub-committee of the Council was formed for Assyrians from Iraq. Simpson, *supra* note 4, at 222–223.

15 However, refugee law was not new, according to Grahl-Madsen. He cites the 1685 Edict of Potsdam and an 1832 French law as examples of prior laws concerning refugees. Atle Grahl-Madsen, 'The Emergent International Law Relating to Refugees: Past – Present – Future,' in *The Land Beyond: Collected Essays on Refugee Law and Policy* 180, 182 (Peter Macalister-Smith and Gudmundur Alfredsson, eds, 2001).

to be considered by governments.[16] At an inter-governmental conference in 1922, called by Dr Nansen,[17] the Arrangement with Regard to the Issue of Certificates of Identity to Russian Refugees was adopted, which provides a common form for the identity certificate as well as conditions related to its issuance and use by a refugee.[18]

Similar concerns about the situation of Armenian refugees led the High Commissioner to consider, at the request of the Council of the League of Nations, the issue of identity certificates for Armenians; Dr Nansen studied the problem and then drafted an agreement concerning identity certificates for this group of refugees.[19] He subsequently initiated an agreement that consolidated and amended the arrangements concerning identity certificates for Russian and Armenian refugees.[20] Other practical problems faced by the refugees resulted in the High Commissioner preparing two instruments that concerned the rights of refugees, which instruments were adopted at an inter-governmental conference in 1928.[21] These arrangements concerned the personal status, legal assistance, expulsion, taxation, and identity certificates of certain groups of refugees.

The fact that the Nansen Office was responsible for the humanitarian rather than the legal and protection work notwithstanding, as already noted, it was, nevertheless, mandated to undertake a function related to the practical application by States of the arrangements instituted by the first High Commissioner. Specifically, the Nansen Office was to '[f]acilitat[e], within the limits of its competence, the application, in particular cases, of the arrangements that have been made for the benefit of the refugees.'[22] This included 'certifying the identity and the position of the refugees', '[t]estifying to the regularity, validity, and conformity with the previous law of their country of origin, of documents issued in such country' among other services.[23] In addition, although not specified in its

---

16 The High Commissioner of the League, Report on the Work accomplished up to 15 March 1922, 3 O.J.L.N. 385–394 (1922).

17 Grahl-Madsen, *supra* note 15, at 182.

18 Arrangement with Regard to the Issue of Certificates of Identity to Russian Refugees, 5 July 1922, 13 L.N.T.S. 237.

19 Plan for the Issue of a Certificate of Identity to Armenian Refugees, 31 May 1924, 5 O.J.L.N. 969–970 (1924). Interestingly, this agreement was merely a plan drafted by the High Commissioner and his staff and then circulated to governments for their signature without an international conference. 39 governments acceded to the agreement. Grahl-Madsen, *supra* note 15, at 182.

20 This agreement was the Arrangement Relating to the Issue of Identity Certificates to Russian and Armenian Refugees, 12 May 1926, 89 L.N.T.S. 47. Report of the Secretary-General, 36 (footnote 2.2), U.N. Doc. A/C.3/527 and Corr.1 (26 October 1949) (hereinafter Report of the Secretary-General).

21 Ibid. These two agreements were the Arrangement Relating to the Legal Status of Russian and Armenian Refugees, 30 June 1928, 89 L.N.T.S. 53, and the Arrangement Concerning the Extension to Other Categories of Refugees of Certain Measures Taken in Favour of Russian and Armenian Refugees, 30 June 1928, 89 L.N.T.S. 63.

22 Statutes of the Nansen International Office for Refugees, 12 O.J.L.N. 309–11 (1931).

23 Arrangement Relating to the Legal Status of Russian and Armenian Refugees, *supra* note 21.

mandate, the Nansen office prepared an agreement, the first one to be legally binding on States, relating to the protection of refugees,[24] the 1933 Convention Relating to the International Status of Refugees.[25]

As for the High Commissioner's Office for Refugees coming from Germany, it was specifically instructed to convoke an intergovernmental conference in order to provide 'a system of legal protection for refugees coming from Germany',[26] which it did in the form of the 1936 Provisional Arrangement Concerning the Status of Refugees Coming from Germany, which concerned certificates of identity, and the personal status and freedom of movement of refugees, among other matters.[27] After the drafting of the 1936 Provisional Arrangement, the Office was instructed by the Assembly of the League of Nations to obtain the accession of States to the Arrangement and 'to prepare an intergovernmental conference for the adoption of an international convention on the status of these refugees.'[28] The result was the 1938 Convention Concerning the Status of Refugees Coming From Germany that replaced the 1936 Arrangement. The 1938 Convention reiterated most of the provisions contained in the 1936 Arrangement, but also covered topics such as labour conditions, welfare and relief, and the education of refugees.[29]

As a result of the creation of a number of agreements for the protection of refugees, when the High Commissioner of the League of Nations for Refugees was appointed in 1938, following the liquidation of the office of the High Commissioner's Office for Refugees coming from Germany and the Nansen Office, the League of Nations Assembly provided it with a specific supervisory responsibility related to international refugee law agreements. The High Commissioner was to 'superintend the entry into force and the application of the legal status of refugees, as defined more particularly in the Conventions of 28 October 1933 and 10 February 1938'.[30] Specifically, the High Commissioner was to ensure that the 1933 Convention relating to the International Status of Refugees concerning Russian, Armenian, Assyran, Assyro-Chaldean, Turkish and other

---

24 Simpson, *supra* note 4, at 211.
25 The Convention Relating to the International Status of Refugees, 28 October 1933, 159 L.N.T.S. 199. This convention provided a further elaboration of the rights contained in the 1928 Arrangement Relating to the Legal Status of Russian and Armenian Refugees.
26 See Report of the Council Committee Appointed to Draw up a Plan for International Assistance to Refugees, *supra* note 13, at 128.
27 Provisional Arrangement Concerning the Status of Refugees Coming From Germany, 4 July 1936, 171 L.N.T.S. 75.
28 Report of the Secretary General, *supra* note 20.
29 Convention Concerning the Status of Refugees Coming From Germany, 10 February 1938, 192 L.N.T.S. 59.
30 See the Mandate of the High Commissioner of the League of Nations for Refugees, Report of the Council Committee Appointed to Draw up a Plan for International Assistance to Refugees, *supra* note 13, ¶ 2(b). The two conventions were the 1933 Convention Relating to the International Status of Refugees, *supra* note 25, and the 1938 Convention Concerning the Status of Refugees Coming From Germany, *supra* note 29.

refugees, and the 1938 Convention Concerning the Status of Refugees Coming From Germany were ratified by States and applied by them within their national systems.

Thus, while the first High Commissioner, Nansen, was given a general mandate for defining the legal status of refugees, the realities of the refugees' situation, in particular, the obstacles they faced, served as the catalyst for the creation of international arrangements concerning identity documents and refugees' legal status. Similarly, while nothing in its mandate provided that it should further develop legal standards for the protection of refugees, the Nansen Office prepared the first convention to be legally binding on States. In creating the High Commissioner for Refugees coming from Germany, States recognized that the protection afforded to certain groups of refugees, such as Russians, Armenians, Turkish, Assyrian, and Assyro-Chaldean refugees needed to be provided to German refugees. Therefore, the High Commissioner for Refugees coming from Germany facilitated the creation of two agreements to provide similar rights to refugees from Germany.

As a result, the first High Commissioner, the Nansen Office, and the High Commissioner for Refugees coming from Germany contributed to the further development of international standards for the protection of the categories of refugees who were of their concern. Their work in this area established an early precedent of involvement by refugee organizations in the development of international refugee law, which would be reflected in the mandate of the International Refugee Organization as well as UNHCR's statutory mandate, as discussed later.

Once international agreements for the protection of refugees had been created, there was a need to ensure that they were adopted and applied by States. The Nansen Office assisted in ensuring the application of such agreements in a practical manner, as most likely did the first High Commissioner. However, it was the High Commissioner of the League of Nations for Refugees that was first assigned specific responsibilities for the supervision of States' ratification and application of agreements for the protection of refugees. Therefore, the activities of these early refugee organizations as well as the mandate of the High Commissioner of the League of Nations, related to the effectiveness of agreements for the protection of refugees, helped establish a basis for the involvement of future organizations in this area, including eventually UNHCR.

1.2.2 Subsequent refugee organizations

The forced mass emigration of Jews from Germany led the United States, which was not a member of the League of Nations, to organize a conference in 1938 of 31 States to discuss co-ordination of support for persons who wished to flee or already had fled Germany because of persecution.[31] As a result, the Intergovernmental Committee on Refugees (IGCR) was created, in 1938, to assist

---

31 Simpson, *supra* note 4. It should be noted that other authors claim that the conference was attended by representatives of 32 States. See for example, Louise Holborn, *Refugees: A Problem*

Jewish persons to leave Germany and resettle in other countries, through negotiations with Germany as well as countries of resettlement,[32] but this work was
obstructed by the outbreak of the Second World War.[33]

Renewed co-operation among States was spurred by the situation of millions
of displaced persons in countries liberated by the Allies at the end of the Second
World War. In 1943, 44 States established the United Nations Relief and Rehabilitation Administration (UNRRA) to provide material assistance to displaced
persons, who also included persons who had fled because of persecution, and to
facilitate the return of displaced persons to their home countries.[34] However,
UNRRA's work became increasingly difficult as a result of the political changes
in Eastern Europe and the Soviet Union, which deterred many displaced persons
from wanting to return. UNRRA then refused to return persons who did not wish
to go back to their home countries.[35] As a result, such persons were stuck in
camps. UNRRA was faced with another significant problem. In 1945, new refugees had begun fleeing from Germany, Austria and Italy, but UNRRA's mandate
provided only for support for repatriation, and therefore, the organization could
not facilitate their settlement in the country in which they had sought refuge or
their resettlement in another country.[36]

States addressed the limitations in UNRRA's capacity by creating the International Refugee Organization (IRO), as a specialized agency of the United
Nations.[37] The mandate of the IRO was 'to bring about a rapid and positive

of Our Time: The Work of the United Nations High Commissioner for Refugees, 1951–1972 18
(1975) and Weis, *supra* note 6, at 209.

32 The League of Nations resolution creating the IGCR, which was adopted by a committee
representing 31 States, is contained in 19 O.J.L.N. 676–677 (1938). Sjöberg states that while 'it
was officially denied' that the IGCR was established with the purpose of assisting only Jewish
persons, he finds that 'there is no doubt that this was in fact the case – at least for all practical
purposes.' Sjöberg, *supra* note 4, at 51.

33 Jacques Vernant, *The Refugee in the Post-War World* 26–27 (1953).

34 Kim Salomon, *Refugees in the Cold War: Toward a New International Refugee Regime in the
Early Postwar Era* 48 (1991). UNRRA 'only incidentally provided assistance for refugees escap-
ing from untenable political situations' according to Leon Gordenker, *Refugees in International
Politics* 23 (1987). For UNRRA's mandate, see Agreement for United Nations Relief and
Rehabilitation Administration, 9 Nov. 1943, 3 Cmd. No. 6491 (1943). In addition, the IGCR's
membership and mandate were extended in 1943 'to include, as far as practicable also those
persons, wherever they may be, who as a result of events in Europe, have had to leave, or may
have to leave, their countries of residence because of the danger to their lives or liberties on
account of their race, religion or political beliefs'. Vernant, *supra* note 33, at 27–28. The IGCR
worked alongside UNRRA in providing protection and assistance to refugees in territory that had
been liberated. Grahl-Madsen, *supra* note 15, at 186.

35 Gordenker, *supra* note 34, at 23.

36 Holborn, *supra* note 31, at 28.

37 For an excellent summary of IRO's work see Louise Holborn, *The International Refugee
Organization: a Specialized Agency of the United Nations – its History and Work 1946–1952*
(1956). IRO's Constitution, an international treaty, was approved by the General Assembly on
15 December 1946, but would only come into effect once 15 States, whose contributions to
IRO amounted to not less than 75% of the total budget, had become parties to the Constitution.

solution of the problem of *bona fide* refugees and displaced persons'.[38] IRO had broad responsibilities for such persons; it was to carry out the 'repatriation; the identification, registration and classification; the care and assistance; the legal and political protection; the transport; and the re-settlement and re-establishment, in countries able and willing to receive them, of persons who are the concern of the Organization'.[39] The IRO even sub-let ships to transport refugees,[40] and its annual budget was four times that of the United Nations.[41]

The IRO essentially assumed responsibility for refugees and displaced persons covered by the mandates of UNRRA and the IGCR[42] as well as new refugees fleeing from Germany, Austria and Italy. The IRO's focus was the repatriation of persons to their home countries. Where such persons objected to their return because of persecution, reasons of a political nature, or compelling family reasons or infirmity or illness, they were to remain under the protection of the IRO and would be assisted with local settlement or resettlement in another country.[43]

1.2.2.1 Responsibilities related to international refugee law

Although the mandates of the IGCR and UNRRA did not contain specific responsibilities related to the development of international refugee law, both organizations initiated agreements related to refugees. IGCR inaugurated what became known as the London Agreement on Travel Documents,[44] promoted accessions

---

Constitution of the International Refugee Organization, and Agreement on Interim Measures to be Taken in Respect of Refugees and Displaced Persons, G.A. Res. 62(I), ¶ 18(b), U.N. Doc. A/RES/62(I) (15 December 1946). Therefore, the work of the IRO was initially carried out by a Preparatory Commission, which assumed responsibility for refugees and displaced persons from the IGCR and UNRRA on 1 July 1947. IRO formally came into existence in August 1948, after the requisite number of States had signed IRO's Constitution, and was abolished in January 1952. 1 Atle Grahl-Madsen, *The Status of Refugees in International Law: Refugee Character* 18 (1966).

38 Constitution of the IRO, in Holborn, *supra* note 37, at Annex 1, art. 1(a).
39 Ibid., at art. 2(1).
40 This information is found in the table of the Planned and Actual Expenditures of IRO from 1947–1952. Holborn, *supra* note 37, at 124.
41 U.N. GAOR, 4th Sess., 265th plen.mtg., ¶ 12 (3 Dec. 1949).
42 See 27 June 1947 Agreement between the IGCR and the PCIRO and the 29 June 1947 Agreement between the PCIRO and UNRRA in Holborn, *supra* note 37, at 591–594.
43 See Constitution of the IRO, in Holborn, *supra* note 37, at art. 2(1)(b) and Annex I, Part I, Section C. The IRO Constitution provided the first comprehensive definition of a 'refugee' in Part I of Annex 1. The wording in Part I, Section A.I clearly served as a basis for the definition of a refugee in the UNHCR Statute and the 1951 Refugee Convention. It provides that a 'refugee' shall apply to a person 'who is outside of his country of nationality or former habitual residence, and who, as a result of events subsequent to the outbreak of the second world war, is unable or unwilling to avail himself of the protection of the Government of his country of nationality or former nationality.' Constitution of the IRO, in Holborn, *supra* note 37, at Annex I, Part I, Section A(1).
44 Agreement Relating to the Issue of a Travel Document to Refugees who are the Concern of the Inter-governmental Committee on Refugees, 15 October 1946, 11 U.N.T.S. 73 (hereinafter London Agreement on Travel Documents). Weis, *supra* note 6, at 212.

to it, and worked to ensure that States implemented the agreement.[45] Similarly, UNRRA committees drafted several agreements. These committees, comprised of government representatives, formulated amendments to modify the 1926 International Sanitary Convention and the 1933 International Sanitary Convention for Aerial Navigation, agreements that arose out of concern about the problems that might arise in connection with the large movements of persons after the war.[46]

In contrast with the IGCR and UNRRA, IRO's constitutional mandate contained several responsibilities related to refugee law. First, instead of detailing specific responsibilities related to prior refugee conventions or the creation of international refugee conventions, IRO's mandate provided a general overarching responsibility. IRO was to provide 'legal and political protection' to refugees.[47] In addition, the IRO mandate authorized the organization to enter into agreements with governments and the occupation authorities in order to ensure assistance to refugees,[48] the protection of their rights,[49] and to arrange mutual assistance in the repatriation of displaced persons.[50] These agreements helped ensure that the IRO obtained the necessary governmental co-operation in matters relating to displaced persons and refugees. Thus, such bilateral agreements covered the specific details of the operations, including the facilities to be provided to IRO in the country, the financing of the operation, and the responsibilities for the provision of material assistance and legal and political protection.

Under the IRO's broadly worded legal and political protection mandate, the IRO made significant contributions to the development of international refugee law. The IRO's concern about the ability of persons to conclusively establish the death of a family member, in order to permit such persons to remarry or inherit, led to the IRO's proposal to the United Nations Economic and Social Council, in 1948, that an International Convention on the Declaration of Death of Missing

45 Weis, *supra* note 6 at 212. The IGCR appointed a Committee of Experts in 1944 that drafted the text and the form of the travel document, which were then adopted on 15 September 1946 at an Intergovernmental Conference. Vernant, *supra* note 33, at 29.

46 A.H. Robertson, 'Some Legal Problems of the UNRRA', 23 *Brit. Y.B. Int'l. L.* 142, 154 (1946). International Sanitary Convention, 21 June 1926, 78 L.N.T.S. 229 and International Sanitary Convention for Aerial Navigation, 12 Apr. 1933, 161 L.N.T.S. 65. These agreements arose out of concern about the problems that might arise in connection with the large movements of persons after the war. Robertson, *Supra* note 46, at 154.

47 Constitution of the IRO, in Holborn, *supra* note 37, at art. 2(1).

48 The IRO 'shall have power ... to enter into contracts and undertake obligations; including contracts with Governments or with occupation or control authorities, whereby such authorities would continue, or undertake, in part or in whole, the care and maintenance of refugees and displaced persons in territories under their authority, under the supervision of the Organization' and 'to conduct negotiations and conclude agreements with Governments'. Ibid., at art. 2.2(d)–(e).

49 The IRO 'shall have power ... to conclude agreements with countries able and willing to receive refugees and displaced persons for the purpose of ensuring the protection of their legitimate rights and interests in so far as this may be necessary'. Ibid., at art. 2.2(j).

50 The IRO 'shall have power... to promote the conclusion of bilateral arrangements for mutual assistance in the repatriation of displaced persons'. Ibid., at art. 2.2(g).

Persons should be drafted.[51] In addition to its contribution to the drafting of the convention, the IRO participated in a number of international conferences concerning refugees' legal position, provided its views on the Universal Declaration of Human Rights and the draft Human Rights Covenant, and was also actively involved in the preparation of the 1951 Convention Relating to the Status of Refugees.[52] Moreover, with its work to increase the number of accessions to the 1946 London Agreement on Travel Documents, the IRO contributed to the actual effectiveness of this agreement.[53]

In sum, the IGCR and UNRRA were both organizations with very specific purposes; essentially, the IGCR was to help Jewish refugees leave Germany and resettle and UNRRA was to provide material assistance to displaced persons and help them return to their home countries. Despite the lack of any reference to legal or protection responsibilities in their mandates, both organizations undertook activities to create agreements that provided protection to the persons they were assisting.

The IRO, however, was explicitly mandated to provide legal and political protection to refugees. The IRO attempted to secure States' protection of refugees by entering into individual agreements with governments concerning refugee protection, such as to ensure refugees' non-discriminatory treatment, access to the labour market and social benefits,[54] rather than promoting the conclusion of treaties among governments that would provide such protection. Most significantly, the IRO actively contributed to the drafting of key international human rights agreements and the 1951 Refugee Convention and thereby assisted in the development of the legal framework that remains essential to the protection of refugees today.

In the area of the development of international refugee law, the work carried out by the IGCR, UNRRA, and IRO, as well as the IRO's legal and political protection mandate, built on the bases established by prior refugee organizations, namely the first High Commissioner, the Nansen Office, and the High Commissioner for Refugees coming from Germany. In addition, in the area of the effectiveness of international refugee law, both the IGCR and the IRO promoted accessions to an agreement providing for documentation for refugees, the London Agreement on Travel Documents, thereby furthering the basis of the role of refugee organizations, established by the previous refugee organizations mentioned above, as well as the High Commissioner of the League of Nations for Refugees. Thus, the need for, and practice of, refugee organizations in the areas of the development and effectiveness of international refugee law were well established prior to the creation of UNHCR.

---

51 Ibid., at 326. Convention on the Declaration of Death of Missing Persons, 6 Apr. 1950, 119 U.N.T.S. 99.
52 Ibid., at 325–327.
53 Weis, *supra* note 6, at 212.
54 Holborn, *supra* note 37, at 318.

1.2.3 The need for a new organization

The IRO, however, was unable to arrange for the repatriation or settlement of all of the refugees and displaced persons from the Second World War due to the political changes that were taking place. The increasing restrictions on rights of persons in the former Soviet Union and many Eastern European countries meant that refugees from those countries were less inclined to return. Western countries also became less willing to return refugees to their home countries. The IRO estimated that on its cessation, scheduled for 30 June 1950, there would remain approximately 292,000 persons in Europe who had not been repatriated to their home country or resettled in a third country.[55] These numbers were substantially augmented by the increasingly large numbers of persons who were fleeing to Western European countries from Eastern European ones as well as the refugee movements in other areas of the world,[56] such as on the Indian subcontinent, the Korean peninsula, in China and Palestine. Thus, given the temporary nature of the organization[57] and the changing political situation, it became clear that the refugee problem could not be solved by the IRO in isolation.

As a result, there was a clear need for a new international organization with a statutory mandate to deal with old and new refugees. In 1949, the UN Economic and Social Council adopted a resolution requesting the United Nations Secretary-General to prepare a plan for a new organization and to propose 'the nature and extent of the legal functions to be performed, taking into consideration the experience of the League of Nations, the Intergovernmental Committee on Refugees and the IRO'.[58] The UN Secretary-General, in his 1949 Report, duly took into account the experience and the mandates of the previous organizations in formulating proposals for the functions, form and financial arrangements of the future refugee organization. Since the Secretary-General's report served as the basis for the discussions about the new organization in the Economic and Social Council, the General Assembly and the third committee of the General Assembly, the report had a determinative influence on the role and responsibilities of the new organization. In particular, the Secretary-General relied on the mandates and work of UNHCR's predecessors in formulating UNHCR's proposed responsibilities. The culmination of the discussions was the creation of a subsidiary organ

---

55 Note by the Secretary-General, U.N. Doc. A/C.3/528, ¶ 12 (26 October 1949).

56 See Loescher, *supra* note 5, at 42.

57 Holborn states that IRO's General Council never lost sight of the temporary nature of the organization. Holborn, *supra* note 31, at 36.

58 E.S.C. Res. 248(IX) A, (1949). ECOSOC did not request the Secretary-General to take into account the experience of UNRRA, in its 6 August 1949 resolution, most likely because it was created with a very specific purpose of providing assistance and facilitating the return of persons displaced by the war.

of the United Nations General Assembly,[59] the office of the United Nations High Commissioner for Refugees.[60]

1.3 Statutory foundations

The United Nations High Commissioner for Refugees was created in December 1950 pursuant to the adoption of its Statute by the General Assembly.[61] The organization began operating in January 1951. UNHCR's Statute remains, even after more than 60 years, the defining document for the organization's structure and powers.

Structurally, as a subsidiary organ of the United Nations General Assembly, UNHCR not only reports to the General Assembly[62] but also may have its mandate modified through General Assembly resolutions. UNHCR's Statute also provides for UNHCR to receive advice from the General Assembly, in the form of resolutions,[63] and from the Executive Committee of the High Commissioner's Programme, an advisory body created by the United Nations Economic and Social Council and comprised of approximately 72 State representatives,[64] in the form of conclusions.

UNHCR's structure and responsibilities were significantly influenced by those of its predecessors, in particular by the IRO. The IRO had been an all-encompassing specialized agency with very broad responsibilities for refugees that required substantial funding. The drafters of UNHCR's Statute did not want UNHCR to be as operationally active or to replace government services as the IRO

---

59 U.N. Charter arts. 7 and 22. Article 7 states: 'Such subsidiary organs as may be found necessary may be established in accordance with the present Charter.' Article 22 states, 'The General Assembly may establish such subsidiary organs as it deems necessary for the performance of its functions.' Refugees were of concern to the General Assembly from its very creation as evidenced by the General Assembly's adoption of a resolution on the refugee problem during its first session as an urgent matter. See G.A. Res. 8(I) (1946).

60 The UNHCR was therefore created to carry out the General Assembly's responsibilities of 'promoting international co-operation in the political field' and 'assisting in the realization of human rights and fundamental freedoms for all with distinction as to race, sex, language, or religion.' U.N. Charter art. 13, para. 1.

61 Statute of the Office of the United Nations High Commissioner for Refugees, contained in the Annex to UN General Assembly Resolution 428(V) of 14 December 1950. G.A. Res. 428(V) (14 December 1950) (hereinafter UNHCR Statute).

62 Ibid., at ¶ 11. UNHCR initially reported to the General Assembly through the UN Economic and Social Council, as provided in paragraph 11 of UNHCR's Statute, but now it submits its Annual Reports directly to the General Assembly. The Notes on International Protection are submitted to EXCOM.

63 Ibid., at ¶ 3, 9.

64 For more information on the Executive Committee's relationship to UNHCR see section 3.2 of Chapter 3. With respect to EXCOM's issuance of guidance to States, it is not at all clear whether EXCOM has the legal authority to issue conclusions directed to States, given that the body was created as an advisory one to UNHCR, even though it has a well-established practice of doing so.

had done.[65] Therefore, UNHCR, unlike the IRO, was not authorized to provide material assistance without the approval of the General Assembly. Instead, UNHCR's role was to be one of 'guidance, supervision, co-ordination and control',[66] and it was envisioned that the High Commissioner would enjoy the same authority and prestige as had Dr Nansen in order to ensure the effective protection of the refugees.[67]

UNHCR's two primary functions, the provision of international protection to refugees and the seeking of permanent solutions for the problem of refugees,[68] built on the work and responsibilities of UNHCR's predecessors. The function of providing international protection to refugees was derived from the mandates of the High Commissioner for Refugees under the Protection of the League of Nations and the IRO that prescribed a 'legal and political protection' responsibility.[69] Even the wording of some of UNHCR's specific protection responsibilities, not only those that concerned international refugee law as elaborated earlier, but also others, can be traced to the mandates of these two organizations.

For example, UNHCR's responsibility to '[keep] in close touch with the governments and inter-governmental organizations concerned' and to 'establish contact in such manner as he may think best with private organizations dealing with refugee questions' repeated obligations that the High Commissioner for Protection under the League of Nations had under his mandate[70] and were

---

65 As the UK representative, Mr. Corley stated: 'Unlike the International Refugee Organization, the High Commissioner with his small staff would not constitute an operational agency; furthermore, he would concern himself with refugee problems of a broader and more universal nature than those faced by the IRO.' U.N. GAOR, 4th Sess., 265th plen.mtg. at ¶ 81 (3 December 1949).

66 Statement of the Representative of France, U.N. GAOR, 4th Sess., 256th plen. mtg. at ¶ 14 (4 November 1949).

67 Statement of the Representative of Mexico, U.N. GAOR, 4th Sess., 257th plen., 3rd cee mtg. at ¶ 40 (8 November 1949). As the UN Secretary-General noted, 'legal and political protection has on the whole been a secondary task, which has been performed largely within the framework of material assistance.' Report of the Secretary-General, *supra* note 20, ¶ 14.

68 Ibid., at ¶ 1. Despite the Statute's pronouncement, in paragraph 1, that UNHCR has two primary functions, the structure and wording of the Statute suggest that the international protection role actually subsumes the search for permanent solutions. Paragraph 8 of the Statute lists activities that further the protection of refugees including that UNHCR is to 'assist governmental and private efforts to promote voluntary repatriation or assimilation within new national communities'. Not only does paragraph 8 include a solutions-type activity under its protection task, but there is no paragraph that elaborates the tasks associated with solutions in the same manner as paragraph 8 does for the international protection of refugees. For a more detailed discussion of the significance of the search for permanent solutions as a separate function of UNHCR, see Marjoleine Zieck, *UNHCR and Voluntary Repatriation of Refugees* 80–81 (1997). Also see Goodwin-Gill and McAdam, *supra* note 1, at 426, noting that 'the provision of international protection is of primary importance'.

69 See Report of the Secretary-General, *supra* note 20, at ¶ 19, fn 1. The Secretary-General proposed the term 'international legal protection of refugees', Ibid., at ¶ 19.

70 See UNHCR Statute, *supra* note 61, ¶ 8(g) and (h) and mandate of the High Commissioner of the League of Nations for Refugees contained in Report of the Council Committee Appointed to Draw Up a Plan for International Assistance to Refugees, *supra* note 13.

similar to IRO's responsibility to 'consult and co-operate with public and private organizations whenever it is deemed advisable'.[71] In addition, UNHCR's responsibility to enter into agreements with governments for 'the execution of any measures calculated to improve the situation of refugees and to reduce the number requiring protection' is similar to obligations that IRO had in its Constitution.[72]

1.3.1 Responsibilities related to international refugee law

UNHCR's specific responsibilities related to international refugee law are contained in sub-paragraph 8(a) of its Statute, which states that 'the High Commissioner shall provide for the protection of refugees falling under the competence of his Office by: (a) [p]romoting the conclusion and ratification of international conventions for the protection of refugees, supervising their application and proposing amendments thereto'.[73] Four distinct responsibilities can be identified in the wording of this sub-paragraph: (i.) the promotion of the conclusion of international treaties concerning refugees; (ii.) the proposal of amendments to such treaties; (iii.) the promotion of ratifications to such treaties; and (iv.) the supervision of the application by States of such treaties.

These four responsibilities, which are considered in detail in Chapter 2, permit UNHCR to work toward securing the existence of international refugee law standards and their effectiveness. The importance of these responsibilities can be ascertained from the fact that they are contained in the first sub-paragraph defining the responsibilities that UNHCR must carry out in order to fulfil its international protection function. They also are consistent with a consideration of international law as not only the basis for the United Nations and the international

---

71 Constitution of the IRO, in Holborn, *supra* note 37, at art. 2.2(f).
72 See UNHCR Statute, *supra* note 61, ¶ 8(b) and Constitution of the IRO, in Holborn, *supra* note 37, at arts. 2.2(g) and (j). In practice, UNHCR would make individual determinations on the eligibility of people for refugee status as the IRO had done and UNHCR's Statute would contain a refugee definition that had its origins in the definition contained in Annex I to the Constitution of the IRO.
73 Paragraph 8(b) also contains wording that could be interpreted as relating to international treaties on refugees. This paragraph states that the High Commissioner also shall promote 'through special agreements with governments the execution of any measures calculated to improve the situation of refugees and to reduce the number requiring protection'. The reference to 'special agreements', however, is not to treaties in the same sense as Paragraph 8(a). The *travaux préparatoires* for the 1951 Convention demonstrate that this sub-paragraph was intended by the drafters to refer to agreements with governments such as repatriation agreements between individual countries and UNHCR as well as co-operation agreements for the establishment of UNHCR offices in countries. Corinne Lewis, 'UNHCR's Contribution to the Development of International Refugee Law: Its Foundations and Evolution', 17 *Int'l. J. Refugee L.* 67, 71–72 (2005).'

relations among States,[74] but also as essential for the maintenance of international peace and security.[75]

Additional sub-paragraphs in paragraph 8 of the Statute facilitate and support UNHCR's responsibilities under sub-paragraph (a). Under sub-paragraph (f), UNHCR is to obtain information from governments concerning the number and situation of refugees and the laws and regulations concerning them. Thus, this paragraph provides a means that facilitates UNHCR's work of supervising States' application of refugee conventions, since it permits UNHCR to obtain the necessary information from States about their treatment of refugees. This provision also would serve as a basis for UNHCR's initially limited role related to States' implementation of their international refugee law obligations. Sub-paragraph (g) lends additional support to UNHCR's responsibilities under paragraph 8(a), since it provides for UNHCR to stay in close touch with governments and thereby foster a good working relationship with States to benefit the refugees UNHCR was mandated to protect.

1.3.1.1 Tracing the historical foundations

As discussed earlier, UNHCR's four statutory responsibilities related to international refugee law[76] are derived from the experiences and mandates of UNHCR's predecessors. In the area of the development of international refugee law, since nearly all UNHCR's predecessors found it necessary to initiate and encourage the conclusion of treaties pertaining to refugees' status and other matters affecting refugees, UNHCR was assigned the responsibility of promoting the conclusion of international treaties concerning refugees.

In addition, States had already seen that the evolution of the refugee situation could necessitate changes in the international agreements related to their protection. The 1926 Arrangement Relating to the Issue of Identity Certificates to Russian and Armenian Refugees[77] amended the 1922 Arrangement with Regard to the Issue of Certificates of Identity to Russian Refugees and the 1924 Plan

---

74 Edvard Hambro, Leland M. Goodrich and Anne Patricia Simons, *Charter of the United Nations* 134 (1969). This approach is reflected in art. 1(1) of the Purposes and Principles section of the UN Charter. Art. 1(1) provides that the United Nations shall 'maintain international peace and security and to that end: ... bring about by peaceful means, and in conformity with the principles of justice and international law, adjustment or settlement of international disputes or situations which might lead to a breach of the peace'.

75 Carl-August Fleischhauer, 'Article 13', in *The Charter of the United Nations: a Commentary* 298, 299 (Bruno Simma, ed., 2nd edn, 2002).

76 The importance of these responsibilities can be seen from the fact that they were included in the earliest drafts of UNHCR's mandate. See for example France: draft resolution, ¶ III(c), U.N. Doc. A/C.3/L.26 (11 November 1949) and United States of America: draft resolution, ¶ 5(b), U.N. Doc. A/C.3/L.28 (11 November 1949).

77 1926 Arrangement Relating to the Issue of Identity Certificates to Russian and Armenian Refugees, *supra* note 20.

for the Issue of a Certificate of Identity to Armenian Refugees.[78] The 1926 Arrangement Relating to the Issue of Identity Certificates to Russian and Armenian Refugees was then extended to other groups of refugees with the 1928 Arrangement Concerning the Extension to Other Categories of Refugees of Certain Measures Taken in Favour of Russian and Armenian Refugees.[79] In addition, the 1938 Convention Concerning the Status of Refugees Coming From Germany, replaced, according to its article 18, the 1936 Provisional Arrangement Concerning the Status of Refugees.[80] Logically, therefore, UNHCR was assigned the responsibility to propose amendments to treaties concerning the protection of refugees.

As concerns the ratification of international refugee law agreements, the Intergovernmental Committee on Refugees and the International Refugee Organization, as already noted, encouraged States to ratify or accede to the London Agreement on Travel Documents[81] and the High Commissioner of the League of Nations for Refugees had been specifically mandated to encourage States to accede to conventions covering refugees. Moreover, the drafters of UNHCR's Statute may have been concerned about the difficulties in obtaining ratifications to previous international conventions concerning refugees.[82] Each subsequent instrument developed for the protection of refugees had a lower number of States parties than the preceding one.[83] In particular, the conventions, as contrasted with the

---

78 1922 Arrangement with Regard to the Issue of Certificates of Identity to Russian Refugees, *supra* note 18. 1924 Plan for the Issue of a Certificate of Identity to Armenian Refugees, *supra* note 19.

79 1928 Arrangement Concerning the Extension to Other Categories of Refugees of Certain Measures Taken in Favour of Russian and Armenian Refugees, *supra* note 21.

80 1938 Convention Concerning the Status of Refugees Coming From Germany, *supra* note 29. 1936 Provisional Arrangement Concerning the Status of Refugees, *supra* note 27.

81 London Agreement on Travel Documents, *supra* note 44.

82 The Report of the Secretary-General notes that further ratifications and accessions could be obtained to the 1938 Convention Concerning the Status of Refugees Coming From Germany and the 1946 Agreement Relating to the Issue of a Travel Document of Refugees who are the Concern of the Intergovernmental Committee on Refugees. Report of the Secretary-General, *supra* note 20, ¶ 24, fn 3.

83 The 1922 Arrangement with Regard to the Issue of Certificates of Identity to Russian Refugees, *supra* note 18, had 53 States parties. The 1924 Plan for the Issue of a Certificate of Identity to Armenian Refugees, *supra* note 19, had 35. The 1926 Arrangement relating to the Issue of Identity Certificates to Russian and Armenian Refugees, *supra* note 20, had 20 States. The 1928 Arrangement relating to the Legal Status of Russian and Armenian Refugees, *supra* note 21, had 11 States. The 1933 Convention Relating to the International Status of Refugees, *supra* note 25, had eight States. The 1936 Provisional Arrangement Concerning the Status of Refugees Coming From Germany, *supra* note 27, had seven States. The 1938 Convention Concerning the Status of Refugees Coming From Germany, *supra* note 29, had three States. UNHCR, Colloquium on the Development in the Law of Refugees with Particular Reference to the 1951 Convention and the Statute of the Office of the United Nations High Commissioner for Refugees held at Villa Serbelloni Bellagio (Italy) from 21–28 April 1965: Background paper submitted by the Office of the United Nations High Commissioner for Refugees, ¶ 28 (1965). Available at http://www.unhcr. org/protect/PROTECTION/3ae68be77.html (accessed 31 October 2011).

arrangements, had very few State parties. The 1933 Convention Relating to the International Status of Refugees was ratified by only eight countries and the 1938 Convention Concerning the Status of Refugees Coming From Germany by a mere three countries.[84]

Most likely, the drafters of UNHCR's Statute would have wanted to ensure that the new convention for the protection of refugees, the 1951 Convention Relating to the Status of Refugees[85] that was being formulated by an ad hoc committee while discussions were taking place on UNHCR's mandate,[86] would be ratified by as many States as possible.[87] Thus, UNHCR's responsibility to promote the ratification of the new convention, the 1951 Refugee Convention, when it was completed, as well as the ratification of any future refugee instruments, would help ensure that such agreements would be legally binding on more States.

Finally, as part of their everyday activities, many of UNHCR's predecessors would have monitored States' conduct to determine whether such conduct conformed to the international standards in place and made representations to governments on issues ranging from non-expulsion, legal protections afforded refugees, detention, and naturalizations procedures.[88] Therefore, it naturally followed from these precedents that UNHCR's drafters would provide UNHCR with a supervisory responsibility related to international conventions for the protection of refugees. The supervisory language of the mandate of the High Commissioner of the League of Nations for Refugees would serve as the basis for the wording of UNHCR's supervisory responsibility.[89]

1.3.1.2 Purpose of responsibilities: international protection

The ultimate purpose of UNHCR's responsibilities related to international refugee law, under paragraph 8 of its Statute, is to ensure international protection, one of UNHCR's primary functions, as noted earlier. However neither paragraphs 1, 8 nor any other paragraph of the Statute, establishes a definition of 'international protection'. Neither does the Statute contain a preamble that would provide the context for the term. Moreover, the meaning of 'international protection' is not self-evident since the terms 'international' and 'protection'

---

84 Ibid.
85 1951 Refugee Convention, *supra* note 2.
86 ECOSOC appointed an ad hoc committee 'consisting of representatives of thirteen Governments, who shall possess special competence in this field'. E.S.C. Res. 248(IX) B (1949).
87 The concern about the ratification of multilateral treaties continues to retain the attention of the United Nations at a general level. For example, in connection with the United Nations Decade of International Law from 1990–1999, G.A. Res. 45/40, Annex I, ¶ 2, A/RES/45/40 (28 November 1990).
88 Vernant, *supra* note 33, at 26.
89 The High Commissioner of the League of Nations was 'to superintend the entry into force and the application of the legal status of refugees'. Report of the Secretary-General, *supra* note 20, at 36, fn 1(b).

have independent meanings[90] and their coupling into a phrase does not provide a separate meaning that stands alone. However, paragraph 8 of the Statute enumerates the activities that UNHCR is to carry out in order to ensure the fulfilment of its international protection function, and therefore, these activities can be examined to determine what they disclose about the meaning of UNHCR's international protection function. Specifically, paragraph 8 states:

> The High Commissioner shall provide for the protection of refugees falling under the competence of his Office by:
>
> (a) promoting the conclusion and ratification of international conventions for the protection of refugees, supervising their application and proposing amendments thereto;
> (b) promoting through special agreements with Governments the execution of any measures calculated to improve the situation of refugees and to reduce the number requiring protection;
> (c) assisting governmental and private efforts to promote voluntary repatriation or assimilation within new national communities;
> (d) promoting the admission of refugees, not excluding those in the most destitute categories, to the territories of States;
> (e) endeavouring to obtain permission for refugees to transfer their assets and especially those necessary for their resettlement;
> (f) obtaining from Governments information concerning the number and conditions of refugees in their territories and the laws and regulations concerning them;
> (g) keeping in close touch with the Governments and inter-governmental organizations concerned;
> (h) establishing contact in such manner as he may think best with private organizations dealing with refugee questions;
> (i) facilitating the co-ordination of the efforts of private organizations concerned with the welfare of refugees.[91]

The list of responsibilities has an eclectic nature rather than a systematic one, but three general areas can be identified. First, UNHCR is to facilitate the admission of refugees to the territories of States where they can be protected; UNHCR does this by promoting the admission of refugees (sub-paragraph d). Second, UNHCR helps ensure that the rights of refugees are respected; UNHCR does so by promoting the conclusion and ratification of international conventions for the protection of refugees, supervising their application and proposing amendments thereto (sub-paragraph a). Third, UNHCR is to work towards finding solutions

---

90 See the definition of 'international' and 'protection' in VII *The Oxford English Dictionary* 1123–1124 (2nd edn, 1989) and XII *The Oxford English Dictionary* 678–679 (2nd edn, 1989).
91 UNHCR Statute, *supra* note 61, ¶ 8.

for refugees; UNHCR therefore concludes special agreements with governments (sub-paragraph b) and assists governments and others to promote 'voluntary repatriation or assimilation within new national communities' (sub-paragraph c). UNHCR also works to ensure that as part of such solutions refugees are permitted to transfer their assets (sub-paragraph e).

UNHCR's responsibilities, to obtain information from governments (sub-paragraph f) and to undertake its work in co-ordination with States and inter-governmental and private organizations (sub-paragraphs g and h) as well as to help co-ordinate the work of private organizations (sub-paragraph i), support all three of the general areas mentioned earlier.

UNHCR's international protection activities follow the path of a refugee from his/her flight to the finding of a solution. A refugee must be admitted to a State in order to obtain an alternative protection to that which would normally have been provided by the country of origin and have his/her rights respected by the country of refuge. Eventually, a refugee should be able to dispense with the protection provided by the state of refuge by either returning to the country of origin or by becoming a national of a new country, thus obtaining the panoply of rights provided to nationals.

The foregoing examination of UNHCR's international protection activities, in order to define 'international protection' more precisely, gives a sense of the practical objectives of international protection, but still does not reveal a clear meaning for the term. UNHCR's international protection function was essentially the performance of activities to ensure that States provide refugees with the necessary legal protection in the absence of such protection from the refugees' home countries. The activities are wide ranging, but include ensuring that States have legal obligations for the protection of refugees and that these obligations are effective. The general manner in which international protection was defined meant that UNHCR would have a great deal of flexibility in defining the parameters and content of its work, as will be seen in subsequent chapters.

1.3.1.3   The essential link to international refugee law: the 1951 Refugee Convention

The initial and foundational link between UNHCR's statutory responsibilities and international refugee law would be laid with the adoption of the 1951 Convention Relating to the Status of Refugees.[92] The Secretary-General proposed the concept of a new refugee convention, what would become the 1951 Refugee Convention, as the second prong of the solution to the problem of refugees after the Second World War. The drafting of the Convention, which began in January 1950 and was completed in July 1951, overlapped with the drafting of UNHCR's Statute.

---

92 Convention Relating to the Status of Refugees, *supra* note 2.

When the drafting of the 1951 Refugee Convention was undertaken, international refugee law was still comprised of the various ad hoc arrangements and agreements described earlier, most of which dated from the League of Nations period. However, these agreements did not cover the various groups of new refugees that were fleeing from Eastern to Western Europe and in other areas of the world. In addition, while the pre-1951 instruments addressed rights that had previously generated serious problems for refugees, the adoption of the Universal Declaration of Human Rights in 1948,[93] with its elaboration of the political, social, economic and cultural rights of persons, meant that a new and firmer basis for the development of the rights of refugees had been provided.

Moreover, in light of the fact that many of the refugees for whom UNHCR assumed responsibility were unable or unwilling to be repatriated, other solutions, such as local integration and resettlement in a third country would need to be applied, thus, requiring an increased focus on rights in a country that would not be a refugee's country of nationality.

The 1951 Refugee Convention was intended therefore 'to revise and consolidate previous international agreements relating to the status of refugees and to extend the scope of and protection accorded by such instruments by means of a new agreement'.[94] The 1951 Refugee Convention would be the first refugee convention for which UNHCR would carry out its responsibilities related to international refugee law. UNHCR would: promote ratifications,[95] obtain information about the laws and regulations implementing the standards in the 1951 Refugee Convention, seek amendment of the 1951 Refugee Convention, and supervise States' applications of the 1951 Refugee Convention's provisions. The durability of the 1951 Refugee Convention is aptly demonstrated by the fact that it serves, even today, as the cornerstone for UNHCR's work related to the development of international refuge law.

1.4 Conclusion

Thus, UNHCR's predecessors, from the first High Commissioner for Refugees through UNHCR's immediate predecessor, the International Refugee Organization, demonstrate that UNHCR was not an entirely new creation. Instead, UNHCR is a continuation of a means used by States, the creation of an organization, to address a specific refugee problem.

93 The Universal Declaration of Human Rights is refered to in the first preambular paragraph of the 1951 Refugee Convention. The drafters of the 1951 Refugee Convention frequently mentioned the UDHR during their discussions. Guy Goodwin-Gill, 'Refugees and Their Human Rights', Barbara Harrell-Bond Lecture, 12 November 2003, Refugee Studies Centre Working Paper No. 17, University of Oxford. Available at http://www.rsc.ox.ac.uk/publications/working-papers/RSCworkingpaper17.pdf (accessed 27 October 2011).
94 1951 Refugee Convention, *supra* note 2, 3rd preambular ¶.
95 As of 1 April 2011, 147 countries are now parties to either the 1951 Convention and/or the 1967 Protocol.

UNHCR's predecessors played a significant role in the development of international refugee law standards; they participated in and facilitated the drafting of legal instruments that articulated the treatment that States were to accord to refugees. UNHCR's mandate reflects this role in providing that UNHCR is to promote the conclusion of international treaties concerning refugees and to propose amendments to such treaties. These precursor organizations also carried out activities to ensure that the early arrangements and agreements were effective. Moreover, it was the mandate of the Office of the High Commissioner of the League of Nations for Refugees, with its explicit responsibility related to States' ratification and application of refugee conventions, that provided the wording for UNHCR's supervisory responsibility.

The work of UNHCR's predecessors also demonstrates how the development of instruments for the protection of refugees was of a gradual nature in reaction to events of the time. The instruments were created to address specific problems encountered by refugees. This incremental approach to resolve new problems also would characterize UNHCR's development of new approaches as will be seen in Chapters 5 and 6.

Thus, States acting through the General Assembly provided UNHCR with a generally worded mandate, which provided the two primary purposes of UNHCR's work, namely, international protection and seeking solutions to the problem of refugees. UNHCR's role was to be one of guidance, supervision, co-ordination and oversight to manage the problem of refugees that States encountered. The primary tool for UNHCR's international protection work vis-à-vis States would be the international refugee law agreement, the 1951 Refugee Convention, which agreement would also serve as the basis for States' protection of refugees.

2 UNHCR's statutory role and work related to refugee law

2.1 Introduction

The United Nations High Commissioner for Refugees was created following the adoption of its Statute by States in the General Assembly in 1950.[1] These States assigned UNHCR the primary function of providing international protection to refugees, and as part of this function, specified certain responsibilities related to the development and effectiveness of international refugee law. These statutory responsibilities were derived from the experiences and mandates of UNHCR's predecessors, as noted in Chapter 1,[2] and were general expressions of such responsibilities rather than a detailed description of the activities UNHCR was to perform.

Given the general wording of UNHCR's responsibilities, States implicitly conferred on UNHCR the task of determining and establishing the content and parameters of these responsibilities through its actual practice. As a result, from the earliest days of its existence, UNHCR developed its autonomy in interpreting its own statute and established the foundations for its role as the co-ordinator for international refugee law matters.

Of UNHCR's four responsibilities related to international refugee law, two of them, the promotion of the conclusion of international treaties concerning refugees and the proposal of amendments to such treaties, concerned the development of international refugee law. The other two responsibilities, the promotion of ratifications to such treaties and the supervision of States' application of such treaties, concerned the 'effectiveness' of international refugee law, a term which is explained in section 2.3.1. This division, between the development and effectiveness of international refugee law, will be utilized throughout this book to structure the examination of UNHCR's responsibilities related to international refugee law.

---

1 UN General Assembly Resolution 428(V) of 14 December 1950. G.A. Res. 428(V) (14 December 1950).
2 See section 1.3.1.1 in this volume.

2.2 UNHCR and the development of refugee law

The general parameters for UNHCR's work related to the development of international refugee law, that is, the creation of legal standards for the protection of refugees as new issues and refugee crises required additional or more elaborated principles, were established by the organization's statutory mandate. However, as shown later, the statutory wording was not completely clear and therefore, the actual work performed by UNHCR is examined in order to convey a clearer picture of the content of UNHCR's responsibilities in this area.

2.2.1 UNHCR's mandate

In the area of the development of international refugee law, UNHCR, under its statutory mandate, was to 'promot[e] the conclusion … of international conventions for the protection of refugees … and propos[e] amendments thereto'.[3] The meaning of this latter responsibility is much clearer from the statutory wording than the former; UNHCR was to propose amendments to States and to relevant international bodies.

However, with UNHCR's responsibility to promote the conclusion of international conventions for the protection of refugees, the term 'promote' has a very broad meaning.[4] The UNHCR Statute does not provide any additional guidance as to the specific activities that UNHCR should perform in order to carry out this activity.[5] Moreover, the *travaux préparatoires* do not contain any detailed discussion, by the drafters of UNHCR's Statute, on UNHCR's promotional role.[6] However, the ambiguity in the meaning of UNHCR's responsibility to promote the conclusion of international conventions for the protection of refugees meant that UNHCR could not only determine how to fulfil this responsibility, but could also carry out a broad range of responsibilities.

---

3 See paragraph 8(a) of the Statute of the Office of the United Nations High Commissioner for Refugees, contained in the Annex to UN General Assembly Resolution 428(V) of 14 December 1950. G.A. Res. 428(V) (14 December1950) (hereinafter UNHCR Statute).

4 To 'promote' means 'to further the growth, progress or establishment of (anything); to help forward (a process or result)' and '[t]o support actively the passing of (a law or measure)'. XII *The Oxford English Dictionary* 616–617 (2nd edn, 1989).

5 For a more detailed analysis utilizing the provisions on treaty interpretation in the 1969 Vienna Convention on the Law of Treaties, see Corinne Lewis, 'UNHCR's Contribution to the Development of International Refugee Law: Its Foundations and Evolution', 17 *Int'l. J. Refugee L.* 67, 72–76 (2005).

6 The drafters focused on issues that engendered significant disagreement. Louise Holborn, *Refugees: A Problem of Our Time: The Work of the United Nations High Commissioner for Refugees*, 1951–1972 65 (1975). For a summary of these issues see Lewis, *supra* note 5, at 74, fn 21.

2.2.2 UNHCR's contribution to international treaties for the protection of refugees

The drafting of the first international convention for the protection of refugees, the 1951 Refugee Convention,[7] overlapped with that of UNHCR's Statute. Therefore, while UNHCR did not participate in the drafting process, it did attend the Conference of Plenipotentiaries, held in Geneva from 2 to 25 July 1951, at which the 1951 Refugee Convention was adopted.[8] UNHCR would, however, play a crucial role in the formulation of the two other key universal refugee agreements, the 1957 Agreement Relating to Refugee Seamen and the 1967 Protocol Relating to the Status of Refugees.

2.2.2.1 1957 Agreement Relating to Refugee Seamen

The 1957 Agreement Relating to Refugee Seamen[9] was the first international agreement for the protection of refugees that UNHCR 'promoted'. This agreement arose out of one of the first significant protection problems that UNHCR had to handle after its creation. Holborn has described this problem very succinctly:

> [S]eamen who sought refuge by serving on ships of states other than their own, or who sought to exercise their calling as seafarers after gaining refuge in a country of asylum, often found themselves in the precarious position of having no country in which they could legally stay, no valid identity or travel documents (or only documents which had expired), and in an irregular status everywhere. Frequently such seamen were not permitted to leave their ships in any port of call for lack of documents, and thus were virtually condemned to sail the seas forever or risk imprisonment when trying to land.[10]

While the 1951 Refugee Convention contains an article that concerns refugee seamen, this article does not establish a fixed standard for determining the State responsible for providing a refugee seaman with travel documents, but only requires States to 'give sympathetic consideration to their [refugee seamen] establishment on its territory and the issue of travel documents to them or their temporary admission'.[11]

In 1953, following a significant number of demands from refugee seamen for UNHCR assistance, UNHCR requested the government of the Netherlands to conduct a study to determine the nature of the problem; out of 700 seamen,

---

7 Convention Relating to the Status of Refugees, 28 July 1951, 189 U.N.T.S. 137 (hereinafter 1951 Refugee Convention).
8 UNHCR, *Report of the UNHCR*, ¶ 32, U.N. Doc. A/2394 (1953).
9 Agreement Relating to Refugee Seamen, 23 November 1957, 506 U.N.T.S. 125.
10 Holborn, *supra* note 6, at 203.
11 1951 Refugee Convention, *supra* note 7, at art. 11.

one-quarter of them did not possess any travel document and another quarter of them were in a 'precarious' position.[12] Following the receipt of this information, UNHCR sent a memorandum to the International Labour Organization suggesting that its governing body consider the problem.[13] UNHCR also attended the conference of eight Western European maritime nations, organized by the Netherlands, as an observer and participated in the discussions of the new agreement, the 1957 Agreement Relating to Refugee Seamen.[14] This agreement essentially turned Article 11 of the 1951 Refugee Convention into a more concrete obligation by providing methods for determining which State is responsible for issuing the travel document to a particular refugee.

2.2.2.2 1967 Protocol Relating to the Status of Refugees

UNHCR's work to modify the definition of a refugee in the 1951 Refugee Convention, and thereby give it a truly international scope, constituted an extremely significant contribution to the development of international refugee law. The definition of a refugee under the 1951 Refugee Convention provided that:

> As a result of events occurring before 1 January 1951 and owing to well-founded fear of persecution for reasons of race, religion, nationality, membership of a particular social group or political opinion, is outside the country of his nationality and is unable or, owing to such fear, is unwilling to avail himself of the protection of that country.[15]

The phrase 'events occurring before 1 January 1951' was to be interpreted, according to the following paragraph in the 1951 Refugee Convention, as either 'events occurring in Europe before 1 January 1951' or 'events occurring in Europe or elsewhere before 1 January 1951'.[16] This meant that the refugee definition in the 1951 Refugee Convention did not apply to all refugees throughout the world. The definition limited the events giving rise to a fear of persecution to events prior to 1 January 1951 and gave States the option of further limiting the scope of such events to those that occurred in Europe. The need for a modification of the refugee definition in the 1951 Refugee Convention became increasingly apparent during the terms of the first three High Commissioners.

---

12 Paul Weis, 'The Hague Agreement Relating to Refugee Seamen', 7 *Intl. & Comp. L.Q.* 334, 339 (1958). UNHCR also had requested, in 1953, the assistance of the International Labour Organization with the refugee seamen and had submitted a memorandum on the problem to the ILO. Ibid., at 338.
13 UNHCR, Report of the UNHCR, ¶ 84, U.N. Doc.A/2648 (1954).
14 UNHCR, Report of the UNHCR, ¶ 244–245, U.N. Doc.A/3123/Rev.1 (1956).
15 1951 Refugee Convention, *supra* note 7, at art. 1.A(2).
16 Ibid., at art. 1B.(1).

G.J. van Heuven Goedhart, who became the first High Commissioner in 1951, envisioned that the 1951 Refugee Convention was to 'become as universal as possible by the accession of the greatest possible number of States' and to include 'any future groups of refugees'.[17] However, in practice, the 1951 Refugee Convention, as well as UNHCR itself, remained an instrument almost exclusively for the protection of refugees as a result of events occurring in Europe before 1951. High Commissioner Goedhart correctly noted the discrepancy between the refugee definition under the 1951 Refugee Convention with the time and optional geographic limitations, on the one hand, and the universal definition of a refugee under UNHCR's Statute, on the other.[18]

UNHCR's determination, of which groups would receive its protection and which only assistance, became increasingly irregular, particularly under Auguste Lindt, who became High Commissioner in 1956 following the death of Goedhart. During Lindt's term, UNHCR applied its mandate and the 1951 Refugee Convention to certain European groups based on an event-effect argument; East Europeans fleeing Communist bloc countries after 1951 were considered to be refugees under UNHCR's mandate and the 1951 Refugee Convention on the basis that the events causing the effect, the flight, had occurred prior to 1951.[19] Similarly, nearly 200,000 Hungarians[20] fleeing Hungary following the invasion of the Soviet Army in November 1956 were recognized as refugees, under UNHCR's mandate and the 1951 Refugee Convention, because the events that gave rise to such flight occurred before 1951.[21]

UNHCR adopted a different approach with respect to Chinese fleeing to Hong Kong, and Algerians. Chinese refugees who escaped to Hong Kong, as a result of the political and economic changes in China particularly during 1945–1952,[22] were given assistance only, pursuant to funds raised by UNHCR under its 'good offices' function, authorized by General Assembly resolutions.[23] UNHCR did not view them as 'refugees' under its statutory mandate due to the political problem of the two Chinas.[24] Algerians fleeing as a result of the Algerian war of

---

17 Gerrit Jan van Heuven Goedhart, 'The Problem of Refugees', 82 *Recueil des Cours*, Hague Academy of International Law 264, 292, 280 (1953).
18 Ibid., at 280.
19 Kazimierz Bem, 'The Coming of a "Blank Cheque" – Europe, the 1951 Convention and the 1967 Protocol', 16 *Int'l. J. Refugee L.* 609, 619 (2004).
20 UNHCR, *Report of the UNHCR*, ¶ 3, U.N. Doc. A/3585/Rev.1 (1957).
21 Also see the discussion of UNHCR's determination that the Hungarians qualify as refugees in section 3.4.1.1. For a good summary of events leading up to the exodus and UNHCR's determination of whether such persons qualified as 'refugees' under the 1951 Convention, see UNHCR, *The State of the World's Refugees 2000: Fifty years of Humanitarian Action* 26–32 (2000).
22 Ivor Jackson, *The Refugee Concept in Group Situations* 90 (1999).
23 See G.A. Res. 1167 (XII) (26 November 1957) and G.A. Res. 1784 (XVII) (7 December 1962).
24 Jackson, *supra* note 22, at 94. For a detailed description of UN deliberations concerning the Chinese refugees in Hong Kong, see Ibid., at 90–94.

independence from 1954–1962 and persecution by the French,[25] were implicitly but unofficially considered by UNHCR to qualify as refugees under its mandate, but UNHCR only provided them with assistance.[26]

Felix Schnyder, the third High Commissioner, led the organization from 1960–1965. He continued to expand UNHCR's use of its 'good offices' in providing assistance to refugees in Africa, who had fled after 1951; however, these refugees were not considered to fall under the protection of the 1951 Refugee Convention.[27] Thus, by the mid-1960s the majority of refugees assisted by UNHCR worldwide did not receive protection under the 1951 Refugee Convention.[28]

High Commissioner Schnyder began to view the disparity, between the number of refugees who benefited from UNHCR's services, but who did not receive the protection of the 1951 Refugee Convention, as a significant problem.[29] He wanted to ensure that the 1951 Refugee Convention would serve as a universal convention, particularly in light of the decision of the then Organization of African Unity (now the African Union) to draft a regional refugee convention.[30]

Under High Commissioner Schnyder, UNHCR studied 'ways and means by which the personal scope of the 1951 Refugee Convention might be liberalized'[31] and proposed a colloquium on this issue.[32] UNHCR representatives attended the

---

25   For a good summary of the events that caused their flight and their situation in countries of asylum see UNHCR, The State of the World's Refugees, *supra* note 21, at 38–43. Cecilia Ruthström-Ruin provides a detailed overview of not only the factual causes of the flight, but also the various internal positions taken by UNHCR on this issue. See Cecilia Ruthström-Ruin, *Beyond Europe: the Globalization of Refugee Aid* 42–98 (1993).

26   Gil Loescher, *The UNHCR and World Politics: A Perilous Path* 100 (2001). Also see Ivor Jackson's analysis that leads to the conclusion that 'the Algerian refugees were considered *prima facie* as a *group* of concern to the High Commissioner under his normal terms of reference.' Jackson, *supra* note 22, at 141.

27   UNHCR, *The State of the World's Refugees*, *supra* note 21, at 53.

28   Ibid.

29   Félix Schnyder, 'Les Aspects Juridiques Actuels du Problème des Réfugiés', 114 *Recueil des Cours*, Hague Academy of International Law 335, 365 (1965). Thus, High Commissioner Schnyder's view evolved considerably during his tenure as High Commissioner. On assuming office, he believed that UNHCR would focus on assistance to refugees in the developing world and that 'his actions in "new" refugee situations should be based on his good offices function and not on his mandate.' Loescher, *supra* note 26, at 106, 112.

30   Holborn, *supra* note 6, at 179. UNHCR, in its 1968 Note on International Protection, espouses a practical justification for its movement from the provision of primarily material assistance to refugees in Africa to that of ensuring their protection. UNHCR states that initially assistance was the more urgent need, that many African countries did not have legislation on employment and social security, among other protections, and that the large number of refugees made it difficult to conduct individual determinations of eligibility for refugee status. The Note adds that due to the fact that more refugees were living in towns and that the legal infrastructure was developing in many African countries, UNHCR was then justified in providing international protection to such refugees. UNHCR, Note on International Protection ¶ 13–15, U.N. Doc. A/AC.96/398 (9 September 1968).

31   UNHCR, *Addendum to the Report of the UNHCR*, ¶ 33, U.N. Doc. A/5811/Rev.1/Add.1 (1964).

32   Schnyder, *supra* note 29, at 444.

colloquium, along with 13 legal experts from various countries and representatives from the Carnegie Endowment for International Peace and the *Institut de Hautes Études* in Geneva, during which they discussed how to modify the 1951 Refugee Convention in order to ensure its applicability to new refugee situations.[33]

UNHCR also drafted a background note for the conference, which extensively considered prior refugee arrangements and conventions and the drafting history of the refugee definition in the 1951 Refugee Convention.[34] UNHCR then assessed the content and the potential forms the document could take, specifically, whether it should be a recommendation or a binding legal instrument.[35] Following the Colloquium's recommendation that the time limitation should be removed completely and that no geographic declarations should be made by States ratifying the Protocol,[36] UNHCR prepared a draft instrument that incorporated States' views. After final modifications were made to the text following suggestions by members of the Executive Committee of the High Commissioner's Programme, UNHCR submitted the 1967 Protocol Relating to the Status of Refugees to the General Assembly, via the Economic and Social Council,[37] where it was adopted.

2.2.3 UNHCR's contribution to other instruments

UNHCR's promotional work was, as its Statute provides, to relate to 'international conventions for the protection of refugees'.[38] However, from very early on, UNHCR's promotional work extended to instruments that were not universal

33 See UNHCR, Colloquium on the Legal Aspects of Refugee Problems (Note by the High Commissioner), Annex I, U.N. Doc. A/AC.96/INF.40 (5 May 1965) for a list of participants in the Colloquium held in Bellagio, Italy from 21–28 April 1965.

34 UNHCR, Colloquium on the Development in the Law of Refugees with Particular Reference to the 1951 Convention and the Statute of the Office of the United Nations High Commissioner for Refugees held at Villa Serbelloni Bellagio (Italy) from 21–28 April 1965: Background paper submitted by the Office of the United Nations High Commissioner for Refugees. Available at http://www.unhcr.org/protect/PROTECTION/ 3ae68be77.html (accessed 27 October 2011).

35 Ibid., at ¶ 128–31. In paragraph 132 of its note, UNHCR proposed:'The possibility cannot be excluded that certain States may still be unwilling to assume future obligations, the extent of which they cannot foresee or to broaden their obligations to cover all existing groups of refugees without limitation. It may thus be necessary to seek a compromise between universality, on the one hand, and effectiveness, on the other. From the point of view of legal technique, it might therefore be desirable for the new obligation, if it is to secure acceptance by the largest possible number of States, either to be limited in itself or to contain the possibility of limitation. Such a limitation could be established (a) *rationae personae*, i.e. according to a particular group, or particular groups, of refugees or (b) *rationae materiae*, i.e. according to particular provisions of the Convention, or the two techniques could be combined.'

36 UNHCR, Colloquium on the Legal Aspects of Refugee Problems, *supra* note 33, ¶ 4, 5.

37 Paul Weis, 'The 1967 Protocol Relating to the Status of Refugees and Some Questions of the Law of Treaties', 42 *B.Y.I.L.* 39, 45 (1967). Protocol Relating to the Status of Refugees, 16 December 1966, 606 U.N.T.S. 267.

38 UNHCR Statute, *supra* note 3, ¶8(a).

international ones, and to instruments that were not solely for the protection of refugees. Thus, UNHCR promoted the inclusion of provisions for the protection of refugees in human rights treaties, conventions on particular topics that affect refugees, and regional instruments.

Although a strict reading of the wording of paragraph 8(a) of UNHCR's Statute, which states that UNHCR is to promote 'international conventions for the protection of refugees', might suggest that UNHCR's promotional work should be limited to refugee conventions, consideration of this phrase in light of UNHCR's overall purpose of helping to ensure the international protection of refugees provides a different perspective. As noted in Chapter 1, the lack of a clear definition of 'international protection' in UNHCR's Statute permits UNHCR a great deal of flexibility in its interpretation and thus, in determining the activities that contribute to furthering international protection. Consequently, UNHCR could be said to have the authorization to promote types of agreements other than universal refugee law conventions.

2.2.3.1 *International human rights treaties*

Since its creation, UNHCR has been active in contributing to the development of standards for the protection of refugees in international human rights instruments. UNHCR actively promoted the inclusion of a right to asylum in the draft Covenant on Civil and Political Rights, worked on by the UN Human Rights Commission (now the Human Rights Council), which work included submission of a memorandum to the Commission[39] and lobbying by the UNHCR Chief Legal Adviser, Paul Weis,[40] although the Commission ultimately rejected the inclusion of such a right. The rejection of such a provision was due to the prevalence of the view that extending asylum to an individual was the right of the State rather than a fundamental right of the individual and to a lack of agreement on the wording of the provision.[41] Thus States considered refugees to be in an exceptional situation that required a problem solving practical approach rather than an international human rights oriented one.

In addition, UNHCR supplied its advice during the work on the draft convention on the reduction of statelessness, the 1961 UN Convention on the Reduction of Statelessness,[42] since refugees may have lost their nationality and become

---

39 UNHCR, Report of the UNHCR, ¶ 42, U.N. Doc. A/2394 (1953).

40 Holborn, *supra* note 6, at 228.

41 See Paul Weis, 'The United Nations Declaration on Territorial Asylum', VII *Can. Y.B. Int'l. L.* 92, 97 (1969). UNHCR also contributed to the drafting of the 1967 Declaration on Territorial Asylum, G.A. Res. 2312 (XXII) (14 December 1967). UNHCR submitted comments on various drafts of the Declaration and provided its views to the Commission on Human Rights, which prepared the Declaration. Weis, ibid., at 99, 101, 103.

42 Convention on the Reduction of Statelessness, 30 August 1961, 989 U.N.T.S. 175. The International Law Commission drafted the 1961 Convention on the Reduction of Statelessness. The issue of statelessness initially subsumed that of refugees. See for example, The Secretary-General,

stateless persons. Specifically, Paul Weis was seconded to the United Nations' legal department to assist the special rapporteur of the International Law Commission with the drafting of the Convention.[43]

UNHCR's involvement in the drafting of international and regional human rights agreements, which as noted, was established very early on in its existence, remains an important part of its promotional work of new conventions for the protection of refugees, particularly given the importance of human rights work to the protection of refugees, as will be seen in Chapter 6. For example, UNHCR contributed to the discussions on the draft of the 1989 Convention on the Rights of the Child.[44] As a result, this Convention specifically mentions refugee children and children seeking asylum and provides that States shall take measures to ensure that they benefit from the rights contained therein.[45] At the regional level, UNHCR provided general and specific comments to the Council of Europe's Ad Hoc Committee on Preventing and Combating Violence against Women and Domestic Violence in connection with their drafting of a Convention on Preventing and Combating Violence against Women and Domestic Violence.[46] UHNCR thereby helped ensure that language on gender related persecution and gender sensitive asylum procedures was included in the convention.[47]

2.2.3.2 *International agreements on particular topics that affect refugees*

UNHCR's work on treaties has been oriented toward ensuring that international agreements on specific topics, which affect the rights of refugees, properly protect refugees' rights. UNHCR's work on such agreements has not only been of a

---

A Study of Statelessness, Submitted to ECOSOC, U.N. Doc. E/1112 (August 1949), although the Secretary-General does distinguish between stateless persons and refugees in pages 7–8 of his report. A 1954 Convention Relating to the Status of Stateless Persons was drafted which provided to stateless persons who are not refugees, similar rights to those of refugees under the 1951 Refugee Convention. Convention Relating to the Status of Stateless Persons, 28 September 1954, 360 U.N.T.S. 117.

43 Paul Weis, 'The United Nations Convention on the Reduction of Statelessness', 1961, 11 *Int'l. & Comp. L.Q.* 1073, 1075 (1962).

44 See UNHCR Memorandum from Gilbert Jaeger (Director of Protection) to the UNHCR Regional Representative at UN Headquarters, New York, concerning 'Possible Convention on the Rights of the Child' (16 October 1978) (available in UNHCR archives and on file with author).

45 Convention on the Rights of the Child, art. 22.1, 20 Nov. 1989, 1577 U.N.T.S. 3.

46 UNHCR, Comments to the First Meeting of the Ad Hoc Committee on Preventing and Combating Violence Against Women and Domestic Violence, 6–8 April 2009. Available at http://www. coe.int/t/dghl/standsetting/violence/UNHCR%20comments%20to%20CAHVIO%20090430. pdf (accessed 27 October 2011). UNHCR, Comments on Articles 48 and 48 bis of the Draft Council of Europe Convention on Preventing and Combating Violence against Women and Domestic Violence, November 2010. Available at http://www.unhcr.org/4cf4fb2d9.html (accessed 27 October 2011).

47 2011 Convention on Preventing and Combating Violence against Women and Domestic Violence, Council of Europe, 11 May 2011, C.E.T.S. 210. Available at https://wcd.coe.int/ViewDoc.jsp?id= 1772191 (accessed 27 October 2011).

varied nature, but also has covered a range of subjects. The following examples illustrate the breadth of UNHCR's involvement.

UNHCR contributed to the creation of the Protocol to the 1952 Universal Copyright Convention,[48] which concerns the rights of authorship to works created by authors, musicians, and others, and provides additional content to article 14 of the 1951 Refugee Convention. UNHCR submitted memoranda and participated as an observer in the Inter-Governmental Copyright Conference concerning the 1952 Universal Copyright Convention and proposed that refugees should be covered by the agreement; while the conference decided not to cover refugees in the primary agreement, it adopted a Protocol covering them instead.[49]

UNHCR also submitted memoranda and participated as an observer in the discussions of the text of the 1956 Convention on the Recovery Abroad of Maintenance Obligations.[50] With respect to the 1963 Vienna Convention on Consular Relations, UNHCR circulated a memorandum related to certain issues under discussion at the UN Conference on the Convention and informally advocated its views to delegations.[51] In connection with the 1982 Maintenance of Social Security Rights Convention, drafted under the auspices of the International Labour Organization, UNHCR participated in the negotiations of the agreement, during which it made interventions, thereby ensuring that the definition of a refugee would be consistent with that in the 1951 Refugee Convention as well as the 1967 Protocol.[52]

More recently, UNHCR was involved in the drafting of two Protocols that supplement the 2000 United Nations Convention against Organized Crime: the 2000 Protocol to Prevent, Suppress and Punish Trafficking in Persons, especially

---

48 Protocol 1, Annexed to the 1952 Universal Copyright Convention, 6 September 1952, 216 U.N.T.S. 132. The 1952 Universal Copyright Convention has been updated with the 1971 Universal Copyright Convention, 24 July 1971, 943 U.N.T.S. 178. Refugees are protected under Protocol 1 to this agreement.

49 UNHCR, Report of the UNHCR and Addendum, ¶ 7, U.N. Doc. A/2126 (1952). UNHCR, Report of the UNHCR, ¶ 37, U.N. Doc. A/2394 (1953).

50 Ibid., at ¶ 41.

51 Memorandum from the UNHCR, submitted to the United Nations Conference on Consular Relations, U.N. Doc. A/CONF.25/L.6 (4 March 1963) and Letter from High Commissioner Schnyder to Ambassador Baron C.H. von Platen, Permanent Representative of Sweden to the European Office of the United Nations (available in UNHCR archives and on file with author). Vienna Convention on Consular Relations, 24 April 1963, 596 U.N.T.S. 261.

52 UNHCR Memorandum from Mr P.M. Moussalli, Director of International Protection, to G.J.L. Coles, Chief, Conference and Treaties Section, concerning Report on the Elaboration of the ILO Convention concerning the Establishment of an International System for the Maintenance of Rights in Social Security (12 July 1982) and attached Memorandum from N. Cronstedt to G.J.L. Coles, Chief, Conference and Treaties Section, concerning Report on the Elaboration of the ILO Convention concerning the Establishment of an International System for the Maintenance of Rights in Social Security (25 June 1991) (both documents are available in UNHCR archives and are on file with author). 1982 Maintenance of Social Security Rights Convention International Labour Organization Convention No. 157. Available at http://www.ilo.org/ilolex/cgi-lex/convde.pl?C157 (accessed 27 October 2011).

Women and Children; and the 2000 Protocol against the Smuggling of Migrants by Land, Sea and Air.[53] UNHCR issued an inter-agency note on the Protocols, delivered an oral statement and informally provided its views to delegations in order to ensure that the Protocols do not negatively affect States' rights under the 1951 Refugee Convention.[54] As a result, both Protocols contain a savings provision which provides that nothing in the Protocols 'shall affect the other rights, obligations and responsibilities of States and individuals under international law, including the 1951 Refugee Convention and the 1967 Protocol and the principle of *non-refoulement* contained therein'.[55]

2.2.3.3 Regional instruments

UNHCR's contributions relating to the creation of international refugee law also have extended to key regional conventions concerning refugees or that affect refugees.[56] UNHCR had been carrying out this work for some time, but EXCOM

53 Protocol to Prevent, Suppress and Punish Trafficking in Persons, especially Women and Children, supplementing the United Nations Convention against Transnational Organized Crime, G.A. Res. 55/25, Annex II, U.N. Doc. A/RES/55/25 (15 November 2000) and Protocol against the Smuggling of Migrants by Land, Air and Sea, supplementing the United Nations Convention against Transnational Organized Crime, G.A. Res. 55/25, Annex III, U.N. Doc. A/RES/55/25 (15 November 2000).

54 See UNHCR, Note by the United Nations High Commissioner for Human Rights, International Organization for Migration, United Nations High Commissioner for Refugees, and the United Nations Children's Fund on the Protocols concerning Migrant Smuggling and Trafficking in Persons (21 February–3 March 2000) (on file with author) and UNHCR, UNHCR Summary Position on the Protocol against the Smuggling of Migrants by Land, Sea and Air and the Protocol to Prevent, Suppress and Punish Trafficking in Persons, Especially Women and Children, supplementing the UN Convention against Transnational Organized Crime (11 December 2000). Available at http://www.unhcr.org/refworld/docid/3ae6b3428.html (accessed 27 October 2011).

55 Protocol to Prevent, Suppress and Punish Trafficking in Persons, especially Women and Children, supplementing the United Nations Convention against Transnational Organized Crime, *supra* note 53, at art. 14 and Protocol against the Smuggling of Migrants by Land, Air and Sea, supplementing the United Nations Convention against Transnational Organized Crime, *supra* note 53, at art. 19.

56 In addition to UNHCR's contributions to regional conventions, UNHCR also has assisted with the drafting of the key non-binding refugee instruments in Central America, the Cartagena Declaration on Refugees, OAS/Ser.L/V.II.66, doc. 10, rev.1, at 190–193 (1984), and for Asia–Africa, the Principles concerning Treatment of Refugees, adopted by the Asian–African Legal Consultative Committee, The Rights of Refugees: Report of the Committee and Background Materials 207–219 (1966). UNHCR cosponsored the colloquium at which the Cartagena Declaration was drafted. See Guy Goodwin-Gill and Jane McAdam, *The Refugee in International Law* 38, fn 119 (3rd edn, 1998). As regards UNHCR's participation in the drafting of the 1966 Principles adopted by the Asian–African Legal Consultative Committee, see pages 3–4 of the Legal Bulletin annexed to UNHCR, Legal Bulletin No. 5, UNHCR/IOM/26/65; UNHCR/BOM/32/65 (15 December 1965) and Asian–African Legal Consultative Committee, The Rights of Refugees: Report of the Committee and Background Materials 3–5, 208–210 (1966). In the case of the former, UNHCR's involvement included the preparation of a working paper for the Colloquium on the Declaration and participation in the Colloquium. See Jackson, *supra* note 22, at 400, 395–396.

and the General Assembly explicitly encouraged UNHCR to become involved in the creation of regional refugee standards in 1997 at the time of the adoption of the Amsterdam Treaty in the European Union.[57] UNHCR's efforts in this area are particularly apparent from its work in Africa and Europe.[58]

In Africa, UNHCR provided substantial input into the 1969 OAU Convention Governing the Specific Aspects of Refugee Problems in Africa.[59] At the time of the drafting of this Convention, the 1951 Refugee Convention, with its time and geographic limitations, did not apply to refugees in Africa. Therefore, with the massive movement of refugees in Africa arising out of problems associated with decolonization and independence struggles, the Organization of African Unity (now the African Union) began a process, in 1964, that would eventually lead to a regional convention to cover refugees in Africa.[60]

UNHCR proposed and was then invited to participate in the process after two unsatisfactory drafts of the convention were completed, and as a result, the Deputy High Commissioner of UNHCR and two staff members from the Legal Division attended the meetings of the Council of Ministers and the Heads of State and Government as observers in October 1965.[61] Therefore, UNHCR was integrally involved in the drafting process.[62] UNHCR's involvement helped ensure that the OAU refugee convention, the 1969 Convention governing the Specific Aspects of Refugee Problems in Africa, complemented rather than conflicted with the 1951 Refugee Convention. UNHCR was successful in reaching this objective since the preamble of the 1969 OAU Refugee Convention states that the

For the latter instrument, UNHCR assisted the secretariat of the Asian–African Legal Consultative Committee with procuring relevant materials and the preparation of a background note which formed the basis for discussions. Asian–African Legal Consultative Committee, The Rights of Refugees: Report of the Committee and Background Materials 3 (1966).

57 EXCOM Conclusion 81, endorsed by the General Assembly, '[e]ncourages States and UNHCR to continue to promote, where relevant, regional initiatives for refugee protection and durable solutions, and to ensure that regional standards which are developed conform fully with universally recognized standards and respond to particular regional circumstances and protection needs'. EXCOM Conclusion 81 (XLVIII), ¶ k, 1997 endorsed by G.A. Res. 52/103, ¶ 1, U.N. Doc. A/RES/52/103 (12 December 1997).

58 UNHCR's work in this area also has extended to the Organization for American States. For example, UNHCR proposed the *non-refoulement* provision contained in the American Convention on Human Rights applicable to Member States of the Organization for American States. See Richard Plender, 'The Present State of Research Carried Out By the English-Speaking Section of the Centre for Studies and Research', in *Right of Asylum*: Hague Academy of International Law 63, 73 (1990).

59 OAU Convention Governing the Specific Aspects of Refugee Problems in Africa, 10 September 1969, 1001 U.N.T.S. 45.

60 Eduardo Arboleda, 'Refugee Definition in Africa and Latin America: The Lessons of Pragmatism', 3 *Int'l. J. Refugee L.* 185, 190–191 (1991).

61 Holborn, *supra* note 6, at 186.

62 Arboleda, *supra* note 60, at 193.

1951 Refugee Convention 'constitutes the basic and universal instrument relating to the status of refugees'.[63]

With respect to European instruments that impact on refugees' rights, UNHCR has played a significant role in the creation of such instruments from its early years up through the present. After the inception of the 1951 Refugee Convention, UNHCR contributed to the creation of European treaties on specific issues such as visa requirements and social security, which also affected refugees. For example, UNHCR undertook efforts toward the codification of a right for refugees to travel between Western European countries without a visa, in a similar manner to nationals, which resulted in the creation of the 1959 European Agreement on the Abolition of Visas for Refugees.[64] UNHCR also contributed to the formulation of protocols to several European social security agreements in order to ensure the extension of such protection to refugees.[65]

Moreover, UNHCR contributed to the drafting of the 1957 European Convention on Extradition.[66] Importantly, UNHCR advocated the inclusion of a provision to protect a refugee from being returned to his/her home country where the home country's request 'for extradition for an ordinary criminal offence has been made for the purpose of prosecuting or punishing a person on account of his race, religion, nationality or political opinion, or that person's position may be prejudiced for any of these reasons.'[67]

UNHCR also provided input into the drafting of the 1990 Dublin Convention[68] agreed to by the 12 States, which were members of the European Economic Community, the forerunner of the European Union.[69] Under the 1990 Dublin Convention, European Economic Community Member States established rules among themselves for determining which State is responsible for considering an application for asylum.

More recently, UNHCR's participation in the European context has related to harmonization of asylum policies by Member States of the European Union.

---

63   Ibid., at 9th preambular ¶. UNHCR continues to participate in the drafting of conventions in this region. For example, UNHCR recently participated in the drafting of the 2009 Convention on the Protection and Assistance of Internally Displaced Persons and the 2006 Protocol on Protection and Assistance to Internally Displaced Persons. In the case of the Convention, UNHCR was a member of the Panel of Experts that worked on the draft and for the Protocol, the Division of International Provision made contributions to the drafting process. Interview of Chaloka Beyani, London School of Economics and Political Science, 13 June 2008.

64   For a good summary of this process see Holborn, *supra* note 6, at 206–210. European Agreement on the Abolition of Visas for Refugees, 20 Apr. 1959, C.E.T.S. 31.

65   Schnyder, *supra* note 29, at 408. Holborn, *supra* note 6, at 220–222. UNHCR, Report of the UNHCR, ¶ 38–39, U.N. Doc. A/2394 (1953).

66   European Convention on Extradition, 13 December 1957, C.E.T.S. 24.

67   Holborn, *supra* note 6, at 217–218.

68   Convention Determining the State Responsible for Examining Applications for Asylum Lodged in One of the Member States of the European Communities, 15 June 1990, C.254 (known as the Dublin Convention).

69   The European Economic Community was established by the Treaty of Rome in 1957. The European Union was created pursuant to the 1992 Maastricht Treaty.

Pursuant to the 1997 Treaty of Amsterdam, the Treaty Establishing the European Community was amended to include a provision whereby Member States agreed to establish directives on certain asylum related topics within a five-year period from the date the Treaty of Amsterdam entered into force, which was 1 May 1999.[70] Directives are not treaties, yet EU Member States are obliged to implement directives, drafted by the European Commission and then amended and approved by the Council of Ministers of the European Union, through their national laws.[71]

As UNHCR was not invited by the EU Member States to participate in the formal discussions of the asylum provisions in the 1997 Treaty of Amsterdam or the various asylum directives, UNHCR used indirect channels to funnel its advice into the discussion processes. For example, with respect to the asylum provisions in the 1997 Treaty of Amsterdam, UNHCR provided its advice in writing and informally through government representatives. UNHCR has worked to influence the content of all of the directives, which thus far include directives on minimum procedural standards for granting and withdrawing refugee status,[72] minimum standards for the determination and content of refugee status and complementary protection[73] and on reception procedures and temporary protection.[74] UNHCR met with Commission staff drafting the directives, provided its comments formally to the Commission and has given advice on amendments. UNHCR also provided its comments directly to Member States, took its comments to European Parliament members to have them advocate UNHCR's positions, and submitted

---

70 The Treaty of Amsterdam Amending the Treaty on European Union, The Treaties Establishing the European Communities and Certain Related Acts, 10 November 1997, 1997 O.J. (C. 340). For the relevant consolidated text see Consolidated Version of the Treaty Establishing the European Community, Title IV, arts. 63, 67, 24 December 2002, 2002 O.J. (C.325).

71 UNHCR also has welcomed South America/Mercosur's Declaration of Rio de Janeiro of 10 November 2000, which expresses the intention of the regional trading bloc organization to harmonize refugee laws in the region. See UNHCR, Briefing Notes: UNHCR Welcomes South America/Mercosur Declaration, 17 November 2000. Available at http://www.unhcr.org/news/NEWS/3ae6b82358.html (accessed 27 October 2011). Mercusor State Members include Argentina, Bolivia, Brazil, Chile, Paraguay and Uruguay.

72 Council Directive on Minimum Standards on Procedures in Member States for Granting and Withdrawing Refugee Status, 2005/85, 2005 O.J. (L 326) 13 (EC).

73 Council Directive on Minimum Standards for the Qualification and Status of Third Country Nationals or Stateless Persons as Refugees or as Persons who Otherwise need International Protection and the Content of the Protection Granted, 2004/83, 2004 O.J. (L 304) 12 (EC).

74 Council Directive laying down Minimum Standards for the Reception of Asylum Seekers in Member States, 2003/9, 2003 O.J. (L31) 18 (EC) and Council Directive on Minimum Standards for Giving Temporary Protection in the Event of a Mass Influx of Displaced Persons and on Measures Promoting a Balance of Efforts between Member States in Receiving such Persons and Bearing the Consequences thereof, Council Directive 2001/55, 2001 O.J. (L212) 12 (EC). Also pursuant to Article 63 of the Consolidated Version of the Treaty Establishing the European Community, the Dublin Convention was replaced by Council Regulation establishing the Criteria and Mechanisms for Determining the Member State Responsible for Examining an Asylum Application lodged in one of the Member States by a Third Country National (EC) No. 343/2003 of 18 February 2003, 2003 O.J.

its views on the general approach taken on asylum to the EU Council of Ministers from time to time. Thus, while UNHCR would have preferred to be included in the formal process, since it was not, it had to resort to influencing a wide variety of actors in the EU context who could impact on the drafting process. UNHCR did derive a number of benefits from its advocacy work; its positions became better known to a wider audience and although these positions were not always adopted, UNHCR established contacts in the EU context and demonstrated its expertise and therefore relevance for further discussions of refugee and asylum matters.

2.3 UNHCR's mandate concerning the effectiveness of refugee law

2.3.1 Effectiveness

UNHCR's international protection function concerns not only the development of conventions for the protection of refugees, discussed earlier, but also actions to ensure that States provide the necessary protection to refugees, in practice, in the absence of protection from their countries of origin. The assurance of such legal protection through refugee law is termed 'effectiveness' herein. The term 'effectiveness' has been utilized consciously, rather than the more traditional term 'compliance' because it is more appropriate to this study. The term compliance, which means 'a state of conformity or identity between an actor's behaviour and a specified rule',[75] is too limited in its scope and too formalistic to adequately capture the comprehensiveness of UNHCR's work and the nature of States' actions.

The traditional approach to compliance involves an evaluation as to whether a State's actions conform to standards contained in an agreement. Thus, with respect to refugee law, the State's conduct would be contrasted primarily with the provisions in the 1951 Refugee Convention. However, the 1951 Refugee Convention contains significant gaps and ambiguities, discussed in detail in Chapter 4, which render the 1951 Refugee Convention's applicable legal standards insufficient in ensuring protection. For example, a State that does not have a refugee status determination procedure or detains asylum seekers who lack legal documents could be considered to be in technical compliance with the standards in the 1951 Refugee Convention, since the 1951 Refugee Convention does not contain any explicit provisions on the procedures that States must adopt and article 31 concerning refugees unlawfully in the country of refuge does not mention detention. Yet, the State would not necessarily be providing sufficient legal protection to the person.

---

75 Kal Raustiala and Anne-Marie Slaughter, *International Law, International Relations and Compliance*, in *Handbook of International Relations* 538, 539 (Walter Carlsnaes, Thomas Risse and Beth A. Simmons, eds, 2002).

The focus on compliance with the 1951 Refugee Convention also overlooks the significance of soft law standards, such as UNHCR doctrinal positions and EXCOM conclusions, and other types of action that are discussed in Chapters 5 and 6. Moreover, since States may comply with a treaty's provisions, even where they have not implemented the provisions in national law, the term is too narrow for the purpose of this study.

The term effectiveness has been most frequently used in the environmental area, where the objective is not to eliminate pollution, as laudable as that might be even if it is not practical at this time, but instead to change States' behaviour with respect to activities that pollute. Scholars use the term in connection with changes in behaviour by States that are caused by and further the goals of the agreement.[76] This book employs the term 'effectiveness' in a manner similar to that used in connection with environmental law. Effectiveness, as used herein, is considered to be the capacity to produce an effect or result. In the case of refugees, the effect or result to be produced is the refugees' enjoyment of their 'fundamental rights and freedoms without discrimination' as stated in the preamble to the 1951 Refugee Convention.[77] While their legal protection starts with the provisions of the 1951 Refugee Convention, it also includes not only other agreements, but also soft law, and a general humanitarian approach by States to refugees. Thus, the effectiveness of refugee law is not just the technical adherence by States to applicable treaty standards, but a more global consideration of whether the protection of refugees is the product of States' actions.

As refugee law forms the basis for UNHCR's interaction with States to ensure protection, refugee law treaties serve as the departure point for UNHCR's work to ensure the effectiveness of refugee law. Then the concept of the effectiveness of refugee law can be divided into three sub-areas that facilitate the evaluation of UNHCR's responsibilities and work: ratification/accession, implementation and application. These categories represent States' commitment to the international obligations (ratification), that such international law obligations are incorporated into national law (implementation), and that States apply the standards in practice (application). Further, these three areas provide a structure for the evaluation of UNHCR's actions relating to the effectiveness of international refugee law. Specifically, UNHCR's mandated responsibilities as well as the work that UNHCR performed in connection with these responsibilities, prior to the refugee crisis in the 1980s, are discussed later.

---

76   David G. Victor, Kal Raustiala and Eugene B. Skolnikoff (eds), *Introduction and Overview*, in *The Implementation and Effectiveness of International Environmental Commitments: Theory and Practice* 8 (1998).

77   1951 Refugee Convention, *supra* note 7, at 1st preambular ¶.

2.3.2 *Ratification of and accession to treaties*

The first step in ensuring the effectiveness of international refugee law is to have States bound by the treaties that provide for the international protection of refugees.[78] Pursuant to its statutory mandate, UNHCR shall provide for the protection of refugees by '[p]romoting the ...ratification of international conventions for the protection of refugees'.[79] This responsibility is derived from the work of UNHCR's predecessors as well as the mandate of the High Commissioner of the League of Nations for Refugees.[80] The General Assembly and EXCOM have adopted resolutions and conclusions, respectively, which reiterate the importance of UNHCR's responsibility, most often specifically mentioning States' accession to the 1951 Refugee Convention and the 1967 Protocol,[81] but do not provide any specifics as to the content of this responsibility.

Yet, the meaning of UNHCR's responsibility to promote the ratification of conventions is much more evident than for UNHCR's responsibility of 'promoting the *conclusion* ... of international conventions'.[82] Since treaty ratification is carried out by States, UNHCR is to encourage States to ratify relevant treaties.[83] In the General Assembly resolution to which UNHCR's Statute was annexed, the General Assembly called on governments to become parties to international conventions for the protection of refugees, as part of their co-operation with UNHCR.[84]

---

78 Some people believe that 'there still may exist expectations which a State, under the principle of good faith and under consideration of international comity, has to fulfil before it decides to make use of its sovereign right not to ratify.' See Hanna Bokor-Szego, *The Role of the United Nations in International Legislation* 158 (Dr Sándo Simon trans., 1978) (citing the UNITAR Study Series No. 2 at 4).

79 UNHCR Statute, *supra* note 3, ¶ 8(a).

80 See section 1.3.1.1. The mandate of the High Commissioner of the League of Nations for Refugees is contained in the Report of the Council Committee Appointed to Draw Up a Plan for International Assistance to Refugees, 19 O.J.L.N. 365–366 (1938).

81 For example, see G.A. Res. 56/137, ¶ 3, U.N. Doc. A/RES/56/137 (19 December 2001); G.A. Res. 55/74, ¶ 4 U.N. Doc. A/RES/55/74 (4 December 2000); and G.A. Res. 53/125, ¶ 3, U.N. Doc. A/RES/53/125 (9 December 1998), which expressly reiterate UNHCR's responsibility in this area. Other General Assembly resolutions have endorsed the EXCOM conclusion that mentions such responsibility. For example, see G.A. Res. 52/103, ¶ 1, U.N. Doc. A/RES/52/103 (12 December 1997), which endorses EXCOM Conclusion 81(XLVIII), ¶ m, 1997. With respect to EXCOM Conclusions see EXCOM Conclusion 90 (LII), ¶ b, 2001 and EXCOM Conclusion 87 (L), ¶e, 1999.

82 See section 2.2.1. Emphasis added.

83 This approach is essentially an interpretation 'in good faith in accordance with the ordinary meaning to be given to the terms of the treaty in their context and in the light of its object and purpose' as provided in Article 31 of the Vienna Convention on the Law of Treaties. Vienna Convention on the Law of Treaties, 22 May 1969, 1155 U.N.T.S. 331. Although the 1951 Refugee Convention was drafted prior to the 1969 Vienna Convention, since the provisions on interpretation in the Vienna Convention are considered to be reflective of customary international law, they can be applied to the 1951 Refugee Convention.

84 G.A. Resolution 428(V), ¶ 2(a) (14 December 1950).

2.3.3 Implementation of treaties in national law

Once a State has ratified or acceded to a convention providing protection to refugees, the convention needs to become part of the State's domestic law.[85] If the obligations undertaken by State signatories of the 1951 Refugee Convention/1967 Protocol are not part of national law, then the protection of refugees' rights cannot be assured within the State. UNHCR, therefore, encourages implementation in order to ensure the protection of refugees and to facilitate its supervisory work. Some countries, such as France and many African countries, have a national rule that provides for the automatic incorporation of a treaty's provisions into national law without the adoption of a national statute, whereas other countries must adopt either specific, such as in the case of the UK and Israel, or general, as in Italy and Germany, national legislation for the treaty's provisions to become effective in national law.[86]

Paragraph 8(a) of UNHCR's Statute, which contains the essential elements of UNHCR's duties related to international refugee law, does not establish any responsibility for UNHCR related to States' implementation of conventions for the protection of refugees.[87] The drafters considered two provisions proposed by the Secretary-General that would have assigned UNHCR an active role in this area. One suggestion was for UNHCR to consult with States in order to further the implementation of their international law obligations.[88] Another draft provision prescribed a reporting obligation by UNHCR concerning States' implementation of rules for the protection of refugees, which implicitly, according to the Secretary-General, would entail obtaining such information from governments.[89]

---

85 As stated by Heinrich Triepel and translated by Antonio Cassese: 'To fulfil its task, international law has to turn continuously to domestic law. Without the latter it is in many respects utterly impotent ... similarly a single rule of international law brings about a number of rules of domestic law, all pursuing the same end: to implement international law within the framework of States'. Antonio Cassese, *Modern Constitutions and International Law,* 192 Recueil des Cours, Hague Academy of International Law 335, 342 (1985).

86 Antonio Cassese, *International Law* 226 (2nd edn, 2005).

87 See section 1.3.1.

88 Specifically, the Secretary-General proposed that UNHCR should 'consult with governments with a view to facilitating the application of conventions'. Despite his use of the word 'application', he was referring to implementation since he noted that with this responsibility, '[t]he international service would be empowered to consult with, and make suggestions to, governments regarding the legislative and administrative measures which might appear necessary to secure the implementation of the provisions of international conventions in force at any one time.' Report of the Secretary-General, 35, U.N. Doc. A/C.3/527 and Corr.1 (26 October 1949) (hereinafter Report of the Secretary-General).

89 The Secretary-General's proposal provided that UNHCR would 'report upon the carrying out of conventions and agreements in force and to further their implementation.' The Secretary-General noted that '[t]his function would involve obtaining information on legislative and administrative measures taken with a view to carrying out the conventions and agreements'. Report of the Secretary General, ibid., at 36.

In the end, the drafters of UNHCR's Statute set aside the Secretary-General's first proposal and adopted a version of his second. However, the ideas of a reporting obligation by UNHCR and its solicitation of information from governments on their implementation of standards for the protection of refugees were placed in two different provisions. With respect to the latter, UNHCR's Statute provides that UNHCR has the responsibility to '[o]btain[] from Governments information concerning ... the laws and regulations concerning' refugees.[90] UNHCR's reporting obligation is contained in a separate provision that provides that the 'High Commissioner shall report annually to the General Assembly through the Economic and Social Council',[91] but does not elaborate at all on the content of such reports. The duty to implement refugee law treaty obligations clearly fell on the States themselves, as expressed in the General Assembly resolution to which the Statute of the Office of UNHCR was annexed; States are to 'tak[e] the necessary steps of implementation' of conventions relating to refugees and provide the High Commissioner with information on 'laws and regulations concerning [refugees]' as part of their co-operation with UNHCR.[92]

The extent to which implementation was viewed at the time as within the sole purview of States, and not an obligation that needed to be articulated, is illustrated by the drafting history of the 1951 Refugee Convention. A proposed article providing an obligation for States to 'take all the legislative or other measures necessary under the rules of their constitution for the application of the present Convention' was considered but rejected during the drafting process.[93] The British representative believed that the article should be deleted since he said it was 'an innovation in international treaties' and that '[i]t was further presupposed that such measures would be taken at the discretion of the State within a reasonable time' and that 'the article was superfluous, since the Convention laid down provisions which, in the case of most countries, were already covered by domestic law'.[94]

The final wording of the 1951 Refugee Convention concerning States' obligations to provide information on their implementation of the Convention creates two separate obligations for States. First, States are to provide UNHCR 'in the appropriate form with information and statistical data requested concerning: ...(b) the implementation of [the 1951 Refugee Convention], and (c) laws, regulations and decrees which are, or may hereafter be, in force relating to refugees'[95] so that UNHCR may 'make reports to the competent organs of the United Nations'.[96] This provision implies that UNHCR must request the information

90 UNHCR Statute, *supra* note 3, at ¶ 8(f).
91 Ibid., at ¶ 11.
92 G.A. Res. 428(V), ¶ 2(a), (h) (14 December 1950).
93 Atle Grahl-Madsen, *Commentary on the Refugee Convention 1951: Articles 2–11, 12–37*, at 256 (UNHCR, ed., 1997).
94 Ibid.
95 1951 Refugee Convention, *supra* note 7, at art. 35(2)(b) and (c),
96 Ibid.

from States; States are not obligated to provide such information automatically to UNHCR. States have a second reporting obligation under the 1951 Refugee Convention; they must provide the Secretary-General, without his/her making a request, with 'the laws and regulations which they may adopt to ensure the application' of the 1951 Refugee Convention.[97] Thus, while the 1951 Refugee Convention does not obligate States to implement the provisions of the agreement, it does provide reporting measures so that implementation of the Convention may be monitored by UNHCR.

2.3.4 *Application*

States' actual application of their international refugee law obligations is the final step in ensuring that international refugee law becomes effective and that the necessary protection is provided to refugees. At the time of the creation of UNHCR, enforcement was not a significant concern of the United Nations; as Oscar Schachter has stated: '[t]he busy world of law-making and law-applying carried on pretty much without serious consideration of means of ensuring compliance. Some international lawyers dismissively referred to enforcement as a political matter outside the law.'[98] Consequently, the drafters of UNHCR's Statute did not provide any sort of structured system to sanction non-compliance.[99] However, they did provide UNHCR with a supervisory responsibility over international conventions for the protection of refugees.

Specifically, as part of its international protection function, UNHCR is to supervise the application 'of international conventions for the protection of refugees'.[100] However, as with the term 'promotion', the meaning of 'supervision' is nowhere defined in UNHCR's Statute and in ordinary usage, has a very general meaning.[101] Therefore, the phrase does not elucidate either the scope or the content of UNHCR's work in this area.

UNHCR has not encouraged either EXCOM or the General Assembly to provide concrete guidance on the scope and precise content of its supervisory work. However, as with UNHCR's 'international protection' function and its responsibility to 'promote[] the conclusion... of international conventions', the lack of concrete guidance on the content of UNHCR's supervisory responsibility allowed

---

97 Ibid., *at art* 36.
98 Oscar Schachter, *The UN Legal Order: An Overview*, in *United Nations Legal Order* 1, 15 (Oscar Schachter and Christopher Joyner, eds, 1995).
99 The critique of the international legal system's lack of enforcement mechanisms is derived from a comparison with domestic legal systems. See for example, Antonio Cassese, who states: '[i]n domestic legal orders enforcement strictly denotes all those measures and procedures, mostly taken by public authorities, calculated to impel compliance, by forcible and other coercive means, with the law.' Cassese, *supra* note 85, at 296.
100 UNHCR Statute, *supra* note 3, ¶ 8(a).
101 To 'supervise' means '[g]eneral management, direction, or control; oversight, superintendence.' XVII *The Oxford English Dictionary* 245 (2nd edn, 1989).

UNHCR to have a great deal of flexibility in determining the parameters and content of the work it could carry out to fulfil the responsibility.

EXCOM has given UNHCR only minimal guidance related to its supervisory responsibility. Specifically, EXCOM noted the 'need for constant advice by UNHCR on the practical application' of the 1951 Refugee Convention and the 1967 Protocol,[102] which naturally flows from UNHCR's responsibility to supervise these agreements. EXCOM also requested UNHCR to ensure 'adequate levels of ... supervision of programmes for prevention and protection from sexual abuse and exploitation, including through physical presence'.[103] This latter reference to UNHCR's supervisory work concerns UNHCR's monitoring work of the physical protection needs of women refugees and asylum seekers in an operational setting.

2.4 UNHCR'S work concerning the effectiveness of refugee law

The work that UNHCR performs in fulfilling its statutory responsibilities related to the effectiveness of international refugee law is not as easily describable as with its contributions to the development of international refugee law, namely the promotion of the conclusion and amendments of international conventions for the protection of refugees. UNHCR's work related to the creation of new agreements and amendments to others can be verified through written documents and most often leads to a concrete result, either a new treaty or provisions protecting the rights of refugees. In the area of effectiveness, in contrast, UNHCR's activities are ongoing, can be formally or informally undertaken, and do not always produce a clear result.

Despite the fluidity between the actions and the consequences of UNHCR's work in the area of effectiveness, a brief overview is provided here of the activities UNHCR has performed concerning State ratification of international conventions for the protection of refugees and State implementation and application of the provisions of such conventions.

2.4.1 Work related to ratifications and accessions

UNHCR has striven, since its creation, to ensure the ratification of, and accession to, the fundamental convention for refugee protection, the 1951 Refugee Convention, and accessions to its 1967 Protocol, which removed the geographic

---

102 See EXCOM Conclusion 19 (XXXI), ¶ d, 1980.
103 See EXCOM Conclusion 98 (LIV), ¶ b(iii), 2003. Also see ¶ a(iv) of the same conclusion, which provides that the 'supervision', among other aspects should be 'designed and implemented in a manner that reduces the risk of sexual abuse and exploitation'. EXCOM Conclusion 98 (LIV), ¶ a(iv), 2003.

and temporal limitations of the Convention.[104] Even in its first annual report to the General Assembly in 1951, UNHCR noted and welcomed the ratification of the 1951 Refugee Convention by States and expressed the hope that other States would do the same.[105]

UNHCR staff members in UNHCR headquarters in Geneva, and in branch offices throughout the world, have undertaken efforts to encourage States to ratify or accede to the 1951 Refugee Convention and the 1967 Protocol. UNHCR also has been instrumental in the creation of General Assembly resolutions and EXCOM conclusions that acknowledge ratifications and accessions and encourage other States to ratify and accede to the 1951 Refugee Convention and the 1967 Protocol[106] as well as EXCOM conclusions that request States to remove reservations to these instruments.[107]

Yet, UNHCR's work in this area has not been limited to the 1951 Refugee Convention and the 1967 Protocol. UNHCR has encouraged States to ratify and accede to other conventions for the protection of refugees, many of which were drafted with UNHCR's input. These include the 1956 Convention on the Recovery Abroad of Maintenance Obligations,[108] the 1957 Agreement Relating to Refugee Seamen, the 1959 European Agreement on the Abolition of Visas for Refugees, the 1954 Convention Relating to the Status of Stateless Persons and the 1961 Convention on the Reduction of Statelessness.[109] Therefore, as with UNHCR's responsibility to promote the conclusion of such agreements, as discussed in section 2.2.3, UNHCR interpreted paragraph 8(a) in its Statute as authorizing its promotion of States' ratification of not just international refugee law agreements, but also other agreements without obtaining clarification from the General Assembly or EXCOM.

---

104 1951 Refugee Convention, *supra* note 7. 1967 Protocol, *supra* note 37.

105 UNHCR, *Report of the UNHCR,* ¶ 42, 44, UN. Doc. A/2011(1951).

106 For example, the General Assembly has adopted resolutions regularly requesting States to accede to the 1951 Convention and the 1967 Protocol. See for a recent General Assembly resolution, G.A. Res. 65/194, ¶ 4, U.N. Doc. A/RES/65/194 (21 December 2010). EXCOM regularly acknowledges accessions to the 1951 Refugee Convention and the 1967 Protocol and calls on other States to do likewise. See for example, EXCOM Conclusion 102 (LVI), ¶ c, 2005 and EXCOM Conclusion 99 (LV), ¶ c, 2004.

107 EXCOM Conclusion 108 (LIX), 3rd preambular ¶, 2008; EXCOM Conclusion 102 (LVI), ¶ c, 2005; EXCOM Conclusion 99 (LV), ¶ c, 2004; EXCOM Conclusion 79 (XLVII), ¶ e, 1996.

108 Holborn, *supra* note 6, at 226.

109 For example, see UNHCR, Note on International Protection, ¶ 11, 14, U.N. Doc. A/AC.96/377 (6 September 1967). In addition, when the Convention on the Declaration of the Death of Missing Persons (1950) entered into force in 1952, High Commissioner Goedhart and the Director-General of the IRO sent a letter 'to governments expressing the hope that more of them would accede to the Convention'. Letter from UNHCR and the Office of the Director-General of the International Refugee Organization (26 Apr. 1951) (UNHCR archives and on file with author).

2.4.2 Work related to implementation

UNHCR has carried out its statutory responsibility to obtain information from governments about their laws and regulations on refugees[110] by requesting the actual legislation and administrative regulations adopted by States, both informally and formally. One of the formal means was a questionnaire sent by UNHCR to all signatory States of the 1951 Refugee Convention and the 1967 Protocol. UNHCR sent questionnaires in both 1970 and 1990. However, only a limited number of States responded to them.[111] In the case of the 1970 questionnaire, which was sent to 63 States, UNHCR had received only 38 replies as of 1974[112] and only 27 States out of nearly 100 States had responded by 1992 to the 1990 questionnaire.[113] Thus, States demonstrated that they did not consider completion of the questionnaires as either significantly important for UNHCR or obligatory and thus few States completed them. This response by States to UNHCR's request implicitly indicated States' unwillingness to have UNHCR integrally involved in assuring States' implementation of refugee law agreements.

In spite of the general view of States, at the time of the drafting of the 1951 Refugee Convention, that the implementation of treaties was a matter to be left to the responsibility of States, UNHCR did carry out activities to encourage States to implement their refugee law obligations. For example, as UNHCR noted in its report to the General Assembly in 1958:

> Largely owing to the close cooperation which has developed between UNHCR Branch offices and the governmental authorities, new legal provisions have been adopted for the benefit of refugees, and measures have continued to be taken for the implementation of important articles of the 1951 Convention.[114]

In UNHCR's 1979 Annual Report to the General Assembly, UNHCR explicitly noted that it was 'encouraging the adoption by States of appropriate legislative and/or administrative measures to ensure that the provisions of these international instruments are effectively implemented.'[115] UNHCR also instigated the adoption by EXCOM, in one of its first conclusions, of a recommendation that UNHCR

---

110 UNHCR Statute, *supra* note 3, ¶ 8(f).
111 The second part of the 1990 questionnaire also treats States' application of international refugee law standards in national law systems. UNHCR, Information Note on Implementation of the 1951 Convention and the 1967 Protocol Relating to the Status of Refugees, UNHCR Doc. EC/SCP/66 (22 July 1991).
112 UNHCR, Note on International Protection Addendum 2: Implementation of the 1951 Convention and 1967 Protocol on the Status of Refugees – Preliminary Report, ¶ 4, U.N. Doc. A/AC.96/508/Add.2 (26 September 1974).
113 UNHCR, Report of the UNHCR, ¶ 13, U.N. Doc. A/47/12 (1992).
114 See for example, UNHCR, Report of the UNHCR, ¶ 11, U.N. Doc. A/3828/Rev.1 (1958).
115 UNHR, Report of the UNHCR, ¶ 12, U.N. Doc. A/34/12 (1979).

'continue to follow up on the ... implementation of the 1951 Refugee Convention and 1967 Protocol'.[116]

Thus, the close relationship between UNHCR and governmental authorities meant that UNHCR could encourage States' implementation of the 1951 Refugee Convention and the 1967 Protocol, despite the lack of an explicit statutory responsibility concerning promotion of such implementation and the fact that UNHCR's responsibility was limited to obtaining information from governments on laws and regulations concerning refugees. The authority for UNHCR to promote States' implementation, as will be seen in Chapter 6, can be derived from its implied powers.

2.4.3 *Work related to application*

UNHCR's supervisory work, which concerns States' application of their international law obligations, has always permeated the organization's international protection role. UNHCR monitors how States treat refugees, what policies they adopt, and the problems that refugees encounter within countries, whether related to their legal status, or to their basic rights, such as shelter, food, and health. UNHCR then must analyze this information to determine whether it is consistent with international law standards. In some cases, it is evident when a violation has occurred; in other cases, UNHCR must conduct a more detailed investigation of the situation and carefully consider the applicable legal standards.

Where there is a violation, then UNHCR must provide some feedback to the concerned State to change its conduct. There is a spectrum of responses that UNHCR can undertake ranging in formality and import. The local office can verbally advise the concerned officials, a *note verbale* can be sent as a formal communication, and/or meetings can be held among UNHCR officers, from local or regional offices or UNHCR headquarters in Geneva, with various levels of government officials. For the most important issues, the matter can be communicated to the UN General Assembly, through UNHCR's Note on International Protection or its Annual Protection Report.

UNHCR's participation in national asylum determination procedures also can be considered as part of UNHCR's supervisory responsibility.[117] UNHCR's role has varied depending on the experience, need, and structure of the State's asylum procedures. For example, in Belgium, UNHCR was the sole determination authority until the responsibility was transferred to the Belgian authorities. Even after the transfer, UNHCR provided its views on issues, on request as well

---

116 EXCOM Conclusion 2 (XXVII), ¶ c, 1976. Also see EXCOM Conclusion 41 (XXXVII), ¶ g, 1986. Moreover, UNHCR was requested by EXCOM to prepare a detailed report on implementation of the 1951 Refugee Convention and the 1967 Protocol for consideration by EXCOM's Sub-Committee of the Whole on International Protection of Refugees. See EXCOM Conclusion 57 (XL), ¶ d, 1989.

117 In addition, UNHCR, like its predecessor, the International Refugee Organization, solely determines whether an individual qualifies as a refugee under its statutory mandate.

as when it deemed it necessary. UNHCR's activities range from the determination of refugee status, in nearly 60 countries,[118] such as in Morocco and Turkey, and involvement of a UNHCR staff member in the government's status determination bodies, to the provision of information and views to the government status determination bodies.

2.5 Conclusion

UNHCR's international law role can be viewed as comprising two distinct areas of responsibility: first, responsibilities related to the development of international refugee law and, second, responsibilities related to ensuring the effectiveness of international refugee law. While States provided UNHCR with duties in each of these two areas, UNHCR's determination of the actual work that it performs in order to fulfil these responsibilities assists in clarifying the parameters and content of UNHCR's role related to international refugee law.

In the area of the development of a refugee law framework, States granted UNHCR the authority, under its Statute, to promote the conclusion of international conventions for the protection of refugees and propose amendments thereto. UNHCR utilized the ambiguity in its Statute related to States' conclusion of 'international conventions for the protection of refugees' to extend the legal framework beyond international refugee law treaties to other conventions that apply to refugees as well as regional refugee instruments. UNHCR did so without obtaining prior formal clarification or authorization from the General Assembly or guidance from EXCOM. This practice is consistent with that of UNHCR's predecessors; these organizations also promoted agreements even in the absence of an explicit mandate to do so, as seen in Chapter 1.

UNHCR exercised a great deal of discretion in determining the content of its responsibilities. Consequently, UNHCR devised a wide-ranging practice of specific means to carry out its work related to the development of international refugee law. These included: identification of the issue that requires a treaty among States, proposing a meeting to discuss the issue, making substantive proposals for the content of the provisions of the treaty, commenting on proposed provisions, participating in the negotiations of the draft agreement, informally and formally communicating its views to States and bodies working on draft agreements, and actually drafting provisions for such agreements.

Thus, UNHCR played a crucial role in the development of early international agreements in the refugee law framework. However, States appeared to be less willing to permit UNHCR to co-ordinate and direct their formulation of standards in regional fora. In both the African and European contexts, UNHCR was not presumed to be a direct participant in the negotiations among States. Thus, States appeared to desire to maintain their control over the formulation of

---

118 In 2010, UNHCR conducted refugee status determination under its mandate in 57 countries. UNHCR, Note on International Protection, ¶ 22, U.N. Doc. A/AC.96/1098 (28 June 2011).

regional instruments. UNHCR managed to became a full participant in the African process. However, the organization was unable to obtain the same status at the European level and was limited to providing its opinions informally during the European harmonization of asylum standards process. The constrained role of UNHCR at the European level meant that the agency had only indirect involvement in, and diminished influence on, the discussions and drafting process, thereby leaving States greater latitude to adopt provisions that restricted the rights granted to asylum seekers and refugees.

In addition, as the drafters of UNHCR's Statute did not wish to leave the assurance of the protection of refugees to the unfettered discretion of States, they provided UNHCR with a crucial role in ensuring the effectiveness of international refugee law, traditionally a domestic domain in which State sovereignty predominates. The term 'effectiveness' is employed in this book to refer to changes in States' behaviour that is caused by international refugee law and further the goal of such laws, the refugees' enjoyment of their fundamental rights and freedoms without discrimination. This term is considered to be more appropriate to a focus on refugees themselves, rather than the term 'compliance', which is more frequently utilized by legal scholars. The concept of the effectiveness of refugee law is considered under three sub-headings: ratification, implementation and application.

UNHCR was assigned the responsibility of promoting States' ratification of international conventions for the protection of refugees and of supervising States' application of such conventions, but was not given any specific responsibility concerning the promotion of States' implementation of these same conventions. UNHCR's mandate in the area of implementation was limited to obtaining information from governments on their laws and regulations relating to refugees. Nevertheless, UNHCR established the precedent of encouraging States to implement the provisions of the 1951 Refugee Convention and the 1967 Protocol. In doing so, UNHCR went beyond the express terms of its mandate to supplement its responsibilities.

UNHCR's work related to ratifications has primarily focused on encouraging the ratification and accession to the 1951 Refugee Convention and accession to the 1967 Protocol. However, UNHCR also encouraged the ratification and accession to other instruments for the protection of refugees within the context of an ambiguous authorization under its Statute and without express authorization from the General Assembly or EXCOM.

UNHCR's supervisory responsibilities, with respect to States' application of their international refugee law obligations, were not given specific content by the drafters of its Statute and UNHCR did not attempt to have the parameters of these responsibilities drawn by the General Assembly and EXCOM. Thus, UNHCR exercised its own discretion to determine how to carry out such supervision. Activities employed by UNHCR ranged from monitoring and gathering information on States' policies, legislation, and actions to raising concerns about inconsistencies with international refugee law informally and through more formal channels, such as the General Assembly. In particular, UNHCR's approach was focused on the 1951 Refugee Convention and on ensuring that once its provisions were given legal force in a State's national laws, the State took actions to comply with its provisions. Compliance by a State with the standards of the 1951 Refugee Convention generally meant that refugee law was effective and that refugees were able to exercise their fundamental rights and freedoms.

UNHCR's traditional activities related to the effectiveness of international refugee law can be characterized as of two types. UNHCR's work to ensure that States ratified/acceded to international conventions for the protection of refugees and implemented the standards from such international agreements into national law was of a promotional nature. UNHCR encouraged States to become parties to the treaties for the protection of refugees so that the provisions of such treaties were binding on States and also encouraged States to incorporate the international treaty law standards into domestic legislation in order to make them binding on the State at the national level. In the area of application of standards to asylum seekers and refugees, UNHCR's work was primarily advisory. Without any enforcement mechanism, UNHCR's efforts to have States apply and respect the provisions of treaties for the protection of refugees rested on UNHCR's persuasive abilities vis-à-vis States. Thus, UNHCR's work related to refugee law was oriented toward influencing States' actions.

In sum, in carrying out activities related to the development and effectiveness of international refugee law, UNHCR established a practice that was responsive to the practical situations it faced in dealing with refugee problems and the reactions by States to those problems. UNHCR's interpretation of the general wording of its statutory responsibilities and its proactive approach to implementation of the 1951 Convention and the 1967 Protocol were not of a radical nature, but rather, more of a gradual adaptation to circumstances in order to more assuredly fulfil its international protection role. In addition, UNHCR's work related to refugee law can be described as a normative one, since its primary focus was on treaties, in particular, the 1951 Refugee Convention. Despite UNHCR's role, States remained the primary actors in the creation of legal instruments for the protection of refugees and in taking measures to ensure the effectiveness of refugee law.

3 Flexibility in UNHCR's international law role

3.1 Introduction

UNHCR's responsibilities and work have undergone significant changes since its creation in 1950. These changes have permitted the organization to evolve within the context of the shifting political dynamics among States and as new refugee flows have emerged. Thus, the organization, which has been in existence for more than 60 years, has been able to adapt and remain relevant for over half a century. Such longevity is in marked contrast to UNHCR's seven predecessor organizations, which collectively were in existence for nearly 30 years, between 1921 and 1950, so for less than half of UNHCR's present tenure.[1] The enduring nature of UNHCR can be attributed to both the political interest of States in shifting the responsibility and burden for refugees to an international organization as well as the shared benefits that States garner from a centralized body to address such problems. The question then becomes, whether States have been the sole agents to facilitate the evolution in UNHCR's responsibilities and work or whether UNHCR also has played a role in such facilitation.

3.2 Statutory means for UNHCR's role to evolve

The drafters of UNHCR's Statute presciently provided UNHCR with several means for its role, including its responsibilities related to international refugee law, to evolve. The first is for the General Assembly to supplement UNHCR's statutory responsibilities by the adoption of a resolution authorizing a new area of work. Specifically, paragraph 9 of UNHCR's Statute states that '[t]he High Commissioner shall engage in such additional activities … as the General Assembly

---

1 These seven organizations, discussed in chapter 1, are the High Commissioner for Russian Refugees, the Nansen International Office for Refugees, the Office of the High Commissioner for Refugees coming from Germany, the High Commissioner of the League of Nations for Refugees, the Intergovernmental Committee for Refugees, the United Nations Relief and Rehabilitation Administration, and the International Refugee Organization. The United Nations Relief and Works Agency is not considered to be a direct predecessor of UNHCR as it was mandated to deal specifically with Palestinian refugees and is still in operation.

may determine'.[2] In doing so, the Statute emphasizes a right to modify UNHCR's mandate that the General Assembly legally has even in the absence of an express statutory provision.[3]

The General Assembly has been quite active in extending UNHCR's mandate both *ratione personae* and *rationae materiae*. It has directed UNHCR to protect and assist certain categories of persons, other than refugees, as defined in the 1951 Refugee Convention, including: (i.) persons fleeing situations of conflict,[4] (ii.) returnees, that is, refugees who have returned to their country of origin,[5] (iii.) persons who have fled to another location within their country as a result of a fear of persecution or situations of conflict, termed 'internally displaced persons', [6] and (iv.) stateless persons.[7] The General Assembly also has added substantial new responsibilities to UNHCR's mandate, including the provision of assistance to refugees and others of concern to UNHCR, the agency's involvement in development oriented assistance, and early warning activities related to new massive flows of refugees and displaced people.[8]

The General Assembly's provision of policy guidance to UNHCR is a second means, furnished by the drafters of UNHCR's Statute, to facilitate the evolution

---

2 See paragraph 9 of the Statute of the Office of the United Nations High Commissioner for Refugees, contained in the Annex to UN General Assembly Resolution 428(V) of 14 Dec. 1950. G.A. Res. 428(V) (14 Dec. 1950) [hereinafter 'UNHCR Statute'].

3 As noted in footnote 56 of chapter 1, the General Assembly has the authority under articles 7 and 22 of the UN Charter to create subsidiary organs, and thus, UNHCR. Therefore, the General Assembly can modify UNHCR's statutory mandate.

4 See, for example, the 1994 General Assembly resolution that calls on States 'to assist and support the High Commissioner's efforts to continue to provide international protection and assistance ... to persons who have been forced to flee or to remain outside their countries of origin as a result of danger to their life or freedom owing to situations of conflict'. G.A. Res. 49/169, ¶ 6, U.N. Doc. A/RES/ 49/169 (23 December 1994).

5 The General Assembly has called on UNHCR to undertake action within the country of origin relating to returnees. A 1994 General Assembly resolution 'calls upon the High Commissioner, in cooperation with States concerned, to promote, facilitate and coordinate the voluntary repatriation of refugees, including the monitoring of their safety and well-being on return'. Ibid., at ¶ 9.

6 See for example, G.A. Res. 47/105, ¶ 14, U.N. Doc. A/RES/ 47/105 (16 December 1992) which welcomes 'efforts by the High Commissioner, on the basis of specific requests from the Secretary-General or the competent principal organs of the United Nations and with the consent of the concerned State, to undertake activities in favour of internally displaced persons'. Also see G.A. Res. 48/116 , ¶ 12, U.N. Doc. A/RES/48/116 (20 December 1993) which '[r]eaffirms its support for the High Commissioner's efforts ... to provide humanitarian assistance and protection to persons displaced within their own country'.

7 See for example, G.A. Res. 3274 (XXIX), ¶ 1 (10 December 1974).

8 UNHCR's Statute provides for it to administer funds that it receives for assistance to refugees and to distribute them to the 'public agencies which [it] deems best qualified to administer such assistance.' UNHCR Statute, *supra* note 2, ¶ 10. However, UNHCR is now authorized to provide assistance to refugees and other categories of persons. See for example, G.A. Res. 39/139, ¶ 7, U.N. Doc. A/RES/ 39/139 (14 December 1984). With respect to UNHCR's role related to development-oriented assistance, see G.A. Res. 39/140, ¶ 7, U.N. Doc. A/RES/ 39/140 (14 December 1984) and with respect to early warning see for example, G.A. Res. 50/182, ¶ 9, U.N. Doc. A/RES/50/182 (22 December 1995).

of UNHCR's role. Pursuant to paragraph 3 of UNHCR's Statute, '[t]he High Commissioner shall follow policy directives given him by the General Assembly'.[9] Such policy directives are legally binding on UNHCR. Thus, the General Assembly has requested UNHCR to take special steps to ensure the protection of certain groups of refugees, such as refugee children, women, and elderly refugees[10] and encouraged UNHCR to improve international burden and responsibility sharing.[11]

Admittedly, the General Assembly does not make any clear distinction in the wording of its resolutions to indicate whether it has assigned additional activities to UNHCR or provided policy guidance. However, for the purpose of attempting to differentiate the two, the former could be characterized as the intention to add new responsibilities and the latter as an elaboration of UNHCR's activities related to its mandated responsibilities.

A third means under UNHCR's Statute to ensure that UNHCR's role remains relevant is through guidance provided to UNHCR by the Executive Committee of the High Commissioner's Programme, generally referred to simply as EXCOM. EXCOM, created in 1958 by the United Nations Economic and Social Council, at the request of the General Assembly, in order to provide advice to UNHCR,[12]

---

9 The United Nations Economic and Social Council may also provide policy guidance to UNHCR, pursuant to paragraph 3 of UNHCR's Statute. However, ECOSOC resolutions related to UNHCR have rarely directed UNHCR to undertake specific action, but have more often recognized UNHCR's work or requested UNHCR to provide information on a particular refugee situation.

10 Recent General Assembly resolutions on refugee children include G.A. Res. 65/194, ¶ 21, U.N. Doc. A/RES/65/194 (21 December 2010); G.A. Res. 64/127, ¶ 20, U.N. Doc. A/RES/64/127 (18 December 2009); G.A. Res. 61/137, ¶ 13, 14, U.N. Doc. A/RES/61/137 (19 December 2006); G.A. Res. 60/129, ¶ 19, U.N. Doc. A/RES/60/129 (16 December 2005); G.A. Res. 58/150, ¶ 10, U.N. Doc. A/RES/58/150 (22 December 2003); G.A. Res. 56/136, ¶ 6, 7, 10, U.N. Doc. A/RES/ 56/136 (19 December 2001) and on refugee women: G.A. Res. 65/194, ¶ 21, U.N. Doc. A/RES/65/194 (21 December 2010); G.A. Res. 64/127, ¶ 20, U.N. Doc. A/RES/64/127 (18 December 2009); G.A. Res. 61/137, ¶ 13, 14, U.N. Doc. A/RES/61/137 (19 December 2006); G.A. Res. 60/129, ¶ 19, U.N. Doc. A/RES/60/129 (16 December 2005) and G.A. Res. 55/74, ¶ 21, U.N. Doc. A/RES/ 55/74 (4 December 2000) and on elderly refugees: G.A. Res. 56/135, ¶ 28, U.N. Doc. A/RES/56/135 (19 December 2001). UNHCR also has been called on to ensure that the refugee's family is protected, 'including through measures aimed at reuniting family members separated as a result of refugee flight'. G.A. Res. 55/74, ¶ 24, U.N. Doc. A/RES/55/74 (4 December 2000).

11 G.A. Res. 61/137, ¶ 24, U.N. Doc. A/RES/61/137 (19 Dec. 2006); G.A. Res. 60/129, ¶ 10, U.N. Doc. A/RES/60/129 (16 December 2005).

12 E.S.C. Res. 672 (XXV), U.N. Doc. E/3123 (1958). G.A. Res. 1166 (XII), ¶ 5, U.N. Doc. A/3805 (26 November 1957). Paragraph 4 of UNHCR's Statute states that the Economic and Social Council may establish 'an advisory committee on refugees, which shall consist of representatives of States Members and States non-members of the United Nations'. Pursuant to this provision, an Advisory Committee on Refugees was established in 1951 with responsibility for providing advice to the High Commissioner, on request. The structure, composition and responsibilities of the advisory committee, foreseen under UNHCR's Statute, have varied during the years. The first advisory committee was created following UNHCR's establishment in 1951 and was called the Advisory Committee on Refugees. It operated until 1954 when it was replaced by the

is presently comprised of representatives from 85 States. Pursuant to its Statute, UNHCR can request EXCOM's advice with respect to its functions.[13] Given that UNHCR's responsibilities related to international refugee law are activities that UNHCR is statutorily mandated to carry out in order to fulfil its international protection function, UNHCR may seek EXCOM's advice that relates to these responsibilities as well.

EXCOM's advice is provided in the form of conclusions on international protection. Although it is not entirely clear from a legal perspective whether EXCOM's conclusions are legally binding on UNHCR[14] without endorsement from the General Assembly,[15] UNHCR acts as though they are by consistently following such advice. EXCOM, like the General Assembly, has provided advice related to groups of refugees, including refugee women, children and elderly persons,[16] and has provided guidance on UNHCR's protection work, on topics

United Nations Refugee Fund Executive Committee (UNREF). UNREF was, in turn, replaced by the present EXCOM.

13 UNHCR Statute, *supra* note 2, ¶ 1. Specifically, paragraph 1 of UNHCR's Statute provides that '[i]n the exercise of [UNHCR's] functions, more particularly when difficulties arise, and for instance with regard to any controversy concerning the international status of these persons, the High Commissioner shall request the opinion of the advisory committee on refugees'. The conclusions sometimes indicate that the guidance is for States or for UNHCR and at other times do not specify to whom it is directed.

14 Holborn states that EXCOM has 'the authority to issue directives to the HC in the field of material assistance programs, but in matters concerning international protection could only give advice' without providing the legal basis for such view. Louise Holborn, *Refugees: a Problem of Our Time: The Work of the United Nations High Commissioner for Refugees, 1951–1972* 92 (1975). Jerzy Sztucki takes the opposite view in finding that '[s]ince the resolutions of the General Assembly on internal matters of the Organization have binding effect, and given that the Committee's involvement in protection matters has been confirmed in practice, such recommendations and requests must be regarded as binding on the High Commissioner, especially bearing in mind General Assembly resolutions 1673(XVI) and 1783(XVII).' Jerry Sztucki, 'The Conclusions on the International Protection of Refugees Adopted by the Executive Committee of the UNHCR Programme', 1 *Int'l. J. Refugee L.* 285, 298–299 (1989).

15 The current practice of the General Assembly is to endorse the EXCOM conclusions, see for example G.A. Res. 65/194, ¶ 1, U.N. Doc. A/RES/65/194 (21 December 2010), which endorses EXCOM's 61st report. In the past, the General Assembly has had a mixed practice of endorsing EXCOM conclusions. At times, it has specifically endorsed certain EXCOM conclusions. For example, see G.A. Res. 45/140, ¶ 15, U.N. Doc. A/RES/45/140 (14 December 1990), which '[e]ndorses the conclusion on the note on international protection' adopted by EXCOM at its 41st session. At other times, the General Assembly has used the content of a particular EXCOM conclusion in its resolution without naming or referring specifically to the conclusion. See, for example, G.A. Res. 48/116, ¶ 16, U.N. Doc. A/48/116 (20 December 1993) which '[r]eaffirms the importance of promoting and disseminating refugee law and principles for the protection of refugees'. This language mirrors the content of EXCOM Conclusion 71 (XLIV), ¶ aa, 1993, although the General Assembly does not specifically cite the conclusion.

16 EXCOM has adopted numerous conclusions specifically addressing concerns about refugee women and children. With respect to refugee women, these include: EXCOM Conclusion 105 (LVII) 2006; EXCOM Conclusion 98 (LIV) 2003; EXCOM Conclusion 73 (XLIV) 1993; EXCOM Conclusion 64 (XLI) 1990; and EXCOM Conclusion 60 (XL) 1989. Conclusions that

ranging from the registration of refugees to solutions, such as resettlement.[17] UNHCR, however, is not a passive recipient of the changes made by the General Assembly to its mandate, or of the policy guidance provided by the General Assembly and EXCOM. UNHCR is an active participant in articulating the changes that should be made as well as the formulation of the changes by the General Assembly. UNHCR plays a similar role in the creation of the policy guidance provided to it by the General Assembly and EXCOM. Staff in UNHCR Headquarters in Geneva actually propose issues and draft proposals for EXCOM conclusions and General Assembly resolutions and therefore, UNHCR plays an important role in determining not only the content of such documents, but also the timing of changes to its mandate and the General Assembly's and EXCOM's provision of policy guidance. However, the adoption and use of conclusions by EXCOM has been under discussion within EXCOM and UNHCR;[18] EXCOM States are beginning to demand a greater role in the choice and content of EXCOM conclusions. Given UNHCR's present in-depth and constructive involvement in the formulation of EXCOM conclusions, it is logical that the organization would follow EXCOM's policy guidance in practice even if such guidance were not legally binding. In the future, more significant control by EXCOM of the topics and content of EXCOM conclusions may alter UNHCR's view of such conclusions.

3.3 UNHCR's interpretation of its international protection function

UNHCR has not just stimulated the adoption of resolutions by the General Assembly and conclusions by EXCOM and contributed to the content of these documents, but also has played an active role in ensuring that its responsibilities, including those related to international refugee law, remain relevant to the needs of refugees and the interests of States. As UNHCR has no explicit authority,

---

specifically cover refugee children include: EXCOM Conclusion 107 (LVIII) 2007; EXCOM Conclusion 105 (LVII) 2006; EXCOM Conclusion 84 (XLVIII) 1997; and EXCOM Conclusion 59 (XL) 1989. UNHCR also addressed issues relating to refugee women and children in its general conclusions as well as in the context of other topics. See, for example, the 2005 conclusion on local integration and the 2004 conclusion on mass influxes, EXCOM Conclusion 104 (LVI), ¶ o–p, 2005 and EXCOM Conclusion 100 (LV), ¶ d, 2004. The elderly have been covered by recent EXCOM conclusions as well. See for example EXCOM Conclusion 104 (LVI), ¶ o–p, 2005 and EXCOM Conclusion 90 (LII), ¶ i, 2001.

17 On the registration of refugees, see EXCOM Conclusion 102 (LVI), ¶ v, 2005 and EXCOM Conclusion 91 (LII), ¶ c and d, 2001, and on resettlement see EXCOM Conclusion 109 (LX), ¶ i, 2009, EXCOM Conclusion 108 (LIX), ¶ p, 2008, EXCOM Conclusion 102 (LVI), ¶ s, 2005, EXCOM Conclusion 99 (LV), ¶ x, 2004 and EXCOM Conclusion 90 (LII), ¶ n, 2001.

18 See UNHCR, Review of the Use of UNHCR Executive Committee Conclusions on International Protection, PDES/2008/03 (UNHCR Policy Development and Evaluation Service, 10 April 2008).

under the terms of its statutory mandate, to modify its responsibilities, UNHCR's approach has been to use informal means.

One of two key means is UNHCR's establishment of its own interpretation of its international protection function. As discussed in Chapter 1, UNHCR's Statute does not establish a definition for the term 'international protection', but only provides a list of the activities that UNHCR should perform in order to provide for the protection of refugees.[19] Thus, at its own initiative, UNHCR has adopted an approach to the concept of international protection that reflects an institutional flexibility, but also contains a core meaning as discussed later.

UNHCR has ascribed various meanings to the concept of 'international protection' over the years. For example, after nearly 10 years of operation, the High Commissioner, Auguste Lindt, described UNHCR's international protection role as helping refugees 'to overcome the disabilities caused by their lack of national protection and ... safeguarding their rights and legitimate interests'.[20] At a time of crisis in international refugee law, UNHCR noted in its 1986 Note on International Protection that:

> International protection involves first of all legal protection, i.e. seeking to ensure that refugees are treated in accordance with internationally accepted standards including protection against *refoulement*, freedom from discrimination and the enjoyment of economic and social rights. Secondly, it entails

19 The meaning of 'international protection' also has been considered by a number of scholars. See Guy Goodwin-Gill, 'The Language of Protection', 1 *Int'l. J. Refugee L.* 6, 6 (1989). In addition, Arthur Helton finds that protection actually means 'legal protection'. See Arthur Helton, 'What is Refugee Protection?', *Int'l. J. Refugee L.* (Special Issue) 119, 119 (1990), and Arthur Helton, 'What is Refugee Protection?: A Question Revisited', in *Problems of Protection: the UNHCR, Refugees and Human Rights* 19, 20 (Niklaus Steiner, Mark Gibney, Gil Loescher, eds, 2003). Walter Kälin has considered UNHCR's protection role as part of his analysis of the content of UNHCR's supervisory role in his note for the Global Consultations process. In the note, Kälin utilizes B.G. Ramcharan's definition of 'international protection' from B.G. Ramcharan, *The Concept and Present Status of the International Protection of Human Rights: Forty Years after the Universal Declaration* 17, 20–21 (1989). 'International protection' denotes 'the intercession of an international entity either at the behest of a victim or victims concerned, or by a person on their behalf, or on the volition of the international protecting agency itself to halt a violation of human rights' or 'to keep safe, defend, [or] guard' a person or a thing from or against a danger or injury.' Walter Kälin, 'Supervising the 1951 Convention on the Status of Refugees: Article 35 and Beyond', in *Refugee Protection in International Law: UNHCR's Global Consultations on International Protection* 613, 619 (Erika Feller, Volker Türk and Frances Nicholson eds, 2003). For an extensive consideration of 'international protection' from an organizational and legal perspective see Guy Goodwin-Gill and Jane McAdam, *The Refugee in International Law* 421–461(3rd edn, 2007).

20 UNHCR, Report of the UNHCR, Appendix I, ¶ 12, U.N. Doc. A/4104/Rev.1 (1959). A similar definition was provided in the Secretary-General's report, concerning the organization and functions of UNHCR. The report states that '[t]he international legal protection of refugees consists essentially of efforts on the part of an international service to ensure that refugees ... shall not be subject to legal and social disabilities arising from their peculiar status.' Report of the Secretary-General, ¶ 19, U.N. Doc. A/C.3/527 and Corr.1 (26 October 1949).

action to promote the development of standards for the treatment of refugees through the adoption of appropriate legal provisions on the international level and/or in national legislation.[21]

On the 50th anniversary of UNHCR's creation, in its Note on International Protection for the year 2000, UNHCR states: 'the challenge of international protection is to secure admission, asylum, and respect by States for basic human rights.'[22] More recently, UNHCR had the General Assembly adopt a resolution that notes that international protection includes:

> the promotion and facilitation of, inter alia, the admission, reception and treatment of refugees in accordance with internationally agreed standards and the ensuring of durable, protection-oriented solutions, bearing in mind the particular needs of vulnerable groups and paying special attention to those with specific needs.[23]

Although these descriptions by UNHCR of its international protection function vary, they nevertheless contain several common features. First, they all have at their core the importance of ensuring respect for the rights of refugees. International protection furnishes refugees, who by definition are people who no longer benefit from the legal protection of their country of origin, a substitute form of legal protection under international law. However, to ensure respect for refugees' rights in practice, the international protection for refugees afforded by international treaties must be transformed into a legal obligation for the State of asylum, through the State's ratification of international treaties for the protection of refugees. Those legal obligations must also be implemented through their encapsulation in national law and then applied in practice by States. Thus, UNHCR must work to ensure that there are international standards to protect refugees and that States, which bear the primary responsibility for the legal protection of refugees,[24] render the standards contained in international law effective at the national level.

Second, the diverse descriptions demonstrate that international protection is more than just a legal notion; it is, as EXCOM has stated, 'both a legal concept

21 UNHCR, Note on International Protection, ¶ 2, U.N. Doc. A/AC.96/680 (5 July 1986).
22 UNHCR, Note on International Protection, ¶ 9, U.N. Doc. A/AC.96/930 (7 July 2000). This Note, written in connection with UNHCR's 50th anniversary, focuses on how UNHCR meets particular protection challenges in order to fulfill its international protection role.
23 G.A. Res. 65/194, ¶ 15, U.N. Doc. A/RES/65/194 (21 December 2010).
24 The primary responsibility of States for the legal protection of refugees was articulated by the General Assembly in the very resolution that created UNHCR. Specifically, the General Assembly recalls the Economic and Social Council request to States 'to provide the necessary legal protection for refugees'. G.A. Res. 319, 3rd preambular ¶ (3 December 1949).

and at the same time very much an action-oriented function'.[25] The General Assembly has reiterated the active nature of international protection:

> International protection of refugees is a dynamic and action-oriented function … that includes, in cooperation with States and other partners, the promotion and facilitation of, inter alia, the admission, reception and treatment of refugees in accordance with internationally agreed standards and the ensuring of durable, protection-oriented solutions.[26]

Walter Kälin, in his final paper for the Global Consultations process, provides a broad range of activities endorsed by EXCOM and agreed to by States as part of UNHCR's international protection role.[27] Not only does international protection permeate UNHCR's fieldwork, but it also is the cornerstone of the organizations' institutional structure. The import of international protection within UNHCR is readily apparent today from the presence of a Deputy High Commissioner for Protection who oversees the Division of International Protection, which is arguably the most influential section within UNHCR.

Most significantly, and of crucial importance to UNHCR's ability to adjust and adapt its role to changing circumstances and needs, these various formulations of 'international protection' by UNHCR convey a sense of the expansive construction given to the term by the organization. As Holborn states: 'from the beginning the practice of the UNHCR has been to ignore the obscurities of par. 8 and to rely instead on the broad phrasing of the paragraph and the general tenor of the Statute to support its contention that international protection should be interpreted broadly.'[28] The general formulation of 'international protection' in UNHCR's Statute, which has at its core the importance of ensuring the rights of refugees, serves as guidance for UNHCR's operational work, but UNHCR exercises a great deal of latitude in deciding what activities are appropriate and conducive to the fulfilment of its international protection role and thus, its international refugee law responsibilities.

Thus, UNHCR's construction of 'international protection' as both a legal and an action oriented function, which has as its base the protection of refugees, provides UNHCR with a sufficiently flexible and expansive meaning for 'international protection'. This broad interpretation permits UNHCR to modify and enhance its activities related to both the development and effectiveness of international refugee law.

---

25 EXCOM Conclusion 95 (LIV), ¶ b, 2003.
26 G.A. Res. 60/129, ¶ 9, U.N. Doc. A/RES/60/129 (16 December 2005).
27 Kälin, *supra* note 19, at 622–624. For example, he includes UNHCR's monitoring, reporting on, and following up on, interventions with governments concerning the situation of refugees, co-operation with States in designing operational responses, and advisory and consultative work with national asylum or refugee status determination procedures, as examples of UNHCR's activities that have been agreed to by States.
28 Holborn, *supra* note 14, at 100.

3.3.1 *Authority for UNHCR to define and perform additional responsibilities: implied powers*

UNHCR, as a subsidiary organization of the United Nations General Assembly, must have the legal capacity to interpret its international protection function and in particular its role and responsibilities related to the development and effectiveness of international refugee law. As UNHCR's statutory mandate does not contain an express authorization for UNHCR to interpret its own mandate, another basis must be found to justify its actions.

The law of international organizations has struggled with the notion of the basis of an organization's actions that extend beyond the express provisions of its constitution or treaty. This struggle epitomizes the inherent tension that exists between two underlying concepts in international organizations law: first, that international organizations are creations of States and are granted authority by States to carry out certain responsibilities but remain subject to the interests of those States; and, second, that once international organizations are created, they have legal personality and autonomy separate from States.

Unlike States, which are presumed to be able to act freely unless international law imposes a limitation, the most prevalent view of international organizations' powers is that international organizations can only act to the extent that they have been granted specific powers.[29] In order to provide a legal imprimatur to organizations' actions beyond such powers, the theory of implied powers is the traditional theory employed. The theory balances States' grant of authority to organizations with the independence needed by such organizations to carry out the purposes assigned to them. Therefore, the prevailing view of international scholars is that the authority of an organization is derived from its constitution or statute, termed express powers, but that the organization has implied powers derived from the express powers that permit it a degree of independence and flexibility in determining what actions it can carry out without having explicit authorization from States for every such action. Implied powers could be said to give effect to the organization's purposes, by reading a term 'into the organization's statute'.[30]

The implied powers theory is legally grounded in several advisory opinions of the International Court of Justice related to the powers of the United Nations organs. The Reparations case is considered the seminal case for the implied powers theory with several subsequent cases, namely the Effect of Awards Case, the Certain Expenses Case, and the Namibia Case, cited as further support by the

---

29 Henry Schermers and Neils Blokker, *International Institutional Law* 157 (5th edn, 2011).

30 Krzysztof Skubiszewski, 'Implied Powers of International Organizations', in *International Law at a Time of Perplexity: Essays in Honour of Shabtai Rosenne* 855; 860 (Yoram Dinstein, ed., 1989). The reading of a term into the organization's statute is not just useful, but necessary, since 'it is never possible to lay down an exhaustive list of powers of the organization in a constitution, *inter alia* because any organization needs to respond to developments in practice which cannot be foreseen when it is created.' Schermers and Blokker, *supra* note 29, at 180–181.

ICJ for the theory.[31] However, the lack of clarity in the Court's articulation of the doctrine has provided much fodder for the debate among scholars as to whether such powers are based on the purposes, the functions, or the explicit responsibilities assigned to the organization[32] and whether the implied power must be of a necessary or essential nature.[33]

While the theory of implied powers became increasingly prominent during the 1990s at a time of significant development of international organizations, some scholars believe it is now on the wane.[34] One of the few alternative theories is that of inherent powers. Under the inherent powers theory, organizations possess the powers necessary to perform all acts related to their purposes. This approach

---

31 In the Reparations for Injuries Suffered in the Service of the United Nations Case, Advisory Opinion, 1949 I.C.J. 174, 182 (11 April) (hereinafter Reparations case), the Court considered whether the UN had the ability to bring a claim for injuries by a State to a UN employee and held that '[u]nder international law, the Organization must be deemed to have those powers which, though not expressly provided in the Charter, are conferred upon it by necessary implication as being essential to the performance of its duties.'

In the Effect of Awards Case, the Court found, in determining whether the General Assembly had the power to establish an administrative tribunal, that it could do so where it was 'essential to ensure the efficient working of the Secretariat ... Capacity to do this arises by necessary intendment out of the Charter'. Effect of Awards of Compensation made by the United Nations Administrative Tribunal, Advisory Opinion 1954 I.C.J. 47, 57 (13 July).

The Court went even further in the Certain Expenses Case, in which it was determined whether expenses for peacekeeping were 'expenses of the Organization' under article 17(2) of the UN Charter. The Court found that 'when the Organization takes action which warrants the assertion that it was appropriate for the fulfillment of one of the stated purposes of the United Nations, the presumption is that such action is not ultra vires the Organization.' Certain Expenses of the United Nations, Advisory Opinion, 1962 I.C.J. 151, 168 (20 July) (hereinafter Certain Expenses Case). Moreover, in the Namibia Case, the Court, in evaluating whether the General Assembly's termination of South Africa's mandate over Namibia was within its competence, also considered the Security Council's powers and noted that 'The only limitations [on its responsibility for the maintenance of peace and security] are the fundamental principles and purposes found in Chapter I of the Charter.' Legal Consequences for States of the Continued Presence of South Africa in Namibia (South West Africa) notwithstanding Security Council Resolution 276 (1970), Advisory Opinion, 1971 I.C.J. 16, 52 (21 June). Note that not all scholars mention the Namibia Case.

32 Schermers and Blokker, *supra* note 29, at 182.

33 Schermers and Blokker, *supra* note 29, at 182. Another three limitations identified by the authors are: (i) the existence of certain explicit powers in the same area, (ii) fundamental rules and principles of international law may not be violated and (iii) the distribution of the functions within the organization may not change as a result of the implied powers. Ibid., at 179–180. Skubiszewski finds for example that this limitation leads to a clearer demarcation of the limits on the scope of implied powers, *supra* note 30, at 861.

34 Jan Klabbers suggests that the 'doctrine has passed its heyday' as evidenced by the ICJ advisory opinion on the World Health Organization's question with respect to the legality of nuclear weapons. Jan Klabbers, *An Introduction to International Institutional Law* 69 (2nd edn, 2009). Legality of the Use by a State of Nuclear Weapons in Armed Conflict, Advisory Opinion, 1996 I.C.J 66 (8 July). The ICJ, after reviewing the object and purpose of the organization, found that the organization did not have the competence to address the legality of the use of nuclear weapons and to ask the Court about such legality. Ibid., at 66. Klabbers also cites recent decisions by the Court of Justice in the European Community.

starts from a presumption that an organization, like a State, has full powers, and is directly contrary to the view that the powers of the organization are derived from the organization's constitution or statute. With the inherent powers theory, the statute or constitution serves as the limitation on the powers as opposed to serving as the basis for the powers under the implied powers theory.

Drawing on the decision of the International Court of Justice in the Certain Expenses case, which is the primary legal basis cited for the inherent powers theory, if the action taken by the organization is 'appropriate for the fulfilment of one of the stated purposes of the UN, the presumption is that such action is not *ultra vires* the Organization'.[35] Thus, to state the latter more clearly by expressing the Court's holding in the alternative, if the organization's action does not fulfil a stated purpose then it is *ultra vires* and is not legally authorized. However, it cannot be presumed that just because the mandate does not explicitly prohibit an activity that the organization is authorized to carry it out[36] and therein lays the greatest weakness in the inherent powers theory.

As the implied powers theory remains the most cohesive legal justification for the actions of an organization that extend beyond the terms of its mandate, it is the approach used in this book. The requirement that such activities be necessary and essential to the performance of the organization's functions or powers, derived from Judge Hackworth's dissent in the ICJ Reparations case,[37] is not utilized in the analysis, however, since this introduces a subjective determination that likely varies depending on whether States or UNHCR make the assessment. With international protection as its primary function, the notion of implied powers affords UNHCR wide discretion to determine what activities will permit it to first, further the responsibilities assigned to it under paragraph 8(a) of its Statute concerning the development and effectiveness of international refugee law, and second, fulfil its purpose of international protection.

3.4 UNHCR doctrine

UNHCR developed a second technique, termed 'UNHCR doctrine' herein, which has significantly contributed to the evolution in UNHCR's role related to the development and effectiveness of international refugee law. UNHCR doctrine is UNHCR's 'voice' on refugee law issues, that is, the articulation by UNHCR of its views on such issues. This approach relies on the meaning of 'doctrine' as used in the French language, to refer to the opinions of those who teach or who

---

35 Certain Expenses case, *supra* note 31. This position has been most notably articulated by Professor Syersted. See Finn Seyersted, *Common Law of International Organizations* 65–70 (2008).

36 Klabbers, *supra* note 34, at 67.

37 Judge Hackworth stated that '[p]owers not expressed cannot freely be implied. Implied powers flow from a grant of express powers, and are limited to those that are "necessary" to the exercise of powers expressly granted.' Reparations case, *supra* note 31, at 198.

write about the law.[38] The term, as used in this book, refers to the views of UNHCR, an organization that writes and instructs on refugee law, of what the law is or should be related to refugees.

UNHCR's doctrinal positions do not arise in a vacuum. They are often formulated as a result of questions posed by States, differing positions taken by States, or positions adopted by States and opposed by UNHCR. The formulation of doctrine by UNHCR is neither simple nor carried out in isolation. UNHCR doctrinal positions can be influenced by numerous factors including: the views of non-governmental organizations, academics, and government officials; political considerations; State practice, and even different views within UNHCR, to name a few. UNHCR may seek the views of a few or many other actors in the refugee law field or may create the position as a result of primarily internal consultations.

In order to understand the authority of UNHCR doctrinal positions for States, it is helpful to attempt to determine their status in international law.[39] In utilizing the traditional determination of sources of law, found in article 38 of the Statute of the International Court of Justice, it can be noted that UNHCR doctrinal positions are not created by States, but by the staff of UNHCR, who are international civil servants. Consequently, they do not constitute one of the traditional sources of international law, such as rules established by treaties, international customary rules, or general principles of law[40] created by States and are not legally binding on States.

The question is then whether UNHCR doctrine is a subsidiary source of international law. The term 'doctrine' is found in the French version of paragraph 1(c) in article 38 of the Statute of the International Court of Justice that refers to subsidiary sources: *'la doctrine des publicistes les plus qualifiés des différentes nations'*, which in English is translated as 'the teachings [*doctrine*] of the most highly qualified publicists of the various nations'.[41] UNHCR can be considered to have an expertise similar to that of academics or publicists. In fact, given the international composition of the UNHCR personnel, the organization may reflect a more diverse and international perspective than a publicist with his/her particular national orientation. However, the difficulty is that UNHCR doctrine is most frequently *lege ferenda*, what the law should be, rather than *lex lata*, what the law is. Therefore, it does not fit well into the definition of subsidiary sources in the

---

38 See Serge Guinchard and Thierry Debard eds, *Léxiques des Termes Juridiques* 318, 19th edn, 2012. The term 'doctrine' finds its etymological basis in the Latin word *doctrina*, derived, in turn, from *docere*, which means to teach in the sense of theoretical study. Denis Allande and Stéphane Rials, *Dictionnaire de la Culture Juridique* 384–387 (2003).

39 French scholars continue to debate whether 'doctrine' is actually a source of French law. Allande and Rials, *supra* note 38, at 385.

40 I.C.J. Statute, art. 38.

41 The French version of article 38, paragraph 1(c) of the Statute of the International Court of Justice reads as follows: '[L]es décisions judiciares et la doctrine des publicistes les plus qualifiés des differentes nations, comme moyen auxiliaire de détermination du droit.'

Court's Statute, which are supposed to evidence what the law is and not what it should be.

Alternatively, UNHCR doctrine may be considered a form of 'soft law'. 'Soft law' in international law is somewhat of a misnomer in the sense that it is not 'law' in a strict sense; this is particularly the case when a strict positivist approach to sources is utilized whereby law is solely created by States. However, while some scholars believe that soft law should not be a concern of lawyers,[42] and that this term belongs to the international relations area, it is nevertheless useful in identifying influences on the development of international law. Although the term has been accorded various interpretations,[43] most soft law must be written.[44] Soft law instruments include not only treaties that contain soft obligations and resolutions of international organizations, but also statements of principles by eminent international lawyers.[45] Such statements of principles by lawyers with expertise can be analogized to UNHCR doctrinal positions drafted by refugee law experts in the organization. UNHCR doctrinal positions, like other forms of soft law, often serve an informative or educational role.[46]

Moreover, in their form as *lege ferenda,* UNHCR doctrinal positions supplement the provisions of the 1951 Refugee Convention and affect the development of the traditional forms of law, as will be shown in Chapter 5. Such positions have the advantage of being in a non-binding form and so do not require States' explicit approval and can be easily modified. In addition, UNHCR can utilize them in connection with existing legal standards to evaluate States' conduct and to provide concrete guidance to States on how they should conform their laws and policies so as to further the protection of refugees, as discussed in Chapter 6.

3.4.1 *Evolution of UNHCR doctrine*

UNHCR began to formulate doctrinal positions shortly after the creation of the 1951 Refugee Convention and continues to do so even today. Generally speaking, the positions have covered an increasing number of topics and the presentation of such positions has become more refined as UNHCR has acquired extensive experience and expertise in issuing such positions during the past 60 years. Doctrinal positions have been a key means used by UNHCR to influence the development of international refugee law, as shown in Chapter 5, and to help ensure that States render international refugee law effective in practice, as shown in Chapter 6.

---

42 See for example José E. Alvarez, *International Organizations as Law-makers* 121 (2005).

43 Tadeusz Gruchalla-Wesierski, 'A Framework for Understanding "Soft Law"' 30 *McGill L.J.* 37, 44 (1984).

44 C. M. Chinkin, *Normative Development in the International Legal System*, in Dinah Shelton, ed., *Commitment and Compliance: The Role of Non-binding Norms in the International Legal System* 21, 25. (2003).

45 C.M. Chinkin, 'The Challenge of Soft Law: Development and Change in International Law', 38 *I.C.L.Q.* 850, 851 (1989).

46 Ibid., at 862.

The special nature of doctrine is best understood through a historical overview of its development by UNHCR. In order to facilitate this overview, the nearly 60-year period since its initial use by UNHCR has been divided into sub-periods based on the evolution in the need and use of doctrine. However, the divisions selected are not intended to be a rigid delineation, but rather a tool for obtaining greater insight into the changes in the content and form of UNHCR doctrine and into the uniqueness of these positions posited by UNHCR.

3.4.1.1 Emergence of UNHCR doctrine: 1950–1966

Following the drafting of the 1951 Refugee Convention, UNHCR's predominant concern was to ensure respect by States of the various political, social and economic rights of refugees contained in the Convention. The underlying thinking was most likely that if refugees' countries of first asylum or resettlement accorded them these rights, then the refugees would be able to integrate into their new countries of residence. UNHCR conveyed its views, concerning these rights, to governments primarily through representations by its branch offices.[47]

UNHCR was particularly preoccupied with problems related to two of the rights contained in the 1951 Refugee Convention, which were considered to be essential to refugees' welfare: the right to work and the provision of a travel document. The provisions on 'gainful employment' in the 1951 Refugee Convention concern the core means by which a person becomes self-supporting and could thereby support not only him- or herself, but also family members, and therefore were of significant importance to refugees. UNHCR's reports to the General Assembly not only express the hope that States, which had not yet ratified the Convention, would do so without a reservation to this provision, but also criticize other States for not giving refugees free access to certain professions.[48]

With respect to travel documents, article 28 of the 1951 Refugee Convention provides that States shall issue travel documents to refugees lawfully staying in their territory. The Final Act of the 1951 Conference, which is an appendix to the 1951 Refugee Convention, explains the importance of such documents in stating that 'the issue and recognition of travel documents is necessary to facilitate the

---

47 As UNHCR stated in its Annual Report for the period June 1952 to May 1953: 'Space would not permit a detailed description of all the representations made by each of the branch offices to the competent authorities to ensure that refugees obtain recognition of their legal rights. These representations cover matters such as the determination of refugee status, regularization of residence, expulsion, the exercise of the right to work, public relief, travel documents, authentication of documentation, personal status, public assistance and social security.' UNHCR, Report of the UNHCR, ¶ 64, U.N. Doc. A/2394 (1953).

48 For example, UNHCR hoped that the Italian government would not make any serious reservations to the right to work and criticized Belgian and French practices. UNHCR, Report of the UNHCR and Addendum, ¶ 70, 87, 100, U.N. Doc. A/2126 (1952).

movement of refugees'.[49] Such movement was undertaken by refugees for a variety of reasons: resettlement, employment, business, education, and to visit relatives or friends. The High Commissioner used the recommendation in the Final Act as a basis for encouraging States to give effect to article 28[50] and encouraged States to use a particular form for the travel document so as to ensure uniformity in the documents issued by States.[51]

The Final Act also served as the basis for UNHCR's positions related to family reunion. Recommendation B in the Final Act recognizes that 'the unity of the family, the natural and fundamental group unit of society, is an essential right of the refugee'. Thus, UNHCR promoted the reunion of family members who were separated as a result of refugee movements.[52]

When situations emerged that raised issues not directly addressed by the 1951 Refugee Convention or the Final Act, UNHCR provided practical advice to countries. The ability to resolve problems in this manner rested on the close relationship UNHCR had with States, one of co-operation, which is further discussed in section 4.2.1. For example, refugees who had been recognized as refugees in one country of asylum were at times moving to another country that was not eager to accept them. Thus, the issue arose, which UNHCR would continue to address over the years, of the first country of asylum. UNHCR sought a solution to this problem with Germany through discussions[53] and then articulated a view in its Second Annual Report: 'These [second] countries cannot undertake to accept indiscriminately refugees who have been given asylum previously in another country.'[54] This position would form the basis for a later doctrinal position on 'first country of asylum' in the 1980s.

The only area in which UNHCR created positions that articulated novel concepts, during this initial period of the emergence of UNHCR doctrine, was with respect to the interpretation of the refugee definition under the 1951 Refugee Convention. Specifically, UNHCR construed the refugee definition in the 1951 Refugee Convention, in addition to its mandate, as applicable to the approximately 190,000 Hungarians who fled primarily to Austria and Yugoslavia in 1956, well after the 1951 temporal limitation. To reach this result, UNHCR advanced the idea that the events leading to the revolution in 1956 had their

---

49 Final Act of the 1951 United Nations Conference of Plenipotentiaries on the Status of Refugees and Stateless Persons, ¶ IV.A, 25 July 1951, 189 U.N.T.S. 137.

50 UNHCR, Report of the UNHCR and Addendum, ¶ 28, U.N. Doc. A/2126 (1952). Also see UNHCR, Report of the UNHCR, ¶ 43, U.N. Doc. A/2394 (1953). The provision of travel documents to refugees was one of the first issues addressed by the first High Commissioner, Fridjtof Nansen, under the League of Nations, as discussed in section 1.2.1.1 of this volume.

51 UNHCR, Report of the UNHCR, ¶ 72, U.N. Doc. A/2648 (1954).

52 See UNHCR, Note on International Protection, ¶ 22, U.N. Doc. A/AC.96/227 (3 March 1964).

53 UNHCR, Report of the UNHCR, ¶ 58, U.N. Doc. A/2648 (1954), UNHCR, Report of the UNHCR, ¶ 57, U.N. Doc. A/2902 and Add.1 (1955).

54 UNHCR, Report of the UNHCR, ¶ 83, U.N. Doc. A/2394 (1953).

genesis prior to 1951.[55] UNHCR utilized the same approach to recognize, as refugees, people fleeing other Eastern European countries after the 1951 date.[56]

In recognizing the Hungarians as refugees under the 1951 Refugee Convention, UNHCR not only provided a distinctive interpretation of the Convention's refugee definition, but also employed a group determination of refugee status. The employment of this concept harkened back to the approach utilized by refugee organizations at the time of the League of Nations. Although group determination of refugee status appears to contrast sharply with the notion of an individual determination under the 1951 Refugee Convention definition of a refugee, the drafters of the 1951 Refugee Convention had discussed a group approach.[57] In addition, UNHCR's Statute provides that its work shall normally relate to 'groups and categories of refugees'[58] and UNHCR had assisted refugees on a group basis in 'good offices' operations. So, while UNHCR was authorised and had worked with groups of refugees, its doctrinal position, on the determination of refugee status under the 1951 Refugee Convention based on a group determination, was new, but was supported by the general wording of its Statute.

3.4.1.2 *Extension of UNHCR doctrine: 1967–1981*

States' adoption of the 1967 Protocol heralded the commencement of a truly international approach to refugees by UNHCR. Consequently, UNHCR was confronted with the need to address the protection situation of refugees in regions other than Europe, initially, in Africa[59] and then in Asia and Central America.[60] UNHCR, therefore, began to issue doctrinal positions on not only the criteria for determining refugee status, but also on the standards for the treatment of refugees. These positions would take new forms as the organization sought to ensure that not only its staff, but also States themselves were apprised of the principles.

While continuing to advocate convention standards,[61] UNHCR articulated its views on new issues related to the assessment of refugee status. For example,

---

55 Ivor Jackson, *The Refugee Concept in Group Situations* 117 (1999). As Grahl-Madsen notes, 'the Ad Hoc Committee interpreted the term "events" as "happenings of major importance involving territorial or profound political changes as well as systematic programmes of persecution which are after-effects of earlier changes"'. Grahl-Madsen agrees with Robinson that this was too restrictive of an interpretation. Atle Grahl-Madsen, *The Status of Refugees in International Law: Refugee Character* 164 (1966).
56 Kazimierz Bem, 'The Coming of a 'Blank Cheque' – Europe, the 1951 Convention and the 1967 Protocol', 16 *Int'l. J. Refugee L.* 609, 619 (2004).
57 Jackson, *supra* note 55, at 85.
58 UNHCR Statute, *supra* note 2, at ¶ 2.
59 UNHCR, Report of the UNHCR, ¶ 2, U.N. Doc. A/7612 (1969).
60 UNHCR, Report of the UNHCR, ¶ 1, U.N. Doc. A/34/12 (1979).
61 See for example, UNHCR, Report of the UNHCR, ¶ 17, U.N. Doc. A/8012 (1970).

UNHCR furnished advice on the eligibility of freedom fighters for refugee status[62] and set forth standards of interpretation for the determination of whether persons associated with organizations that advocate violence could obtain refugee status.[63] UNHCR also drew on international principles to address the situation of the extradition of asylum seekers and refugees.[64] UNHCR's views in these areas were initially provided to staff members via internal memoranda. However, the memoranda served as the basis to ensure uniformity of views among UNHCR's offices and for UNHCR staff members to provide consistent advice to governments and others.

Most significantly, in order to address the problem of different interpretations of the refugee definition,[65] UNHCR clarified, in 1979, how the definition should be applied in a standalone document, the Handbook on Procedures and Criteria for Determining Refugee Status.[66] This document, which has become one of the most important doctrinal documents ever created by UNHCR, is still used today by UNHCR, lawyers, and refugee status determination bodies, among others. The Handbook not only provides a clause-by-clause interpretation of the definition, but also interprets the principle of family unity by examining to whom it applies and in what circumstances. Furthermore, the Handbook establishes procedures for the determination of refugee status. Of particular importance to the development of UNHCR doctrine is the fact that the Handbook was not limited to providing guidance on existing standards. It also enunciated new principles such as that of agents of persecution and group determination in large-scale influxes, criteria for cancellation of refugee status, and the standard for the burden of proof in establishing refugee status (the benefit of the doubt), topics that are not explicitly mentioned in the 1951 Refugee Convention.[67]

UNHCR also used documentation furnished to EXCOM and the General Assembly to set forth its positions. In particular, UNHCR expressed its views in its Notes on International Protection. Following the creation of the Sub-Committee of the Whole on International Protection of EXCOM, in 1975, UNHCR's notes to the Sub-Committee on particular topics became a key means for UNHCR to document and elaborate its doctrinal views and bring those views

62 UNHCR, Question of 'Freedom Fighters' and Liberation Movements in Africa, UNHCR/IOM/22/68; UNHCR/BOM/26/68 (June 1968).
63 UNHCR, Determination of Refugee Status of Persons connected with Organizations or Groups which Advocate and/or Practise Violence, UNHR/IOM/16/78; UNHCR/BOM/16/78 (5 April 1978).
64 UNHCR, Extradition, UNHCR/IOM/23/68; UNHCR/BOM/29/68 (26 June 1968).
65 UNHCR was concerned about the uniform application of the refugee definition even during the first decade of its work. See for example, the Statement by the High Commissioner in Annex II of UNHCR, Report of UNHCR, ¶ 9, U.N. Doc. A/3828/Rev.1 (1958).
66 UNHCR, *Handbook on Procedures and Criteria for Determining Refugee Status*, HCR/IP/4/Eng./Rev.1 (January 1992). The Handbook was originally published in 1979.
67 Ibid., at ¶ 65, 44, 117, 196, 203–204.

to the attention of States.[68] For example, UNHCR advocated procedural standards for handling asylum claims in its 1976 Note on International Protection and in a 1977 Note to the Sub-Committee of the Whole on International Protection.[69]

UNHCR's provision of its views to the Sub-Committee then served as the basis for the formulation of EXCOM conclusions on protection issues, which would become an ideal means for UNHCR to have its doctrinal positions endorsed by States. For example, UNHCR established that a State's determination of refugee status should normally not be questioned by another State unless the person 'manifestly does not fulfil the requirements of the Convention'.[70] UNHCR extended the protection offered against the expulsion of refugees under article 32 of the 1951 Refugee Convention by asserting that refugee delinquents cannot be expulsed, but should be treated in the same manner as national delinquents[71] and advised on the content of the provisions in refugee travel documents and their renewal.[72]

UNHCR also utilized EXCOM conclusions to provide procedural guidance on the determination of refugee status and to advance principles for the treatment of asylum seekers,[73] since the 1951 Refugee Convention contains few explicit provisions for the protection of asylum seekers, except article 31, concerning penalties for illegal entry and freedom of movement, and article 33, on *non-refoulement*. Moreover, after having established that asylum seekers in large-scale influxes should receive 'at least temporary refuge' in EXCOM conclusions in 1977 and 1978, a 1979 EXCOM conclusion more forcefully advocated that '[i]n cases of large-scale influx, persons seeking asylum should always receive at least temporary refuge.'[74] Subsequently, UNHCR encouraged EXCOM to articulate the

---

68 The Sub-Committee was established in order to 'study in more detail some of the technical aspects of the protection of refugees'. EXCOM Conclusion 1 (XXVI), ¶ h, 1975. The Sub-Committee met for the first time in 1976. UNHCR selected the topics for discussion by the Sub-Committee and served as the secretariat for the Sub-Committee. UNHCR, Review of Selected Issues for Future Consideration of the Sub-Committee of the Whole on International Protection, UNHCR Doc. EC/SCP/56 ¶ 6, (28 July 1989). The Sub-Committee was replaced by the Standing Committee in 1995.

69 UNHCR, Note on International Protection, ¶ 30, U.N. Doc. A/AC.96/527 (20 September 1976), UNHCR, Note on Determination of Refugee Status under International Instruments, ¶ 16, UNHCR Doc. EC/SCP/5 (24 August 1977).

70 EXCOM Conclusion 12 (XXIX), ¶ g, 1978.

71 EXCOM Conclusion 7 (XXVIII), ¶ d, 1977. This conclusion relates to article 32 of the 1951 Refugee Convention.

72 EXCOM Conclusion 13 (XXIX), ¶ c–d, 1978.

73 EXCOM Conclusion 8 (XXVIII), ¶ e, 1977. EXCOM Conclusion 15 (XXX) 1979.

74 EXCOM Conclusion 5 (XXVIII) 1977, EXCOM Conclusion 11 (XXIX), ¶ d, 1978, EXCOM Conclusion 15 (XXX), ¶ f, 1979. The concept of temporary protection was not a new concept at the time. The idea of asylum is that it should be of a temporary nature with refugees returning to their country of origin or eventually becoming integrated in the country of residence or a third country. The concept was included in Article II.5. of the 1969 OAU Convention Governing the Specific Aspects of Refugee Problems in Africa, 10 September 1969, 1001 U.N.T.S. 45 (hereinafter 1969 OAU Refugee Convention).

standards that should apply to the treatment of refugees who receive temporary protection.[75]

Another area in which UNHCR asserted its own doctrinal views was with respect to the cessation clauses to refugee status in UNHCR's Statute and the 1951 Refugee Convention. UNHCR initially declared the application of the cessation clauses to refugees from two former Portuguese colonies, Guinea-Bissau and Mozambique.[76] Although such declaration under the Statute follows naturally from UNHCR's responsibility to determine whether individuals are eligible for refugee status, nothing in the 1951 Refugee Convention, which is between States, assigns UNHCR this role.

UNHCR, as in prior years, also continued to interpret its mandate in light of changing circumstances. For example, UNHCR adopted the doctrinal position that it is responsible for persons fleeing armed conflict or serious and generalized disorder and violence.[77] Thus, UNHCR extended its mandate beyond refugees having a fear of persecution to include persons who qualified as refugees under regional instruments, specifically, under the 1969 OAU Refugee Convention and the 1984 Cartagena Declaration.

By the end of the 1970s, UNHCR had established the practice of providing guidance on the application of the refugee definition, further developed existing refugee law standards, and addressed new issues not specifically derived from the standards in the 1951 Refugee Convention. The most significant step taken by UNHCR was the publication of the Handbook, which essentially contained UNHCR's doctrinal positions on the interpretation and application of the refugee definition.

UNHCR formulated its doctrinal views in a way to reach an increasing number of States. UNHCR no longer solely responded to individual requests from States for UNHCR's views based on its internal memoranda, but increasingly employed documentation prepared for EXCOM and the General Assembly, bodies comprised of States, to express its views. EXCOM conclusions became a means for obtaining endorsement by States of UNHCR's views. The provision of such doctrinal views, however, was by and large limited to States. Even the Handbook was intended for use outside of UNHCR only by government officials; distribution of the Handbook to non-governmental organizations and others, such as academics and the media, was restricted.[78]

---

75 EXCOM Conclusion 19 (XXXI), ¶ e, 1980. EXCOM Conclusion 22 (XXXII) 1981. This latter conclusion followed a report of the Group of Experts on temporary refuge in situations of large-scale influx, which met in Geneva from 21–24 April 1981.

76 UNHCR, Status of Guineans (Bissau) Abroad, UNHCR/IOM/38/75; UNHCR/BOM/48/75 (1 December 1975) and UNHCR, Status of Mozambicans Abroad after 25 June 1975, UNHCR/IOM/36/75; UNHCR/BOM/47/75 (14 November 1975).

77 UNHCR, Note on International Protection, ¶ 17, U.N. Doc. A/AC.96/593 (31 July 1981). Also see EXCOM Conclusion 22 (XXXII), ¶ 1, 1981.

78 UNHCR, *Handbook on Procedures and Criteria for Determining Refugee Status*, UNHCR/BOM/66/80 (31 October 1980).

3.4.1.3 Expansion of use of UNHCR doctrine: 1982 to the present

3.4.1.3.1 1982–1989

During the 1980s, UNHCR intensified its formulation and issuance of doctrinal positions through means well established in the 1970s: internal memoranda, documents to EXCOM and the General Assembly, and EXCOM conclusions. The import of certain UNHCR doctrinal positions was strengthened by UNHCR's procurement of the General Assembly's endorsement of specific EXCOM conclusions, which contained UNHCR doctrine.[79]

Provisions of the 1951 Refugee Convention continued to receive clarification and elaboration through UNHCR doctrine. UNHCR doctrinal documents established elements for the determination of the refugee status of persons connected with organizations that advocate or practice violence and persons in civil war situations[80] and elements for the consideration of issues relevant to the 'membership of a particular social group' grounds in the inclusion clauses of the refugee definition.[81]

With respect to standards for protection in the 1951 Refugee Convention, UNHCR doctrine clarified the topic of detention, related to article 31 of the 1951 Refugee Convention. Specifically, UNHCR suggested standards on detention for refugees and asylum seekers in its 1984 Note on International Protection, which were then articulated in an EXCOM conclusion.[82] UNHCR even expressed the view that the principle of *non-refoulement* had acquired the character of a peremptory rule of international law.[83] In addition, UNHCR continued to elaborate on the principle of family unity, contained in the Final Act annexed to the 1951 Refugee Convention, with an interpretation of types of family reunification.[84]

Importantly, UNHCR continued its formulation of doctrinal positions on issues not covered in the 1951 Refugee Convention. UNHCR articulated principles for the application of the cancellation of refugee status,[85] an option not mentioned in

---

79 See for example G.A. Res. 40/118 ¶ 7, U.N. Doc. A/RES/40/118 (13 December 1985) and G.A. Res. 42/109 ¶ 5, 6, U.N. Doc. A/RES/42/109 (7 December1987).
80 UNHCR, Determination of Refugee Status of Persons connected with Organizations or Groups which Advocate and/or Practise Violence, UNHCR/IOM/78/88; UNHCR/FOM/71/88 (1 June 1988); UNHCR, Refugees in Civil War Situations, UNHCR/IOM/138/89; UNHCR/FOM/114/89 (18 December 1989).
81 UNHCR, Membership of a Particular Social Group, UNHCR/IOM/132/89; UNHCR/FOM/110/89 (12 December 1989) and EXCOM Conclusion 39 (XXXVI), ¶ k, 1985.
82 UNHCR, Note on International Protection, ¶ 26-30, U.N. Doc. A/AC.96/643 (9 August 1984). EXCOM Conclusion 44 (XXXVII) 1986.
83 EXCOM Conclusion 25 (XXXIII), ¶ b, 1982.
84 UNHCR, The Reunification of Refugee Families, UNHCR/IOM/52/83; UNHCR/FOM/49/83 (18 July 1983).
85 UNHCR, Note on Loss of Refugee Status Through Cancellation (4 July 1989). Available at http://www.unhcr.org/refworld/docid/441045d44.html (accessed 27 October 2011).

the 1951 Refugee Convention but provided for in the Handbook.[86] The solution of voluntary repatriation, also not mentioned in the 1951 Refugee Convention, received clarification by UNHCR. UNHCR articulated the doctrinal principle that repatriation should take place at the freely expressed wish of the refugee in an EXCOM conclusion,[87] prepared guidelines on voluntary repatriation,[88] at the request of EXCOM,[89] and subsequently, articulated key standards in its 1987 Note on International Protection.[90] UNHCR also provided procedural guidance on the determination of manifestly unfounded applications in two conclusions,[91] and expressed principles for when asylum seekers could be returned to their first country of asylum,[92] a concept initially addressed by UNHCR in the early 1950s.

3.4.1.3.2   1990s

In the 1990s, UNHCR began to provide its views much more publicly.[93] The European Union's harmonization process was a key factor that pushed UNHCR to develop its positions well beyond standards contained in the 1951 Refugee Convention and to issue them in a publicly available, non-restricted manner. Thus, UNHCR issued doctrinal positions on such issues as reception standards, temporary protection, and complementary protection, among others in connection with the European Commission's drafting of directives on various asylum topics.[94]

UNHCR increasingly began to provide doctrinal positions in standalone documents rather than primarily in its reports submitted to EXCOM and the General Assembly. For example, UNHCR announced doctrinal positions on the eligibility

---

86 UNHCR Handbook, *supra* note 66, at ¶ 117.

87 EXCOM Conclusion 40 (XXXVI), ¶ b, 1985.

88 UNHCR, Voluntary Repatriation: Principles and Guidelines for Action, UNHCR/IOM/5/87; UNHCR/FOM/5/87 (10 February 1987).

89 EXCOM Conclusion 40 (XXXVI), ¶ m, 1985. Pursuant to this paragraph, UNHCR was called on to elaborate an instrument 'reflecting all existing principles and guidelines relating to voluntary repatriation for acceptance by the international community as a whole'.

90 UNHCR, Note on International Protection, ¶ 47, U.N. Doc. A/AC.96/694 (3 August 1987).

91 EXCOM Conclusion 28 (XXXIII) 1982, EXCOM Conclusion 30 (XXXIV) 1983.

92 EXCOM Conclusion 58 (XL), ¶ f, 1989.

93 This is likely due to the crisis in international refugee law, which is treated in detail in Chapter 4. UNHCR had become quite concerned about refugee protection, which was 'seriously jeopardized in certain situations as a result of denial of access, expulsion, refoulement and unjustified detention, as well as other threats to … [refugees'] physical security, dignity and well-being'. EXCOM Conclusion 71(XLIV), ¶ f, 1993.

94 For a compilation of UNHCR's positions on draft directives, see UNHCR, Tool Boxes on EU Asylum Matters: Tool Box 2: The Instruments (September 2002). Available at http://www.unhcr. org/publ/PUBL/406a8c432.pdf (accessed 27 October 2011).

of draft evaders and military deserters,[95] agents of persecution,[96] and the exclusion and cessation clauses of the refugee definition in its own independent documents.[97] Moreover, UNHCR expressed its views on issues that were not covered by the 1951 Refugee Convention. These positions included the topic of complementary protection,[98] and a range of issues interpreted by States in a manner so as to deny asylum seekers protection as refugees: internal relocation as a reasonable alternative to seeking asylum,[99] safe country of origin and safe country of asylum notions,[100] the safe third country concept,[101] visa requirements and carrier sanctions,[102] and agents of persecution.[103]

For the first time, UNHCR doctrinal positions did not just elaborate principles, but also overtly criticized certain approaches adopted by States. Thus, UNHCR stated that the fiction of 'international zones' in airports was used to 'avoid obligations toward refugees', that 'carrier sanctions pose a threat to basic principles of refugee protection', and that the use of the concept of safe country of origin essentially 'preclude[d] access to status determination procedures as a de facto reservation to art. 1 A(2) of the Convention'.[104]

UNHCR also developed doctrinal principles concerning the protection of refugee children and women, issues that were fairly uncontroversial for States in light of the global concern about these groups. In the case of refugee children, UNHCR utilized the 1989 Convention on the Rights of the Child, which has near universal

---

95 UNHCR, UNHCR's Position on Certain Types of Draft Evasion, (22 January 1991). Available at http://www.unhcr.org/refworld/docid/441025c44.html (accessed 27 October 2011).

96 UNHCR, Agents of Persecution – UNHCR Position (14 March 1995). Available at http://www. unhcr.org/refworld/docid/3ae6b31da3.html (accessed 27 October 2011).

97 On exclusion, see UNHCR, The Exclusion Clauses: Guidelines on Their Application (2 December 1996). Available at http://www.unhcr.org/refworld/docid/3ae6b31d9f.html (accessed 27 October 2011); UNHCR, Note on the Exclusion Clauses, UNHCR Doc. EC/47/SC/CRP.29 (30 May 1997); and UNHCR, Background Paper on the Article 1F Exclusion Clauses, (June 1998) (on file with author). On cessation, see UNHCR, Note on Cessation Clauses, UNHCR Doc. EC/47/SC/ CRP.30 (30 May 1997) and UNHCR, The Cessation Clauses: Guidelines on Their Application (26 April 1999). Available athttp://www.unhcr.org/refworld/docid/3c06138c4.html (accessed 27 October 2011).

98 UNHCR, Protection of Persons of Concern to UNHCR who Fall Outside the 1951 Convention: A Discussion Note, UNHCR Doc. EC/1992/SCP/CRP.5 (2 April 1992).

99 UNHCR, UNHCR Position Paper: Relocating Internally as a Reasonable Alternative to Seeking Asylum (The So-Called 'Internal Flight Alternative' or 'Relocation Principle') (9 February 1999). Available at http://www.unhcr.org/refworld/docid/3ae6b336c.html (accessed 27 October 2011).

100 UNHCR, Background Note on the Safe Country Concept and Refugee Status, UNHCR Doc. EC/ SCP/68 (26 July 1991).

101 UNHCR, Considerations on the 'Safe Third Country' Concept (July 1996). Available at http:// www.unhcr.org/refworld/docid/3ae6b3268.htm (accessed 27 October 2011).

102 UNHCR, UNHCR Position: Visa Requirements and Carrier Sanctions (September 1995). Available at http://www.unhcr.org/refworld/docid/3ae6b33a10.html (accessed 27 October 2011).

103 UNHCR, Agents of Persecution – UNHCR Position (14 March 1995) (on file with author).

104 UNHCR, Current Asylum Issues, UNHCR/IOM/28/92; UNHCR/FOM/29/92 (13 March 1992).

ratification by States,[105] to further define principles for the treatment of refugee children and for unaccompanied children seeking asylum.[106] Several UNHCR Notes to EXCOM concerning refugee women not only established policy approaches for dealing with refugee women but also procedural requirements with respect to the treatment of asylum claims by women and particular grounds for their persecution.[107]

The ability of UNHCR to issue doctrinal documents was not totally unlimited, however. UNHCR had to remain aware of and sensitive to States' interests as suggested by UNHCR's experience in attempting to have EXCOM adopt a conclusion on detention that built on the initial position it articulated in the 1986 EXCOM Conclusion.[108] In 1999, UNHCR issued Revised Guidelines on the Detention of Asylum-Seekers. UNHCR then prepared a paper titled 'Detention of Asylum-Seekers and Refugees: The Framework, the Problem and Recommended Practice' for the 1999 EXCOM session with the intention that EXCOM would adopt a conclusion on this topic.[109] However, insufficient support in EXCOM resulted in no conclusion on the topic.

3.4.1.3.3 2000 TO THE PRESENT

UNHCR's creation of doctrinal positions accelerated significantly at the beginning of the second millennium. UNHCR produced papers on various topics that not only explored the context and the different approaches adopted by States, but also established doctrinal principles. These included papers on gender related persecution, complementary protection, and the interpretation of article 1 of the 1951 Refugee Convention.[110]

---

105 Somalia and the United States remain the only countries that have not yet ratified this convention.

106 See for example, EXCOM Conclusion 84 (XLVIII) 1997 and UNHCR, UNHCR Policy on Refugee Children, UNHCR Doc. EC/SCP/82 (6 August 1993) and UNHCR, Guidelines on Policies and Procedures in Dealing with Unaccompanied Children Seeking Asylum (February 1997). Available at http://www.unhcr.org/refworld/docid/3ae6b3360.html (accessed 27 October 2011).

107 See UNHCR, Note on Certain Aspects of Sexual Violence Against Refugee Women, U.N. Doc. A/AC.96/822 (12 October 1993) and UNHCR, Note on Refugee Women and International Protection, UNHCR Doc. EC/SCP/59 (28 August 1990). Also see EXCOM Conclusion 64 (XLI), ¶ a (iii), 1990 and EXCOM Conclusion 73 (XLIV), ¶ a, 1993.

108 EXCOM Conclusion 44 (XXXVII) 1986.

109 UNHCR, Detention of Asylum-Seekers and Refugees: The Framework, The Problem and Recommended Practice, UNHCR Doc. EC/49/SC/CRP.13 (4 June 1999). In particular, see paragraph 26, which sets forth recommended practices that would have served as the basis for an EXCOM conclusion.

110 See UNHCR, Gender-related Persecution (January 2000). Available at http://www.unhcr.org/refworld/docid/3bd3f2b04.html (accessed 27 October 2011); UNHCR, Complementary Forms of Protection (April 2001) (on file with author), and UNHCR, Interpreting Article 1 of the 1951 Convention Relating to the Status of Refugees (April 2001). Available at http://www.unhcr.org/refworld/docid/ 3b20a3914.html (accessed 27 October 2011).

The present formulation of doctrine by UNHCR takes the Global Consultations process, launched by UNHCR in late 2000, as its starting point. Two significant anniversaries, the 50th anniversary of UNHCR in 2000 and the 50th anniversary of the 1951 Refugee Convention in 2001 were the stimuli for this process. UNHCR decided to mark these key dates with a process that would reinvigorate the principles and standards that assure protection to refugees. During the consultations, which were undertaken during an 18-month period among governments, intergovernmental and non-governmental organizations, UNHCR and refugee experts,[111] numerous protection issues were discussed.[112]

The outcome of these discussions was UNHCR's creation of an Agenda for Protection, approved by EXCOM, which specifies that UNHCR shall 'produce complementary guidelines to its Handbook on Procedures and Criteria for Determining Refugee Status' and that UNHCR is to 'explore areas that would benefit from further standard-setting'.[113] Since the adoption of the Agenda for Protection, UNHCR has formulated a number of guidelines, including on the topics of the exclusion clauses, the cessation clauses, and refugee women as a particular social group.[114]

In addition, during this period, the legal value of UNHCR doctrine contained in EXCOM conclusions has been further strengthened. The General Assembly now regularly endorses EXCOM's annual report, which contains the EXCOM conclusions.[115] Thus, all of the EXCOM conclusions adopted each year are endorsed by the General Assembly.

3.4.2 *Authority for UNHCR's issuance of doctrine*

As is evident from a review of UNHCR's Statute, there is no wording that suggests that UNHCR is to issue doctrinal positions. Moreover, the General Assembly has not issued any resolution that refers to UNHCR's creation of doctrinal positions. The lack of any specific mandatory wording or any General Assembly resolution mentioning UNHCR's issuance of doctrinal positions is not surprising; the General Assembly merely establishes UNHCR's responsibilities

---

111 UNHCR, Agenda for Protection 9 (2003).
112 Ibid., at 85–93.
113 Ibid., at 38.
114 UNHCR, Guidelines on International Protection No. 5, Application of the Exclusion Clauses: Article 1F of the 1951 Convention Relating to the Status of Refugees, HCR/GIP/03/05 (4 September 2003); UNHCR, Guidelines on International Protection No. 3: Cessation of Refugee Status under Article 1C(5) and (6) of the 1951 Convention Relating to the Status of Refugees (the 'Ceased Circumstances' Clauses) HCR/GIP/03/03 (10 February 2003); UNHCR, Guidelines on International Protection No. 2: 'Membership of a Particular Social Group' Within the Context of Article 1A(2) of the 1951 Convention and/or its 1967 Protocol Relating to the Status of Refugees, HCR/GIP/02/02 (7 May 2002).
115 See for example, G.A. Res. 61/137, ¶ 1, U.N. Doc. A/RES/61/137 (19 Dec. 2006) and G.A. Res. 62/124, ¶ 1, U.N. Doc. A/RES/62/124 (18 December 2007).

and the general parameters of UNHCR's work. Yet, UNHCR clearly believes that:

> [UNHCR] has a doctrinal responsibility to work for the progressive develop-
> ment of international refugee law. In essence, this function involves promot-
> ing, interpreting, safeguarding and developing the fundamental principles
> of refugee protection. The immediate goal is to strengthen international
> commitments to receive refugees, as well as to combat discrimination and
> negative practices jeopardising refugees and to search for durable solutions
> to their problems which give prime importance to humanitarian considera-
> tions and respect for basic rights. For the longer term, the objective is to
> develop and promote a far-reaching regime of refugee protection based on
> solid legal foundations and internationally recognized principles.[116]

So, the question remains: what is the source of authority for UNHCR's issuance of doctrinal positions? Such authority can be found in a number of sources depending on the nature of the doctrinal work. In some cases, UNHCR has been asked to create a doctrinal document by EXCOM. For example, UNHCR drafted the Handbook pursuant to an explicit request by the Executive Committee to 'consider the possibility of issuing – for the guidance of Governments – a hand-book relating to procedures and criteria for determining refugee status ... – with due regard to the confidential nature of individual requests and the particular situations involved'.[117] UNHCR's development of guidelines on voluntary repat-riation also was undertaken following a request by EXCOM.[118] Furthermore, EXCOM requested UNHCR to promote the development of criteria and guidelines with respect to refugee women.[119]

More generally worded EXCOM conclusions can be considered as the basis for UNHCR's issuance of other doctrinal positions not authorized by one of the foregoing methods. EXCOM has encouraged 'the continued development and elaboration of refugee law in response to the new and changing humanitarian and other problems of refugees and asylum-seekers'[120] and recognized the contributions

---

116 UNHCR, *Note on International Protection*, ¶ 3 U.N. Doc. A/AC.96/728 (2 August 1989).

117 EXOM Conclusion 8 (XXVIII), ¶ g, 1977.

118 EXCOM Conclusion 40 (XXXVI), ¶ m, 1985. Ten years passed between EXCOM's request
    and UNHCR's issuance of the guidelines, which suggests that it was not easy for UNHCR to
    prepare guidelines which conformed to UNHCR's protection standards but yet would be accept-
    able to States. See UNHCR, Handbook: Voluntary Repatriation: International Protection, 1996.
    Available at http://www.unhcr.org/pub/PUBL/ 3bfe68d32.pdf (accessed 27 October 2011).

119 See EXCOM Conclusion 77 (XLVI), ¶ g, 1995, which '[c]alls *upon* the High Commissioner to
    support and promote efforts by States towards the development and implementation of criteria
    and guidelines on responses to persecution specifically aimed at women'. Also see EXCOM
    Conclusion 79 (XLVII), ¶ o, 1996 which recalls the 1995 conclusion.

120 EXCOM Conclusion 25 (XXXIII), ¶ i, 1982. The wording of paragraph (i) in EXCOM
    Conclusion 25 does not expressly state that UNHCR must take action, however, since EXCOM's

made by UNHCR through its activities.[121] EXCOM also acknowledged that UNHCR's work related to 'the development ... of basic standards for the treatment of refugees' is part of UNHCR's international protection function.[122] This development of standards should be carried out 'by maintaining a constant dialogue with Governments, non-governmental organizations and academic institutions and of filling lacunae in international refugee law', according to EXCOM.[123]

One of the most noteworthy EXCOM conclusions in this area suggests an involved and substantive role for UNHCR in the creation of principles within international refugee law; specifically, UNHCR is to 'explor[e] the development of guiding principles' to ensure international protection to all who need it.[124] This guidance from EXCOM could be construed as a direct reference to UNHCR doctrine. Although it is not legally binding, as noted in section 2 above, UNHCR does follow the guidance provided by EXCOM conclusions in practice.

UNHCR's articulation of its doctrinal views, in reports submitted to the General Assembly[125] and EXCOM, can be considered as an inherent and normal aspect of its reporting obligation. Any UNHCR doctrinal position, which cannot be considered as authorized by either an EXCOM conclusion or as part of UNHCR's reporting responsibility, can be justified on the basis of UNHCR's implied powers that are derived from its express powers, discussed in section 3.3.1. Consequently, UNHCR's authority to issue doctrinal positions can be said to be derived from its international protection function and linked to two of its statutory responsibilities: first, the promotion of the creation of international conventions for the protection of refugees by States and, second, the supervision of States' application of existing international refugee conventions. Doctrinal positions have become an integral and necessary component of UNHCR's international protection work, and, more specifically, its efforts to ensure the development and effectiveness of international refugee law, as will be seen in more detail in Chapters 5 and 6.

3.5 Conclusion

UNHCR's Statute provides for the possibility for States, through the means of UN General Assembly resolutions, to supplement UNHCR's statutory responsibilities.

---

purpose is to provide advice to UNHCR, as already noted in section 2, it can be implied that this advice is directed to UNHCR.
121 EXCOM Conclusion 29 (XXXIV), ¶ k, 1983.
122 EXCOM Conclusion 29 (XXXIV), ¶ b, 1983.
123 EXCOM Conclusion 29 (XXXIV), ¶ j, 1983. As with EXCOM Conclusion 25 (XXXIII), ¶ i, 1982 cited in footnote 120, it can be assumed that although the conclusion does not specify that UNHCR must take action, it is nevertheless directed to UNHCR.
124 EXCOM Conclusion 77 (XLVI), ¶ f, 1995 and EXCOM Conclusion 81 (XLVIII), ¶ p, 1997 endorsed by G.A. Res. 52/103, ¶ 1, U.N. Doc. A/RES/52/103 (12 December 1997).
125 UNHCR Statute, *supra* note 2, at ¶ 11.

The Statute also specifies that the General Assembly and EXCOM may provide policy advice to UNHCR. While these statutory provisions would suggest that UNHCR is on the receiving end of such decisions and advice, in practice, UNHCR not only initiates the requests for the General Assembly to assign it additional responsibilities and to provide it with policy guidance, but also formulates the content of the relevant resolutions. Similarly, in the case of guidance from EXCOM, UNHCR seeks EXCOM's advice, which then takes the form of an EXCOM conclusion, when there is a need to have a clear articulation of the action that UNHCR is to undertake or of a principle for States to follow as well as the support of States for UNHCR's work. States' participation in this process has grown in recent years, in particular since the crisis in refugee protection and law discussed in Chapter 4, but UNHCR still has a strong and stable influence on the process.

States clearly left the discretion as to the determination of the content of UNHCR's statutory responsibilities to UNHCR. UNHCR utilized its own initiative to broadly interpret its international protection function in order to alter and extend its responsibilities related to international refugee law. In addition, UNHCR's broad definition of international protection has allowed it a great deal of latitude in the daily work that it performs and also enables the organization to further refugee protection, specifically, to work to ensure that States' ratify/ accede and implement treaties relevant to asylum seekers and refugees and apply and respect such treaty provisions in practice. The authority for UNHCR to define international protection in a way that permits the agency to adopt additional responsibilities related to international refugee law can be based on the notion of implied powers.

The second technique, which permits UNHCR to continue to play a key role in ensuring international protection for refugees and has been progressively developed by UNHCR over the years, is that of UNHCR's 'voice' on refugee law issues, referred to as 'UNHCR doctrine' in this book. The authority for UNHCR to articulate doctrinal positions varies in accordance with the nature of the doctrinal work. Such authority may emanate from EXCOM's specific requests for such positions, generally worded EXCOM conclusions, or be an inherent characteristic of its reporting work to the General Assembly and EXCOM. Such authority may also be derived from UNHCR's implied powers linked to its statutory responsibilities to promote the creation of international refugee law as well as its supervisory responsibilities.

UNHCR's doctrinal positions have significantly changed during the more than 60 years of UNHCR's work. The content has evolved from an initial reiteration of standards contained in the 1951 Refugee Convention to the articulation of new principles as well as the further development of the refugee definition and standards contained in the 1951 Refugee Convention. The form of these positions has been transformed from internal memoranda to include documents drafted by UNHCR for EXCOM and the General Assembly, including EXCOM conclusions, and most importantly, independent documents provided not only to governments, but also to non-governmental organizations and academics, among others.

UNHCR has enhanced the availability of its positions to all interested persons, by making such documents available on its website. However, it has not yet publicly disseminated a comprehensive compilation of such doctrinal positions. Thus, government officials, researchers and others must still sift through the rather daunting number of UNHCR position papers, handbooks and training manuals, and other documents to find relevant positions taken by UNHCR.

The evolution in the nature of UNHCR's doctrinal positions has been very marked since the 1980s. This coincided with the need for UNHCR to undertake a greater role in shaping the development of international refugee law, particularly in light of the emergence of the crisis in refugee protection and law, a topic discussed in the next chapter.

4   The crisis in refugee protection

4.1 Introduction

Those concerned with refugees generally speak of 'refugee crises', that is, flows of refugees. In the 1980s, however, the crisis became a 'crisis in refugee protection'. States demonstrated not only a pronounced unwillingness to ensure the protection of refugees as generously as they had previously, but also manifested their desire and intent to resume control over, what they considered to be, the refugee problem. Such assertion of control divested UNHCR of the extensive practical authority it previously had to manage the problem of refugees on behalf of States and shifted responsibility for refugees more squarely into the domain of States.

Consequently, the relationship between States and UNHCR, based on co-operation, would become marked by significant differences in views. The domain for the formulation of these different views would be international refugee law. As a result, the weaknesses in the refugee law framework and in the means for ensuring the effectiveness of the 1951 Refugee Convention standards became increasingly apparent and of crucial importance.

4.2 UNHCR's changing relationship with states

4.2.1 Co-operation

In theory, UNHCR's role related to the international protection of refugees is to complement that of States. States bear the primary responsibility for not only creating international refugee law standards, but also for taking the necessary steps to ensure that those standards are effective at a national level. In order to execute this relationship in practice, a close and co-operative relationship between UNHCR and States is essential.

The essential obligation of co-operation, for both UNHCR and States, was articulated at the time of the drafting of UNHCR's Statute. UNHCR is to stay 'in close touch with the Governments … concerned'[1] and States are 'to co-operate

---

1   See paragraph 8(g) of the Statute of the Office of the United Nations High Commissioner for Refugees, contained in the Annex to UN General Assembly Resolution 428(V) of 14 December 1950. G.A. Res. 428(V) (14 December 1950) (hereinafter UNHCR Statute).

with the United Nations High Commissioner for Refugees in the performance of his functions'.[2] The importance of such co-operation is reflected in the wording of the sixth preambular paragraph of the 1951 Refugee Convention[3] and is reinforced by article 56 of the UN Charter.[4] Moreover, pursuant to article 35 of the 1951 Refugee Convention, States are to 'undertake to co-operate with' UNHCR 'in the exercise of its functions, and shall in particular facilitate its duty of supervising the application of the provisions' of the 1951 Refugee Convention.[5]

However, this co-operative relationship is a dynamic one affected by refugee crises, and the changing political, social and economic situation within States. The number of asylum seekers seeking protection, their countries of origin, their reasons for flight, and their needs can vary and affect States' willingness to grant them asylum. States' treatment of asylum seekers and refugees constantly fluctuates due to a complex, but inevitable interplay between States' concern about refugees and their national interests.[6] This interaction between States' humanitarian concerns for refugees and political interests is not new; it existed well before the drafting of the 1951 Refugee Convention. For example, when Western European countries, which would eventually form the core contingent of signatory States of the 1951 Refugee Convention, were trying to avoid a war in

2 G.A. Res. 428(V), ¶ 2 (14 December 1950).
3 Convention Relating to the Status of Refugees, 6th preambular ¶, 28 July 1951, 189 U.N.T.S. 150 (hereinafter 1951 Refugee Convention). This preambular paragraph states that: 'Noting that the United Nations High Commissioner for Refugees is charged with the task of supervising international conventions providing for the protection of refugees, and recognizing that the effective co-ordination of measures taken to deal with this problem will depend upon the co-operation of States with the High Commissioner.'
4 U.N. Charter, art. 56.
5 1951 Refugee Convention, *supra* note 3, at art. 35(1). Protocol Relating to the Status of Refugees, art. II(1), 16 December 1966, 606 U.N.T.S.267. Regional instruments relating to refugees also contain provisions on co-operation with UNHCR. For example, the 1969 OAU Convention Governing the Specific Aspects of Refugee Problems in Africa provides that 'Member States shall co-operate with the Office of the United Nations High Commissioner for Refugees.' OAU Convention Governing the Specific Aspects of Refugee Problems in Africa, art. VIII.1, 10 September 1969, 1001 U.N.T.S. 45. Similarly, the 1984 Cartagena Declaration, a non-binding instrument that has significant moral force in Central America, 'acknowledges with appreciation the commitments with regard to refugees included in the Contadora Act on Peace and Co-operation in Central America, the bases of which the Colloquium fully shares' and which include '[t]o support the work performed by the United Nations High Commissioner for Refugees (UNHCR) in Central America and to establish direct co-ordination machinery to facilitate the fulfilment of his mandate'. The Cartagena Declaration on Refugees, ¶II.e, OAS/Ser.L/V.II.66, doc. 10, rev.1, at 190–193 (1984). In Europe, Declaration 17 to the Treaty of Amsterdam provides for consultations to be established with UNHCR 'on matters relating to asylum policy'. Declaration No. 17 on article 73k of the Treaty of Amsterdam Amending the Treaty on European Union, the Treaties establishing the European Communities and certain Related Acts, 2 October 1997, 1997 O.M. (C 340).
6 See Guy Goodwin-Gill, *The Politics of Refugee Protection*, Lecture given on 19 October 2007 at the Workshop 'UNHCR and the Global Cold War, 1971–1984' (on file with author).

the 1930s, they refused to accept Jewish persons as refugees.[7] British refugee policy since 1905, according to some, has been generous to refugees 'as much the result of guilt, economic self-interest and international power politics (including, to a lesser extent, international law) than of notions of "natural justice" *per se.*'[8]

UNHCR, as part of its supervisory responsibility, has always had to address States' actions that are inconsistent with international refugee law. Situations of non-fulfilment by States of their obligations under the 1951 Refugee Convention have preoccupied UNHCR since its creation.[9] However, where States' approaches are underpinned by a commitment to the protection of refugees and a general humanitarian spirit, workable resolutions to such situations are more readily formulated in a co-operative manner with UNHCR.

With the end of the Second World War, there was a convergence between States' concern about refugees and States' national interests, which resulted in the creation of UNHCR and the drafting of the 1951 Refugee Convention. At that time, States were attempting to resolve a collective problem: the situation of the estimated 292,000 persons in Europe who had not been repatriated to their home countries or resettled in third countries[10] as well as the new refugees who were arriving from Eastern European countries.[11] Their interest in protecting refugees did not arise exclusively from a humanitarian spirit. There also was a very practical and political side to States' willingness to guarantee the protection of refugees. As the President of the International Refugee Organization noted in 1950, during discussions on the draft Convention, States would be willing to accept refugees to the extent that they needed labour.[12] Indeed, this was the primary

---

7 Laura Barnett, 'Global Governance and the Evolution of the International Refugee Regime', 14 *Int'l. J. Refugee L.* 238, 243 (2002).
8 Tony Kushner and Katharine Knox, *Refugees in an Age of Genocide: Global, National and Local Perspectives during the Twentieth Century* 399 (1999).
9 For example, see UNHCR, Report of the UNHCR and Addendum, 1952, U.N. Doc. A/2126 (1953), which includes a review of the protection problems of refugees in different countries.
10 Note by the Secretary-General, U.N. Doc. A/C.3/528, ¶ 12 (26 October 1949) (hereinafter Note by the Secretary-General). U.N. GAOR, 4th Sess., 265th plen.mtg. at ¶ 12 (3 December 1949).
11 Gil Loescher, *The UNHCR and World Politics: A Perilous Path* 42 (2001).
12 During the discussions of the draft Statue of UNHCR, accusations were made by Eastern European countries that Western European countries were willing to accept healthy refugees who could provide needed labour. See for example, statements by the Representative of the Ukranian Soviet Socialist Republic, U.N. GAOR, 4th Sess., 258th plen., 3rd cee mtg. at ¶ 47, (9 November 1949) and Mr. Zebrowski, Poland, U.N. GAOR, 4th Sess., 264th plen. mtg. at ¶ 165–166 (2 December 1949). The memorandum of the International Refugee Organization, addressed to the General Assembly, essentially confirms the view of the Eastern European States by stating that approximately 150,000 persons cared for by the IRO 'are in circumstances which have so far made resettlement difficult, if not impossible, for them. They consist of people left alone in the world, unable to support themselves, requiring hospital accommodation or permanent care, or of individuals or whole families who, on grounds of age, health, occupation etc., have not as yet been resettled in other countries.' Note by the Secretary-General, *supra* note 10, at ¶ 14.

approach taken by States that accepted Eastern European refugees after the creation of UNHCR.[13]

4.2.2 Divergence

At present, there is a widespread perception that States are less willing to receive refugees, and to provide them with international protection. Thus, a significant divergence between UNHCR's and States' views of how asylum seekers and refugees should be treated has emerged.[14] Pinpointing when and why States' interest in providing protection to refugees no longer converged with their political, economic and social interests is not easy. There has been no comprehensive study done of the causes of such crisis, but various theories have been advanced. Chimini finds that the end of the Cold War meant that refugees no longer had 'ideological or geopolitical value' for developed States.[15] Loescher cites the 'steep rise in European unemployment combined with high immigration levels' that resulted in 'increasing concern about being flooded by foreigners.'[16] Gilbert Jaeger, a former Director of UNHCR's Division of International Protection, believes that the end of legal immigration, except for family reunification, in Western Europe in 1973–1974, also played a significant role.[17] Grahl-Madsen situates the problem in an even broader context of a stagnating world economy and man's increasing awareness of global limitations in such areas as raw materials, energy and the capacity to reabsorb pollution, as well as rising unemployment.[18]

At the beginning of the refugee protection crisis, UNHCR noted that:

It cannot be overlooked that various problems related to asylum have acquired an increasingly complex character due to continuing large influxes

---

13 As Jan and Leo Lucassen have noted, the refugees fleeing from Eastern to Western Europe 'were ostensibly welcomed by western countries for ideological and humanitarian reasons. In practice, however, each country tried to select the most able and best educated among the refugees. No one was interested in people who were elderly, sick, or disabled.' Jan Lucassen and Leo Lucassen, *Migration, Migration History, History: Old Paradigms and New Perspectives* 16 (1997).

14 There have been numerous articles analyzing the causes and effects of such crisis and making proposals for the way forward. See for example, Guy Goodwin-Gill, 'The International Protection of Refugees: What Future?', 12 *Int'l. J. Refugee L.* 1 (2000) and James Hathaway, 'Making International Refugee Law Relevant Again: A Proposal for Collectivized and Solution-Oriented Protection', 10 *Harv. Hum. Rts. J.* 115 (1997).

15 See B.S. Chimini, 'The Meaning of Words and the Role of UNHCR in Voluntary Repatriation', 5 *Int'l. J. Refugee L.* 442, 443–444 (1993).

16 Loescher, *supra* note 11, at 235.

17 Gilbert Jaeger, 'Are Refugees Migrants? The Recent Approach to Refugee Flows as a Particular Aspect of Migration', *in* OIKOUMENE, Special Issue, Refugees and Asylum Seekers in a Common European House, 18, 20 (Commission on Inter-Church Aid and World Council of Churches, eds, August 1991) (on file with author).

18 Atle Grahl-Madsen, *Refugees and Refugee Law in a World in Transition*, in *The Land Beyond: Collected Essays on Refugee Law and Policy*; 138 138–139 (Peter Macalister-Smith and Gudmundur Alfredsson, eds, 2001).

of asylum-seekers experienced by developed and developing countries alike. The higher level of economic opportunities in certain countries has prompted the mass movement from lesser developed areas of persons who voluntarily leave their country of origin drawn by the prospect of economic betterment. Current recessionary trends in the developed world have however limited the capacity of such countries to absorb large numbers of new arrivals. An additional and related factor is a perceptible resentment against aliens – including refugees – who are seen as competing for reduced economic opportunities. In the face of increasingly restrictive admission practices resulting from declining immigration quota – many of the persons included in these migrationary flows attempt to circumvent immigration rules by endeavouring to gain admission as asylum-seekers. These various developments must also be seen against the background of a general decline in public sympathy for the situation of the asylum-seeker, an unfortunate development that has been described as 'compassion fatigue'.[19]

Clearly, the declining economies in developed countries combined with increasing numbers of asylum seekers left the public as well as officials with a less welcoming approach to refugees. One indication of the impending changes in countries' approaches to asylum was the unsuccessful attempt to turn the 1967 Declaration on Territorial Asylum into a Convention. The Universal Declaration of Human Rights provides that '[e]veryone has the right to seek and to enjoy in other countries asylum from persecution'[20], but in reality, the concept of asylum has been viewed as the prerogative of the State, rather than the right of the individual. A convention on territorial asylum would have given individuals such a right. However, despite more than five years of work with a significant contribution by UNHCR, States could not reach agreement on the text.[21] The failure of States to adopt a text did not augur well for States' humanitarian approach to refugees. Since then, States have not adopted any additional refugee law instruments of a universal stature.

Signs of change clearly emerged in States' treatment of refugees in the 1980s. UNHCR's 1981 annual report to the General Assembly was quite positive. It notes that the general protection situation was 'somewhat more encouraging than in previous years', with no large-scale measures of *refoulement*; States were

---

19 UNHCR, *Note on International Protection*, ¶ 10, U.N. Doc. A/AC.96/609 (26 August 1982).

20 Universal Declaration of Human Rights, G.A. Res. 217A, art.14(1), U.N. Doc. A/810 (12 December 1948).

21 The final death knoll for the draft Convention occurred at the United Nations Conference on Territorial Asylum held from January to February 1977 at which only a few of the draft articles were discussed in a harsh political climate. Atle Grahl-Madsen, *Territorial Asylum* 8–10 (1980). An honest assessment of the reasons for the failure of the conference are given in Gervase Coles, *Recent and Future Developments in International Refugee Law* 5–8 (paper submitted to the Seminar on Problems in the International Protection of Refugees, University of New South Wales, 2–3 August 1980) (on file with author).

generally applying liberal practices as regards the admission of asylum seekers.[22] However, in UNHCR's 1982 annual report, UNHCR notes that '[t]here are indications that Governments in different areas of the world are adopting an increasingly restrictive approach', such as by assuming 'that certain groups of asylum-seekers were a priori ineligible for refugee status' and adopting 'more onerous standards of proof' for certain categories of asylum seekers.[23] These initial restrictive measures would develop into a pronounced trend, which became the dominant focus of UNHCR's concern about international protection. As a result, the 1983 Note on International Protection was essentially devoted to the deterioration in international protection, in particular with respect to States' admission policies and their treatment of refugees.[24]

In essence, the crisis concerned the effectiveness of international law, that is, the actual protection of refugees' rights by States in practice. States were trying to adapt the system of protection, namely the laws, to their own needs. Thus, they attempted to disregard or narrowly interpret their international legal obligations and to develop more detailed national standards. This trend, which began in the early 1980s, still characterizes States' policies and practices toward refugees today. Countries, particularly those in the developed world, have continued to devise restrictive measures. They attempt to limit the number of refugees reaching their territory, including through the sealing off of borders with electric fences, direct or indirect *refoulement*, non-embarkation of asylum seekers arriving by boat, visa requirements, carrier sanctions,[25] and detention,[26] and have even proposed to screen asylum seekers outside the country of asylum.[27] States also have attempted to limit the number of persons eligible for refugee status through various approaches. They have applied narrow interpretations of the refugee definition and exclusion clauses, and limited rights to appeal.[28] They have

---

22 UNHCR, Report of the UNHCR, ¶ 7, U.N. Doc. A/36/12 (1981). However, the situation was not completely rosy as certain problems encountered in previous years, such as difficulties for refugees of finding a country of asylum, *refoulement* of individuals, unjustified detention, threats to personal safety, piracy, abduction and armed attacks, continued. Ibid., at ¶ 14.

23 UNHCR, Report of the UNHCR, ¶ 9, 47, U.N. Doc. A/37/12 (1982).

24 UNHCR, Note on International Protection, ¶ 10–19, U.N. Doc. A/AC.96/623 (31 July 1983).

25 See UNHCR, Note on International Protection, ¶14-15, U.N. Doc. A/AC.96/750 (27 August 1990).

26 See UNHCR, Note on International Protection, ¶ 13, U.N. Doc. A/AC.96/989 (7 July 2004). Also see UNHCR, Note on International Protection, ¶ 38, U.N. Doc. A/AC.96/1085 (30 June 2010), which provides that the '[d]etention of refugees and asylum-seekers remained a concern, especially when there are no exceptional grounds; when access to detention facilities by UNHCR or partners is denied; or when the conditions of detention are below acceptable standards. Penal-like conditions, including the use of handcuffs, hooding and shackles, are not uncommon.'

27 This issue received considerable attention when a draft United Kingdom document, see CO/HO Future of Migration Project, *A New Vision for Refugees*, Final Report, 4 (January 2003), was leaked to the UK press. See Alan Travis, 'Shifting a Problem back to its Source – Would-be Refugees may be sent to Protected Zones near Homeland', *The Guardian*, 5 February 2003.

28 See UNHCR, Note on International Protection, ¶ 11, U.N. Doc. A/AC.96/609/Rev.1 (26 August 1982). Chaloka Beyani finds that 'a narrow construction of refugee law has emerged by reference

provided alternative categories for refugee status, such as 'humanitarian status', 'B status', and 'de facto status',[29] delayed the determination of refugee status in the expectation that the country situation would change, and adopted principles, such as first country of asylum, safe third country and safe country of origin.

Developing countries also have adopted restrictive measures, such as: the obligation that refugees live in camps, prohibitions on seeking or accepting work, and restrictions on education for children. They have increased their use of the arrest and detention of refugees, restricted movement outside refugee camps, and reduced food rations, and opportunities for generating income.[30]

In the developed world, today, the refugee issue is intertwined with States' preoccupation about migration issues, on the one hand, in particular illegal immigration and smuggling activities, and security concerns, on the other, particularly following the terrorist acts of 11 September 2001.[31] Issues of race, or as others term it, the north–south problem, also complicate the situation. Concerns in the developing world, which have received much less attention from the press and refugee scholars, primarily revolve around human security issues related to economic security, social and political security, and physical security.[32]

At the same time that States were adopting measures, some of which actively violated the provisions of the 1951 Refugee Convention/1967 Protocol and others, which although not an express breach of a provision were nevertheless contrary to the humanitarian spirit of those agreements, UNHCR's influence and ability to curb such approaches was diminishing. States' various internal difficulties, mentioned earlier, meant that they were less willing to follow UNHCR's guidance, particularly in the absence of an international refugee law that contradicted or contravened their conduct, and were unable or unwilling to preserve the more humanitarian approach of previous years.

UNHCR could no longer simply advise States how to remedy a refugee issue and count on States' co-operation in doing so. UNHCR's frustration was apparent in its 1988 Note on International Protection when it noted that its international protection function was a 'fundamental, humanitarian responsibility ... [which] requires UNHCR to stand between the endangered individuals and a state authority.'[33] Many of the policies and actions taken by States capitalized on the weaknesses in refugee law and the methods for ensuring the effectiveness of

to the mechanical process of status determination under domestic legal procedures and case law.' Chaloka Beyani, 'The Role of Human Rights Bodies in Protecting Refugees', in *Human Rights and Refugees, Internally Displaced Persons and Migrant Workers: Essays in Memory of Joan Fitzpatrick and Arthur Helton* 269, 271 (Anne Bayefsky, ed., 2006).

29 UNHCR, Complementary Forms of Protection: Their Nature and Relationship to the International Refugee Protection Regime, ¶2, UNHCR Doc. EC/50/SC/CRP.18 (9 June 2000).

30 See UNHCR, Note on International Protection, ¶ 7, U.N. Doc. A/AC.96/1008 (4 July 2005).

31 Ibid., at ¶ 9.

32 See Chapter 1 titled 'Safeguarding Human Security' in UNHCR, The State of the World's Refugees: A Humanitarian Agenda (1997).

33 UNHCR, Note on International Protection, ¶ 1, U.N. Doc. A/AC.96/713 (15 August 1988).

international refugee law. As a result, the content of refugee law became the source for the points of contention between UNHCR and States and the effectiveness of refugee law became a dominant concern for UNHCR.

Although UNHCR acknowledged, in its 1983 Note on International Protection, that the principles of international protection needed to be 'strongly reaffirmed, effectively implemented and, where necessary, further developed',[34] a valid concern can be raised as to whether this has actually occurred and in particular, whether UNHCR has been sufficiently committed to strengthening the principles of international protection. UNHCR's relationship with States is a complicated one that often requires factoring in States' views and their willingness to support UNHCR's actions. However, UNHCR's organizational autonomy, coupled with its mandate, provides the organization with the necessary foundations to assure that legal principles of protection remain the centrepiece for its work and indeed, its very existence.

4.3 Weaknesses in the treaty framework

The difficulties, which emerged in the 1980s with States' protection of refugees, brought the weaknesses in the traditional refugee law framework to the forefront. This traditional framework is based on the 1951 Refugee Convention and is supplemented by the 1967 Protocol and several other specific international refugee law instruments, namely, the 1957 Refugee Seamen Agreement and the Universal Copyright Convention, which supplement articles 11 and 14, respectively, of the 1951 Refugee Convention[35] as well as regional refugee instruments. As the 1951 Refugee Convention contains the most comprehensive elaboration of States' obligations to refugees and had been only minimally supplemented by other agreements, the gaps and ambiguities relate primarily to the provisions of this convention.

While in 1983, UNHCR acknowledged the insufficiency of standards relating to the obligation of governments towards refugees and asylum seekers,[36] nearly 20 years later such inadequacies would lead to claims by some government officials that the 1951 Refugee Convention is no longer relevant and that a new convention should be drafted.[37] In particular, the weaknesses in this traditional

---

34 UNHCR, Note on International Protection, ¶ 27, U.N. Doc. A.AC.96/623 (31 July 1983).
35 Agreement Relating to Refugee Seamen, 23 November 1957, 506 U.N.T.S. 125, which was updated with the 1973 Protocol to the Agreement Relating to Refugee Seamen, 12 June 1973, 965 U.N.T.S. 445; Protocol 1 to the Universal Copyright Convention, 6 September 1952, 216 U.N.T.S. 132; and Protocol 1 Annexed to the Universal Copyright Convention as Revised at Paris on 24 July 1971, concerning the Application of that Convention to Works of Stateless Persons and Refugees, 24 July 1971, 943 U.N.T.S. 178.
36 UNHCR, Note on International Protection, ¶ 27, U.N. Doc. A/AC.96/623 (31 July 1983).
37 For example, in 2000, the UK Home Secretary, Jack Straw, indicated an interest in completely revising the 1951 Refugee Convention. See Alan Travis, 'Straw Aims to Rewrite Treaty on Refugees', *The Guardian*, 8 June 2000 at 1–2. Presidency of the European Union, Austrian Strategy Paper

refugee law framework include gaps and ambiguities in the treaty standards and different regional standards.

4.3.1 Gaps and ambiguities

In the 1980s, States' treatment of asylum seekers and refugees resulted in new legal issues that exposed gaps in the traditional legal framework, comprised of the 1951 Refugee Convention, other international refugee agreements, and regional refugee instruments. For example, States prevented asylum seekers, who arrived by boat, from disembarking in their territory. States argued that the 1951 Refugee Convention only applied once the asylum seeker had reached the territory of a State party to the Convention. Also, in the absence of legal standards concerning voluntary repatriation, States attempted to return refugees to their countries of origin by adopting measures to pressure them into returning and frequently returned them without any guarantees as to their treatment on return.

In addition, States adopted more restrictive approaches in their treatment of refugees, in particular with respect to asylum seekers. Only two articles in the 1951 Refugee Convention directly apply to asylum seekers; article 31 prohibits States from imposing penalties on a person based on her illegal entry, and article 33 bars States from undertaking the *refoulement* of a person.[38] Thus, States limited the rights of asylum seekers in their territories in order to discourage additional arrivals. UNHCR also was confronted by States' adoption of approaches and concepts that had not previously existed, such as those of 'safe third country' and 'first country of asylum', which were intended to limit the number of refugees for which countries of asylum were responsible.

States' tendency to adopt narrow interpretations of the 1951 Refugee Convention's provisions also made ambiguities in the provisions of the traditional legal framework more apparent, and highlighted areas in which the 1951 Refugee Convention's provisions required clarification. These included: the meaning of 'particular social group' in the refugee definition, the application of the cessation and exclusion clauses,[39] the content of States' obligation not to impose penalties on asylum seekers for their illegal entry or presence, and the

---

    on Immigration and Asylum, ¶ 102, 9809/98 (13 July 1998) proposing that the Convention should be supplemented, amended or replaced.

38 1951 Refugee Convention, *supra* note 3, at arts. 31(1), 33(1). The first paragraph of Article 31 provides that:'The Contracting States shall not impose penalties, on account of their illegal presence, on refugees who, coming directly from a territory where their life or freedom was threatened in the sense of Article 1, enter or are present in their territory without authorization, provided they present themselves without delay to the authorities and show good cause for their illegal entry or presence.'

    The first paragraph of Article 33 provides that:

    'No Contracting State shall expel or return (*'refouler'*) a refugee in any manner whatsoever to the frontiers of territories where his life or freedom would be threatened on account of his race, religion, nationality, membership of a particular social group or political opinion.'

39 1951 Refugee Convention, *supra* note 3, at arts. 1A, 1C, 1F.

extent of the obligation imposed on States by the provision that they 'shall as far as possible facilitate the assimilation and naturalization of refugees.'[40]

The 1951 Refugee Convention provides only general guidance when addressing new issues or clarifying the content of the Convention's provisions. Specifically, the preamble to the 1951 Refugee Convention states that the Charter of the United Nations and the Universal Declaration of Human Rights affirm the principle 'that human beings shall enjoy fundamental rights and freedoms without discrimination.'[41] The Final Act,[42] of the UN Conference that completed the drafting and adopted the 1951 Refugee Convention, also contains some limited principles, specifically those of family unity, the extension of treatment provided by the Convention to other persons not covered by the Convention, and international co-operation among States in order to ensure that refugees find asylum.

Thus, when States adopted measures, which exploited the gaps and ambiguities in the refugee law framework, UNHCR had difficulty alleging that such actions were breaches of specific 1951 Refugee Convention standards. UNHCR's problem, in addressing States' actions through the provisions of the 1951 Refugee Convention, was compounded by the fact that the Convention does not provide a mechanism for the further development of its standards. The general principles in the preamble of the 1951 Refugee Convention and the Final Act only serve as a general guide to the tenor and approach that should be taken to clarify such ambiguities or to fill in gaps.

4.3.2 *Different standards for different states*

The 1951 Refugee Convention, with the 1967 Protocol, furnished the foundations for refugees to be treated in a similar manner regardless of the country of asylum, but the presence of the 1969 OAU Refugee Convention and, from 1984, the Cartagena Declaration, meant that different standards applied to refugees in different regions. For example, in OAU Member States and Latin American States, every person had a right to seek and obtain asylum.[43] States outside these two regions, however, were only bound by the 1951 Refugee Convention's prohibition on the *refoulement* of a refugee.[44]

The presence of regional instruments also meant that even the definition of who is a refugee depended on where the person was located. Latin American States, under the 1984 Cartagena Declaration, and OAU (now African Union) States, under the 1969 OAU Refugee Convention, recognized a broader category

---

40 Ibid., at arts. 31, 34.
41 1951 Refugee Convention, *supra* note 3, at 1st preambular ¶.
42 Final Act of the 1951 United Nations Conference of Plenipotentiaries on the Status of Refugees and Stateless Persons, 28 July 1951, 189 U.N.T.S. 137.
43 African Charter on Human and Peoples' Rights, art.12(3), 27 June 1981, 21 I.L.M. 58 (1982) and American Convention on Human Rights, art. 22(7), 22 November 1969, 1144 U.N.T.S. 123.
44 1951 Refugee Convention, *supra* note 3, at art. 33.

of refugees than States relying solely on the refugee definition in the 1951 Refugee Convention. The former group of States recognized not only persons fleeing persecution, but also persons fleeing internal conflict or war or other causes that perturbed public order.[45] Although UNHCR recognized such persons as refugees,[46] no international convention of a universal stature enshrined the larger refugee definition.

Recently, a further regional disparity in who may qualify as a refugee was introduced by the European Union's limitation of the definition of a 'refugee' to third country nationals.[47] As a result, persons who originate from an EU Member State country are excluded from obtaining refugee status; only persons coming from a non-EU Member State are eligible for refugee status within an EU country.

Temporary protection is another concept whose application was dependent on the location of the person; persons in the OAU (now African Union) could obtain temporary protection, but not persons in other States. For Member States, the 1969 OAU Refugee Convention provides that refugees may be accorded temporary asylum where the 'refugee has not received the right to reside in any country of asylum', but does not elaborate the obligations States have to refugees in such cases or any other details.[48] There is no universal refugee convention, however, that contains the concept of temporary protection, although from a common sense standpoint, it could be said that asylum was always meant to be a temporary solution to the situation of refugees.

Another regional approach to the issue of temporary protection was introduced by the European Union with the EU Council Directive 2001/55 on temporary protection. This Directive establishes certain obligations of EU Member States towards persons receiving temporary protection, including the length of time of the temporary protection, and the ability of persons receiving temporary protection to submit an asylum application.[49] However, unlike the 1969 OAU Refugee Convention, EU Council Directive 2001/55 does not clearly state when States may utilize temporary protection.

Thus, in the absence of a universal harmonization of international legal standards applicable to refugees, the treatment of an asylum seeker or refugee depends

45 1969 OAU Refugee Convention, *supra* note 5, at art. I.2 and 1984 Cartagena Declaration, *supra* note 5, at III.3.
46 UNHCR, Note on International Protection, ¶ 17, U.N. Doc. A/AC.96/593 (31 July 1981). Also see EXCOM Conclusion 22 (XXXII), ¶ 1, 1981.
47 Council Directive on minimum standards for the qualification and status of third country nationals or stateless persons as refugees or as persons who otherwise need international protection and the content of the protection granted, art. 2(c), 2004/83, 2004 O.J. (L 304) 12 (EC) (hereinafter Qualification Directive).
48 1969 OAU Refugee Convention, *supra* note 5, at Art. II.5.
49 Council Directive on Minimum Standards for Giving Temporary Protection in the Event of a Mass Influx of Displaced Persons and on Measures Promoting a Balance of Efforts Between Member States in Receiving Such Persons and Bearing the Consequences Thereof, Council Directive 2001/55, 2001 O.J. (L212) 12 (EC).

on the location of such person. From a general perspective, the legal framework also becomes less universal and more regionalized, thereby leaving inconsistent standards. Additionally, there is a risk that States begin to view the legal framework for refugee protection as one based on their own regional interests rather than a common international one.

4.3.3 Obstacles to the completion of the treaty framework

Logically, if the treaty law framework is deficient and incomplete, then why has it not been modified and supplemented to address the gaps, ambiguities, and differences in standards? There are a number of reasons, both political and institutional, why it has not.

From a political perspective, there has not been a new refugee convention adopted at the international level following States' inability to reach agreement on a convention on territorial asylum. As noted in section 4.2, the changes in the political, social and economic situation of States have meant that States are not interested in expanding the rights of refugees, but rather in limiting such rights and the number of refugees who reach their territories. Thus, UNHCR has never pursued an update of the 1951 Refugee Convention as it realized that States were unlikely to adopt new instruments to meet these situations.[50] Moreover, if States could agree on additional standards, that would provide further clarification and elaboration of the legal protection for refugees, they would likely reduce the protection standards for refugees rather than enhance them.

Recent developments in regional refugee law standards in the European Union attest to the fact that countries are more interested in limiting the rights of refugees. UNHCR initially welcomed the important initiative of the European Union to harmonize asylum law as an opportunity to have similar, elaborated and it was hoped, high level protection for refugees. However, as the process continued, UNHCR, non-governmental organizations and others concerned about refugees became increasingly alarmed by the propensity to adopt standards that harmonized Member States' laws at the 'lowest common denominator'[51] and that provided opt-out provisions, which permit States not to apply certain substantive provisions.

For example, as noted earlier, the refugee definition in the EU Council Directive on minimum standards for the qualification and status as refugees is

---

50 UNHCR, Note on International Protection, ¶ 44, U.N. Doc. A/AC.96/830 (7 September 1994). According to Schachter '[T]he prevailing practice of seeking consensus or near unanimity to adopt a convention has led to highly ambiguous or vacuous provisions.' Oscar Schachter, 'The UN Legal Order: An Overview', in *The United Nations And International Law* 3, 7 (Christopher Joyner, ed., 1997)

51 UNHCR, Aide Memoire: Directive on Minimum Standards on Procedures for Granting and Withdrawing Refugee Status (18 November 2003). Available at http://www.unhcr.org/protect/PROTECTION/43661fd62.pdf (accessed 27 October 2011).

more restrictive than the definition contained in the 1951 Refugee Convention, since it is limited to 'third country nationals'.[52] Moreover, the EU Directive introduces two additional criteria for excluding an asylum applicant from refugee status that are not contained in the 1951 Refugee Convention.[53]

From an institutional perspective, there is no body at the international level with responsibility for the creation of refugee law in a manner similar to legislatures and parliaments that create law at a national level. Within the United Nations, the General Assembly does not have any legislative powers, but rather is to 'encourag[e] the progressive development of international law and its codification'.[54] The International Law Commission, created by the General Assembly to assist it in furthering the progressive development of international law,[55] was assigned, as part of its initial list of subjects to be codified, the topic of the right to asylum. However, the ILC did not consider this topic ready for codification. Consequently, the ILC has never codified the right to asylum or any other refugee law topic.[56] However, the ILC decided to include the topic on the expulsion of aliens in its programme in 2004. The draft articles on this topic contain a specific provision barring the expulsion or return of a person whose right to life or liberty is in danger due to reasons of his or her 'race, religion, nationality, membership of a particular social group or political opinions'.[57]

The ILC not only consolidates existing law but also contributes to its progressive realization and, in doing the latter, assists in making significant advancements in areas of law that it considers. States, however, are not ready for significant advancements in connection with either asylum or refugee law in general since they view these areas as within their domain and refugees a *problem* to be resolved through national control rather than international co-ordination. Thus, the General Assembly has not evidenced any recent interest in assigning refugee law related issues to the ILC or another body for drafting.

52 Qualification Directive, *supra* note 47, at art. 2(c).

53 Ibid., at art. 14 (4–5).

54 U.N. Charter art. 13, para. 1(a). In fact, a proposal to permit the General Assembly to adopt conventions, in a manner similar to that of the ILO Conference, was defeated at the San Francisco conference on the drafting of the UN Charter. D.W. Bowett, *The Law of International Institutions* 344 (4th edn, 1982).

55 G.A. Res. 174(II) (21 November 1947).

56 Arthur Watts, *The International Law Commission: 1949–1998* 5-6 (1999).

57 Draft article 14(1) on the 'Obligation to ensure respect for the right to life and personal liberty in the receiving State of persons who have been or are being expelled' provides: No one may be expelled or returned (refoulé) to a State where his or her right to life or personal liberty is in danger of being violated because of his or her race, religion, nationality, membership of a particular social group or political opinions.

See footnote 1250 in para. 124 on page 275 of the Report of the International Law Commission for its session of 3 May–4 June and 5 July–6 August 2010. International Law Commission, *Report of the International Law Commission,* 62nd Session (2010) U.N. GAOR, 65th Sess., Supp. No. 10, A/65/10.

Neither is there an administrative body that is empowered to adopt binding interpretative formulations on refugee law issues as in certain national legal systems.[58] The Executive Committee of the UNHCR is the closest analogy that exists in refugee law to an administrative body with such interpretative authority. EXCOM does adopt conclusions on protection issues addressed to States, but these are not legally binding on them.[59] In addition, EXCOM cannot be said to be a fully representative body since not all State parties to the 1951 Refugee Convention or the 1967 Protocol are members of EXCOM.[60] However, from a practical standpoint, EXCOM conclusions often address areas where there is a lack of standards or ambiguities in existing standards. Even though Member States of EXCOM would not adopt such conclusions if they did not believe that States should abide by them, there is no follow-up mechanism to evaluate compliance. Endorsement of EXCOM's conclusions by the General Assembly does provide the conclusions with additional significance, but does not turn them into legally binding obligations for States.[61]

Thus, States remain the decisive force and the key to the international community's failure to complete the gaps and clarify ambiguities in refugee law. As former Director of the Division of International Protection in UNHCR has stated: 'some States have actively resisted' the development of refugee law while 'others have given clear precedence to perceived political or national interests'.[62] The lack of action by States may be preferable, however, to the updating of the 1951 Refugee Convention in a manner that diminishes States' obligations to accord rights to refugees. A risk exists that they would adopt an approach similar to that applied by the ILC with respect to the rights of aliens who are to be expelled; namely, that while the International Court of Justice has recognized States' obligation to respect human rights, the ILC found that 'it seemed to be realistic and consistent with State practice to limit the rights guaranteed during

---

58 In fact, no human rights treaty has such a body. However, note that several UN specialized agencies do have mechanisms for creating standards without the explicit approval of all Member States. For example, the International Civil Aviation Organization can adopt international standards and recommended practices as annexes to the Chicago Convention. See Frederic Kirgis, 'Specialized Law-Making Processes', in *The United Nations and International Law* 65, 70–72 (Christopher Joyner, ed., 1997).

59 The General Assembly and ECOSOC resolutions creating EXCOM, discussed in section 3.2, do not expressly authorize EXCOM to provide advice to States. EXCOM's role was to advise the High Commissioner.

60 Only 85 States are represented on EXCOM and not all of them are parties to the 1951 Refugee Convention or 1967 Protocol.

61 General Assembly resolutions are not normally binding on Member States of the United Nations, except with respect to the budget of the United Nations, under article 17 of the UN Charter, and certain internal matters, such as decisions on membership.

62 Dennis Macnamara and Guy Goodwin-Gill, 'UNHCR and International Refugee Protection', Refugee Studies Centre Working Paper No. 7, at 6 (Refugee Studies Centre, University of Oxford, ed., June 1999). Available at http://www.rsc.ox.ac.uk/publications/working-papers/RSCworkingpaper2.pdf (accessed 27 October 2011).

expulsion to the fundamental human rights and to those rights the implementation of which was required by the specific circumstances of the person being
expelled'.[63]

4.4   Weaknesses in the means for ensuring the effectiveness of international refugee law

States' employment of restrictive measures toward refugees highlighted not only
problems in the refugee law framework, but also weaknesses in the means for
ensuring the effectiveness of international refugee law standards for the protection of refugees. As already noted, the crisis in the 1980s can be termed not only
a 'crisis in international protection' but also a 'crisis in international refugee law'.
In particular, the difficulties with ensuring States' ratification and accession of the
1951 Refugee Convention and the 1967 Protocol and States' implementation and
application of their international refugee law obligations under these agreements,
assumed greater importance.

4.4.1   Problems with ensuring ratifications and accessions

International refugee law is founded on a treaty law basis, that of the 1951
Refugee Convention, with its 1967 Protocol. Since the 1951 Refugee Convention
was the primary international agreement providing protection to refugees prior to
the crisis in refugee law and protection, and remains the central agreement today,
it is essential that all Member States of the United Nations become parties to the
1951 Refugee Convention with its 1967 Protocol.

The drafters of UNHCR's Statute, who provided UNHCR with a promotional
role related to States' ratification of international conventions for the protection
of refugees, as discussed in section 1.3.1.1, were indeed justified in their concern
about States' ratification of the 1951 Refugee Convention. Eleven years passed
before all original signatories to the 1951 Refugee Convention had ratified the
1951 Refugee Convention, with Turkey being the last signatory to ratify it
in 1962. No mechanism exists to oblige States to submit the 1951 Refugee
Convention for ratification within a certain time frame or requires States that have
not yet ratified to report on measures toward ratification or the problems delaying
ratification. Such mechanisms do exist under the constitutions of the International
Labour Organization, the World Health Organization, and the United Nations
Educational, Scientific and Cultural Organization,[64] but these are organizations

---

63 See paragraph 93 on page 318 of the Report of the International Law Commission on the work of
    session from 4 May–5 June and 6 July–7 August 2009. International Law Commission, *Report of
    the International Law Commission*, 61st Session, 2009, U.N. GAOR, 64th Sess., Supp. No. 10,
    (A/64/10).
64 See for example, Constitution of the International Labour Organization, art. 19(5), which
    provides that States will take action on the convention or agreement within one year and

that are UN specialized agencies with constitutions that are treaties rather than, in the case of UNHCR, a General Assembly resolution.

The process of turning the 1951 Refugee Convention into a treaty universally applicable, through accessions to it and its 1967 Protocol, has been a slow process. As of April 2011, there were still nearly 50 countries that had not become parties to one or both treaties.[65] This means that about one-quarter of the world's countries are still not bound by the 1951 Refugee Convention standards.

Most States that are not parties to these refugee instruments are located in Asia and the Middle East. Quite a few of these countries, such as Iraq, Jordan, Pakistan and Thailand, have hosted or are currently hosting large numbers of refugees. However, while there is a regional declaration on refugees in Asia, the Bangkok Principles on Status and Treatment of Refugees,[66] no binding regional convention exists for Asia. In the Middle East, an Arab Convention on Regulating Status of Refugees in the Arab Countries was adopted in 1994, but is not used.[67]

From a legal standpoint, the fact that the State does not accede to the 1951 Refugee Convention or the 1967 Protocol does not mean that the State cannot protect refugees' rights in practice. But if the State has no international legal obligation then there are fewer incentives for it to adopt the requisite national

even where formal ratification is not obtained by a State, the State must report periodically on its law and practice relative to matters dealt with in the convention. Constitution of the International Labour Organization. Available at http://www.ilo.org/ilolex/english/constq.htm (accessed 27 October 2011) (hereinafter ILO Constitution). Under article 20 of the Constitution of the World Health Organization, each State must take action to accept a convention or agreement within 18 months and if it does not accept such instrument within this time limit, then the State must furnish information as to the reasons for non-acceptance. Constitution of the World Health Organization. Available at http://www.who.int/governance/eb/who_constitution_en.pdf (accessed 27 October 2011) (hereinafter WHO Constitution). In addition, under article IV(4) of UNESCO's Constitution, each Member State shall submit recommendations or conventions to its competent authorities within a year. UNESCO Constitution. Available at http://www.icomos.org/unesco/unesco_constitution.html (accessed 27 October 2011). The International Maritime Organization has a mechanism to ensure that amendments to treaties come into effect relatively quickly; when an amendment is adopted by the IMO, States are obligated to accept such amendments after the passage of a certain period of time. See Nagendra Singh, 'The UN and the Development of International Law', in *United Nations, Divided World: the UN's Roles in International Relations* 384, 411–2 (Adam Roberts and Benedict Kingsbury, eds, 2nd edn, 1993).

65 See UNHCR, States Parties to the 1951 Convention Relating to the Status of Refugees and the 1967 Protocol (as of 1 November 2007). Available at http://www.unhcr.org/protect/PROTECTION/3b73b0d63.pdf (accessed 27 October 2011).

66 Asian–African Legal Consultative Organization (AALCO), Principles Concerning Treatment of Refugees, Asian–African Legal Consultative Committee ('Bangkok Principles'), 31 December 1966. Available at http://www.unhcr.org/refworld/docid/3de5f2d52.html (accessed 27 October 2011).

67 1994 Arab Convention on Regulating the Status of Refugees in Arab Countries, adopted by the League of Arab States in 1994. Available at http://www.unhcr.org/publ/PUBL/455c733b2.pdf (accessed 27 October 2011).

legislation and to comply with such obligations. Consequently, accession remains the essential first step in ensuring the effectiveness of international refugee law.

Even where a State is a party, States may use reservations to limit the effectiveness of the refugee treaties. For example, Madagascar, Monaco and Turkey still maintain the geographic restriction contained in the 1951 Refugee Convention.[68] Other States, such as Botswana, Mexico, and Papua New Guinea, have made reservations to key provisions of the 1951 Refugee Convention, such as article 31 on illegal entry and article 32 concerning the expulsion of refugees. No means exist to review and require the State concerned to remove its reservation.

As a result, in the case of countries that have not acceded to the 1951 Refugee Convention or the 1967 Protocol and countries that maintain a geographic restriction, UNHCR is left without the 1951 Refugee Convention as the key instrument for sanctioning actions that violate refugees' rights and for diplomatically or vociferously demanding a change in such conduct. In addition, reservations made by countries to key provisions of the 1951 Refugee Convention also pose challenges to UNHCR's work to ensure that the full range of obligations contained in the Convention are binding on States at an international level.

In sum, the ratification and accession of the key conventions for the protection of refugees, the 1951 Refugee Convention and the 1967 Protocol, have been matters left to the discretion of States, with UNHCR's traditional role being merely one of promoting ratifications and accessions, as seen in Chapter 2.

4.4.2 *Problems with implementation*

The 1951 Refugee Convention and the 1967 Protocol remain dead letter law unless their provisions, for the protection of refugees, are incorporated into national law. The only legal obligations of States related to their implementation of international refugee law standards are furnishing UNHCR with information about 'the implementation' of the 1951 Refugee Convention and the 1967 Protocol as well as 'laws, regulations and decrees' relating to refugees and providing the UN Secretary-General with 'the laws and regulations which they may adopt to ensure the application' of the 1951 Refugee Convention.[69] However, while States have an affirmative obligation to apprise the UN Secretary-General of the national laws and regulations that implement their international obligations, such information is to be provided to UNHCR following UNHCR's request. Moreover, the obligations to provide such information are not very stringent, particularly as they do not establish a time frame within which this information

---

68 UNHCR, States Parties to the 1951 Convention Relating to the Status of Refugees and the 1967 Protocol, *supra* note 65.

69 1951 Refugee Convention, *supra* note 3, at arts. 35(2) and 36, 1967 Protocol, *supra* note 5, at arts. II(2), III.

must be provided, as is the case with some of the UN specialized agencies[70] and under certain international human rights instruments.[71]

UNHCR has understandably taken the initiative to request information on States' national laws and rules that implement their international refugee law obligations. However, when UNHCR requested information from States about their implementation of the 1951 Refugee Convention through questionnaires, many States failed to respond, as discussed in section 2.4.2. Even where States responded, the information provided was not always sufficiently detailed or accurate,[72] since States are usually unwilling to criticize themselves.[73]

States' approach, increasingly visible in the 1980s, of discouraging the arrival of more asylum seekers and of making the lives of those asylum seekers already on their territories objectionable, has taken concrete form in the national legislation adopted by States. Therefore, UNHCR has been confronted with national legislation that actually violates the standards of the 1951 Refugee Convention, such as with provisions for the detention of all asylum seekers arriving without visas at airports. In other cases, national legislation or administrative measures may contain provisions, such as the safe third country concept, which do not expressly violate the 1951 Refugee Convention's standards but are nevertheless contrary to the humanitarian spirit of the convention and the notion of refugee protection. Yet, no UNHCR or international mechanism exists to sanction the content of States' national rules.

Some States simply fail to incorporate the provisions of international conventions for the protection of refugees into their national laws. This clearly suggests reluctance, on their part, to give full effect to the rights that they are legally obligated to accord to refugees under international law. Here again, there is no means provided to require States to incorporate their international legal obligations to refugees into national standards.

---

70 Under the ILO Constitution each Member State must report annually 'on the measures it has taken to give effect to the provisions of Conventions to which it is a party'. ILO Constitution, *supra* note 64, at art. 22. Under the WHO Constitution, each member must report annually on action taken with respect to recommendations and conventions, and provide 'important laws, regulations, official reports and statistics pertaining to health which have been published in the State'. WHO Constitution, *supra* note 64, at arts. 62–63.

71 See for example, article 9(1) of the 1965 International Convention on the Elimination of All Forms of Racial Discrimination, which provides a time within which States must report on the 'legislative, judicial, administrative or other measures which they have adopted and which give effect' to the Convention's provisions and provides for regular reporting 'thereafter every two years and whenever the Committee so requests'. International Convention on the Elimination of All Forms of Racial Discrimination, 21 December 1965, 660 U.N.T.S. 195.

72 See for example, UNHCR, Note on International Protection Addendum 2: Implementation of the 1951 Convention and 1967 Protocol on the Status of Refugees – Preliminary Report, ¶ 4, U.N. Doc. A/AC.96/508/Add.2 (26 September 1974).

73 Henry Schermers and Niels Blokker, *International Institutional Law* 882 (5th edn, 2011) citing Niels Blokker and Sam Muller, eds, *Towards More Effective Supervision by International Organizations*, in *Towards more Effective Supervision by International Organizations: Essays in Honour of Henry G. Schermers* 281–282 (1994).

Thus, traditionally and prior to the crisis in international protection and refugee law, implementation of international conventions for the protection of refugees was primarily left to the discretion of States, with UNHCR's responsibility consisting of obtaining information from States about actual administrative and legislative measures that States had adopted.

4.4.3 Problems with application

Prior to the 1980s and the onset of the refugee law crisis, when States' and UNHCR's perceptions of the importance of protecting refugees were in greater alignment, UNHCR could provide informal advice to States and States were more likely to undertake the necessary steps to modify their actions. As noted earlier, a greater sense of co-operation prevailed between UNHCR and States before the mid-1980s. Since then, the question of how to ensure the application of international legal standards for the protection of refugees has become a predominant concern of UNHCR.

Enforcement mechanisms are the normal means relied on in law to ensure compliance.[74] In the area of international refugee law, the International Court of Justice offers two possible avenues to sanction a State's actions that violate the 1951 Refugee Convention. First, UNHCR can make a request to the International Court of Justice for an advisory opinion related to the interpretation of the 1951 Refugee Convention, pursuant to article 65 of the ICJ Statute.[75] UNHCR has never done so. Alternatively, under article 38 of the 1951 Refugee Convention, States can bring a dispute to the ICJ that concerns the interpretation or application of the 1951 Refugee Convention.[76] However, this dispute mechanism has not yet been invoked by any State. In fact, the ICJ has only heard two cases related to refugee law, both of which it decided prior to the adoption of the 1951 Refugee Convention.[77]

No other multinational mechanism exists, in relation to the provisions of the 1951 Refugee Convention, to sanction non-compliance. UNHCR's statutory responsibility, to supervise States' application of international conventions for the protection of refugees, remains the primary means of ensuring compliance by States. However, UNHCR does not have the authority, in contrast to the treaty

---

74 See Carl-August Fleischhauer's distinction between enforcement and compliance. Carl-August Fleischhauer, 'Inducing Compliance', in *United Nations Legal Order* 231, 232 (Oscar Schachter and Christopher Joyner, eds, 1995).

75 U.N. Charter, art. 65.

76 1951 Refugee Convention, *supra* note 3, at art. 38.

77 Asylum Case (Colombia v. Peru) 1950 I.C.J. 266 (20 November) and Haya de la Torre (Columbia v. Peru) 1951 I.C.J. 71 (13 June). These cases, between Columbia and Peru, involved the issue of the grant of diplomatic asylum by the Colombian Ambassador in Lima, Peru in 1949 to Mr Haya de la Torre, the head of a political party in Peru. Both cases involve the interpretation of a provision in the 1928 Havana Convention on Asylum concerning asylum in a country's embassy to political refugees of the country in which the embassy is located.

bodies to the key human rights agreements, to receive and hear complaints from States or individuals concerning non-compliance with the 1951 Refugee Convention's provisions.

States' obligation to co-operate with UNHCR, under the 1951 Refugee Convention and/or the 1967 Protocol, includes 'in particular [to] facilitate [UNHCR's] duty of supervising the application of the provisions of this Convention'.[78] The question is then what States must do to 'facilitate' UNHCR's supervision. UNHCR has not provided a response to this question, although Walter Kälin, in his final report on UNHCR's supervisory responsibility for the Global Consultations process, finds that such co-operation imposes:

> [a] treaty obligation on States Parties (i) to respect UNHCR's supervisory power and not to hinder UNHCR in carrying out this task, and (ii) to cooperate actively with UNHCR in this regard in order to achieve an optimal implementation and harmonized application of all provisions of the Convention and its Protocol. These duties have a highly dynamic and evolutive character.[79]

As UNHCR does not have a means to enforce or ensure that States comply with their international refugee law obligations, UNHCR's key tools for its supervisory work are soft ones, those of persuasion, coercion, and inducement with the objective of obtaining States' compliance. UNHCR can bring the matter to the attention of EXCOM, the Council on Human Rights, the UN Economic and Social Council or the UN General Assembly. However, the positions taken by these bodies on States' actions, in conclusions, in the case of EXCOM, or resolutions, in the case of the Council on Human Rights, ECOSOC and the General Assembly, are not binding on States. Thus, while UNHCR can call on States to take certain actions, States ultimately decide whether and to what extent they will comply with such requests.

Moreover, given the nature of the 1951 Refugee Convention, as a human rights treaty, States do not derive mutual benefits from the observance of its provisions and therefore have little incentive to supervise one another's conduct.[80]

---

78 1951 Refugee Convention, *supra* note 3, at art. 35(1).
79 Walter Kälin, 'Supervising the 1951 Convention on the Status of Refugees: Article 35 and Beyond', in *Refugee Protection in International Law: UNHCR's Global Consultations on International Protection* 613, 617 (Erika Feller, Volker Türk and Frances Nicholson, eds, 2003).
80 As the first High Commissioner, Gerrit Jan van Heuven Goedhart, stated in his lecture at the Hague Academy of International Law:'Conventions concerning refugees are, from the point of view of international law, of a special character inasmuch as they are "pacta in favorem tertiorum": normally the Contracting States derive rights from international conventions and undertake obligations under them; in this case, however, the beneficiaries of the Convention are the refugees, persons who do not enjoy national protection. Since they themselves do not directly derive any enforceable rights from the Convention, the international community has considered it desirable that the international organ charged with the protection of refugees should also supervise its application to the beneficiaries – the refugees.'Gerrit Jan van Heuven Goedhart, *The Problem of Refugees*, 82 Recueil des Cours, Hague Academy of International Law 261, 293 (1953).

Thus, essentially, the refugee system has been, and continues to be, primarily a system of voluntary compliance with international refugee law by States.

Clear violations of international refugee law are not the only ones that pose a challenge to a refugee regime without an enforcement mechanism. States' adoption of policies and measures, which attempt to diminish the number of refugees obtaining access to their territories and reduce the rights accorded asylum seekers and refugees but do not explicitly violate refugee law, present a different, but still significant problem. In the case of an explicit violation of the 1951 Refugee Convention by a State, other States, UNHCR, non-governmental organizations and other concerned parties can clearly identify the legal standard that has been breached. States may choose not to condemn such action publicly, but they still can clearly identify the violation. Where States' policies, legislation, and actions limit refugees' access to asylum and reduce their rights but do not violate an international law standard, it is more difficult for States and others to determine if a violation exists. If they wish to do so, they have the added difficulty of not having an explicit standard from the 1951 Refugee Convention to cite to condemn the offensive policy, legislation or action.

UNHCR, in particular, faces a significant difficulty when confronted with States' actions, which negatively impact on the rights of refugees, but do not expressly violate the 1951 Refugee Convention. In such cases, UNHCR lacks a clear standard with which to criticize the action by the State and to use as a basis to request a modification in treatment of the refugees. Moreover, restrictive measures by States not only diminish the actual protection afforded to refugees, but also set a negative precedent, which other States may follow. There also is a risk that restrictive measures adopted by other States may eventually develop into a new customary law.

4.5 Conclusion

The relationship between States and UNHCR is based on co-operation. The concept of co-operation is expressed in both UNHCR's Statute and the General Assembly resolution to which the Statute was annexed. However, while the General Assembly's creation of UNHCR is legally binding on States,[81] neither UNHCR's Statute nor the General Assembly resolution to which UNHCR's Statute was annexed is binding on them.[82]

---

81 The general view taken by international institutional law authors is that General Assembly resolutions creating subsidiary organs, pursuant to article 22 of the UN Charter and which concern the internal workings of the UN, are binding. As Rosalyn Higgins has stated, 'the *Expenses Case* established that lawfully established subsidiary bodies – that is to say, bodies established with the objects and purposes of the UN Charter and given tasks not specifically prohibited thereunder – generate financial and legal obligations for UN members.' Rosalyn Higgins, *Problems and Process: International Law and How to Use it* 25 (1994).

82 The issue of whether UNHCR's Statute is binding on States was considered by several authors in the late 1970s to mid-1980s. See, for example, Maynard and Garvey who believe UNHCR's

States are legally bound, however, to co-operate with UNHCR pursuant to the 1951 Refugee Convention and the 1967 Protocol, or if not a party to either of these agreements, then pursuant to article 56 of the UN Charter. States are to co-operate with UNHCR in the exercise of its international protection function, which includes UNHCR's international refugee law responsibilities. These responsibilities, under UNHCR's Statute, include: UNHCR's promotion of the conclusion and ratification/accession to conventions for the protection of refugees, its obtainment of information concerning the laws and regulations concerning refugees, and its supervision of conventions for the protection of refugees. Yet, the specific content of what States must do to co-operate with UNHCR in connection with its international protection function remains undefined. Vagueness in the content of such co-operation posed no difficulty to UNHCR's work until the 1980s since States operated with a humanitarian approach, which was responsive to UNHCR's formal and informal suggestions as to how to improve protection for refugees.

In the 1980s, the underlying premise of co-operation between States and UNHCR eroded as a result of significant changes in the approach of States to refugee protection. Although it is not entirely clear what the exact causes of these changes were, declining economies in developed countries, which brought about a reduced need for labour and lead to more restrictive admissions policies, and the increasing number of asylum seekers were essential elements. Public sentiment against more arrivals also influenced the political response of States.

The decline in States' interest in assuring the protection of refugees clearly emerged in the 1980s and has continued up until the present day. States in all parts of the world have adopted measures, in the form of policies, legislation, and even actions toward refugees that contradict UNHCR's views. In some cases, the measures specifically violate provisions of the 1951 Refugee Convention, while others, although not express breaches of the 1951 Refugee Convention, are contrary to the humanitarian spirit and the notion of international protection that underpin the 1951 Refugee Convention. These measures essentially attempt to

Statute is recommendatory and non-binding. P.D. Maynard, 'The Legal Competence of the United Nations High Commissioner for Refugees' 31 *Int'l & Comp. L.Q.* 415, 416 (1982) and Jack Garvey, 'Toward a Reformulation of International Refugee Law' 26 *Harv. Int'l. L.J.* 483, 488 (1985). For the contrary view see Hartling, a former High Commissioner of UNHCR, and Professor Grahl-Madsen, an international lawyer who spent 18 months as a Special Consultant in the Office of UNHCR. Poul Hartling finds that since UNHCR's Statute was adopted pursuant to a General Assembly resolution, it is 'therefore valid in all States Members of the United Nations.' Poul Hartling, 'Concept and Definition of "Refugee" – Legal and Humanitarian Aspects', 48 *Nordisk Tidsskrift for International Ret* 125, 129 (1979). Grahl-Madsen notes the responsibilities of the General Assembly under article 55 of the UN Charter and finds that the UNHCR Statute 'may consequently be construed as an international convention adopted by delegated authority. Consequently the Member States are contractually bound to recognize the competence of the High Commissioner as defined in the Statute'. Atle Grahl-Madsen, *The Status of Refugees in International Law: Refugee Character* 31–32 (1966).

limit refugees' access to States' territory, the number of asylum seekers eligible for refugee status, and the rights of asylum seekers and refugees.

The various measures taken by States took advantage of the weaknesses in refugee law to reduce their responsibilities toward asylum seekers and refugees. Their maintenance of such measures, despite UNHCR's objections and requests to modify such conduct, were assertions of States' interest in placing refugee matters back under the national domain. UNHCR no longer had the same degree of influence over States' policies and approaches to refugee matters and thus, would have its liberty of action circumscribed by States in a manner that it had not previously experienced. UNHCR also no longer had the same degree of organizational independence to adopt initiatives to address refugee problems and to develop refugee law principles since States were less willing to give their support, both financial and political, unless States clearly perceived a benefit to themselves, primarily, the reduction in the number of refugees requiring protection in their territories.

Consequently, international refugee law became, and today remains, the basis for the points of contention between UNHCR and States. This meant that the weaknesses in the refugee law framework became more clearly exposed. The gaps and ambiguities in the provisions of the 1951 Refugee Convention resulted in a refugee law framework that did not adequately cover new refugee law issues. In addition, the presence of regional laws and directives created disparate and sometimes contradictory standards, and detracted from the universal nature of refugee protection, that is, the treatment and respect accorded the refugee varied greatly depending on the country in which the person had obtained asylum. As a result, the fact that 'the legal rules linking governments are far from being a coherent, uniform body covering all situations and all needs', as High Commissioner Schnyder recognized in the mid-1960s,[83] become a significant impediment for the protection of refugees with the onset of the refugee crisis in the 1980s.

Following the emergence of the crisis in refugee law and refugee protection, States have not demonstrated any interest in extending the rights of refugees. In the absence of a body at the international level, which has responsibility for creating international refugee law, or even an administrative body that could adopt interpretative decisions on refugee law issues, the adoption of new universal refugee law treaties has come to a standstill.[84]

---

83 Felix Schnyder, 'Les Aspects Juridiques Actuels du Problème des Réfugiés', 114 *Recueil des Cours*, Hague Academy of International Law 335, 347 (1965). Translation from French into English by author.

84 The weaknesses in international refugee law, however, are not unique. As Castañeda has noted with respect to international law in general: 'The absence of permanent legislative organs and, in general, the unspecialized and uninstitionalized nature of the process by which international law is created, gives rise to a lack of stability, precision, and definiteness in many nonconventional rules, to frequent contradictions among certain rules, and to the relatively numerous lacunae observed in that normative order.' Jorge Castañeda, *Legal Effects of United Nations' Resolutions* 169–170 (1969).

In addition, the question of how to ensure the effectiveness of refugee law, that is the actual protection of refugees, became a dominant concern for UNHCR. At the time of the onset of the crisis in refugee law and protection, the 1951 Refugee Convention and 1967 Protocol had not been acceded to by all States and some States maintained reservations to key provisions in the Convention. Not all States had fully incorporated the standards in the 1951 Refugee Convention into their national legislation, while the legislation of other States expressly violated provisions of the 1951 Refugee Convention, or contravened the spirit of this agreement. Thus, refugee protection lacked an adequate expression in the very States that were supposed to provide protection to refugees. States' obligation to provide UNHCR with information, on the implementation of the 1951 Refugee Convention and the laws, regulations and decrees relating to refugees, was a weak mechanism for inciting States to adopt adequate national legislation to ensure refugees' rights.

The crisis in refugee law also highlighted the fact that States' actual application of international refugee law standards remains one almost exclusively within their discretion. The existing mechanisms, by which the International Court of Justice could hear an advisory claim by UNHCR or a dispute between States parties to the 1951 Refugee Convention, have never been utilized in practice. UNHCR's supervisory responsibility was the conventional means used to obtain States' compliance with international refugee law standards, but is based on soft means of persuasion.

Thus, UNHCR would need to adapt its role and responsibilities in order to ensure a more complete legal framework and the effectiveness of refugee law. The steps UNHCR has taken in order to do so are explored in Chapters 5 and 6.

5 UNHCR's approaches to address weaknesses in the treaty framework

5.1 Introduction

As the crisis in refugee protection unfolded in the 1980s, UNHCR was confronted with States that were increasingly assertive about their own interpretation of the 1951 Refugee Convention and that were adopting national laws in conflict with both the letter and the spirit of the Convention. UNHCR, as an organization funded by many of the very same States that were diminishing the protections afforded refugees, had to determine how to respond. UNHCR could not simply ignore States' attempts to reduce the number of refugees and the protections afforded them. If UNHCR had done so, it would have forfeited its leadership role in developing international refugee law and allowed States to establish widely disparate standards that reduced the level of protection provided to refugees. Yet, UNHCR's criticism of States that failed to support the protection of refugees was insufficient to force States to change their behaviour.

UNHCR was practically unable to promote the conclusion of new universally applicable international conventions for the protection of refugees and to propose amendments to such conventions, both of which are mandated responsibilities under its Statute.[1] States were uninterested in extending the refugee law framework or refugee protection. Instead, UNHCR's role, in the area of the development of refugee law, was one of trying to counteract States' attempts to reduce refugee protection. UNHCR, therefore, adopted several proactive approaches, at its own initiative, that were intended to strengthen the legal standards for protection and thereby reduce the weaknesses in the refugee law framework.

---

1 See paragraph 8(a) of the Statute of the Office of the United Nations High Commissioner for Refugees, contained in the Annex to UN General Assembly Resolution 428(V) of 14 December 1950. G.A. Res. 428(V) (14 December 1950) (hereinafter UNHCR Statute).

5.2 Weaving a more complete framework

Since the drafting of the 1951 Refugee Convention, only two international refugee law agreements had been created to complement the Convention.[2] The 1967 Protocol[3] removed the date and geographic restrictions of the 1951 Refugee Convention and the 1957 Refugee Seamen Agreement, with its 1973 Protocol,[4] clarified article 11 of the 1951 Refugee Convention as to which State should serve as the asylum State and provide the refugee with a travel document.[5]

At the time of the crisis in international refugee law, UNHCR viewed several other international instruments as supplemental agreements to the 1951 Refugee Convention and thus part of the refugee law framework.[6] Protocol 1 to the Universal Copyright Convention[7] provided additional content to article 14 of the 1951 Refugee Convention on artistic rights and industrial property. The Convention on the Recovery Abroad of Maintenance[8] facilitated the recovery of maintenance by a claimant in a State from a person in another State, and was therefore important where a refugee's family members were separated. In addition, the regional refugee convention in Africa, the 1969 OAU Refugee Convention, and the 1954 and 1961 conventions concerning stateless persons, with their provisions applicable to refugees who were stateless, were also included in this framework.[9]

In order to expand the limited refugee law framework, by means other than through the creation of new treaties or amendments of existing treaties, since States had not demonstrated any collective interest in the creation of new international instruments, UNHCR utilized existing international instruments, in particular human rights law agreements, to supplement the traditional legal framework.

2   Convention Relating to the Status of Refugees, 28 July 1951, 189 U.N.T.S. 150 (hereinafter 1951 Refugee Convention).
3   Protocol Relating to the Status of Refugees, 16 December 1967, 606 U.N.T.S. 267.
4   Refugee Seamen Agreement, 23 November 1957, 506 U.N.T.S. 125 and Protocol to the Agreement Relating to Refugee Seamen, 12 June 1973, 965 U.N.T.S. 445.
5   Pursuant to article 28 of the 1951 Refugee Convention, States are to 'issue to refugees lawfully staying in their territory travel documents for the purpose of travel outside their territory'. 1951 Refugee Convention, *supra* note 2, at art. 28.
6   UNHCR, Report of the UNHCR, Annex II, U.N. Doc. A/5511/Rev.1 (1964).
7   Protocol 1 to the Universal Copyright Convention, 6 September 1952, 216 U.N.T.S. 132 and Protocol 1 Annexed to the Universal Copyright Convention as Revised at Paris on 24 July 1971, concerning the Application of that Convention to Works of Stateless Persons and Refugees, 24 July 1971, 943 U.N.T.S. 178.
8   Convention on the Recovery Abroad of Maintenance, 20 June 1956, 268 U.N.T.S. 3.
9   OAU Convention Governing the Specific Aspects of Refugee Problems in Africa, 10 September 1969, 1001 U.N.T.S. 45. Convention Relating to the Status of Stateless Persons, 28 September 1954, 360 U.N.T.S. 117. Convention on the Reduction of Statelessness, 30 August 1961, 989 U.N.T.S. 175.

5.2.1 Human rights instruments

Despite the reference in the preamble of the 1951 Refugee Convention to the Universal Declaration of Human Rights and the fundamental rights of individuals[10] and UNHCR's acknowledgement that these human rights principles should be applied by States to refugees,[11] UNHCR's full embrace of human rights standards in its doctrinal positions did not occur until the 1990s. The UNHCR Handbook, for example, notes that serious violations of human rights would constitute persecution,[12] but does not specify which instruments provide standards for these rights. In addition, while UNHCR articulated, in the early 1980s, that the rights of refugees are human rights,[13] it did not always specify the precise standards to which it referred.

The evolution in UNHCR's use and citation of international human rights instruments is apparent in its doctrinal positions in the area of detention. For example, in its 1984 Note on International Protection, UNHCR suggested standards for detention, and then in 1986, provided more detailed standards in an EXCOM conclusion.[14] However, while the 1984 Note provides that 'asylum-seekers in detention should be treated according to certain minimum standards, including the due process of law and the possibility of access to legal advice and/or to UNHCR' and the 1986 conclusion provides that the conditions of detention should be 'humane',[15] they do not reference any legal instruments for the basis for these standards. In contrast, UNHCR's 1999 Guidelines on

10 Universal Declaration of Human Rights, G.A. Res. 217A, art.14(1), U.N. Doc. A/810 (12 December 1948). The preamble to the 1951 Refugee Convention states that 'the United Nations has, on various occasions, manifested its profound concern for refugees and endeavoured to assure refugees the widest possible exercise of [the] fundamental rights and freedoms' contained in the 1948 Universal Declaration of Human Rights and provides that 'the Charter of the United Nations and the Universal Declaration of Human Rights ... have affirmed the principle that human beings shall enjoy fundamental rights and freedoms without discrimination'. 1951 Refugee Convention, *supra* note 2, at 2nd, 1st preambular ¶. Thus, the preamble places the rights of refugees within the overall human rights framework and references the Universal Declaration of Human Rights as the basis for such rights.

11 In 1965, High Commissioner Schnyder, in a speech to the Hague Academy, stated that UNHCR not only supervises governments' application of international refugee law, but also principles contained in the Declaration of Human Rights. *'En outre, Le Haut Commissairiat se trouve dans une situation unique en ce sens qu'il remplit le rôle d'une autorité internationale qui, dans l'exercice de ses fonctions de protection des réfugies, supervise l'application par les gouvernements de certains principes de droit international et de la Déclaration des droits de l'homme.'* Felix Schnyder, 'Les Aspects Juridiques Actuels du Problème des Réfugiés', 114 *Recueil des Cours*, Hague Academy of International Law 335, 347 (1965).

12 UNHCR, *Handbook on Procedures and Criteria for Determining Refugee Status*, ¶ 51, HCR/IP/4/Eng./Rev.1 (January 1992).

13 UNHCR, Note on International Protection, ¶ 30, U.N. Doc. A/AC.96/623 (31 July 1983).

14 UNHCR, Note on International Protection, ¶ 30, U.N. Doc. A/AC.96/643 (9 August 1984) and EXCOM Conclusion 44 (XXXXVII) 1986.

15 UNHCR, 1984 Note on International Protection, *supra* note 14. EXCOM Conclusion 44, *supra* note 14, at ¶ f.

Detention explicitly cite international human rights standards, in connection with the reasons for detention, the detention of children, and the conditions of detention.[16]

Notably, since the 1990s, UNHCR has encouraged EXCOM and the General Assembly to make greater reference to human rights law in relation to the protection of refugees[17] and has urged its staff to use human rights more extensively in their own work. As an example, UNHCR issued the 'Human Rights and Refugee Protection' training module in 1995 to permit its staff to become more familiar with the use of human rights instruments and mechanisms in their work.[18] This document was then revised, expanded, and reissued in 2006.[19]

Moreover, in 1995, UNHCR issued a 'Collection of International Instruments and Other Legal Texts Concerning Refugees and Others of Concern to UNHCR'[20] that updated its 1979 'Collection of International Instruments Concerning Refugees'.[21] The 1995 two-volume set reflects UNHCR's emphasis on human rights instruments as tools for the protection of refugees. It includes international and regional human rights documents in addition to other instruments of relevance to refugees. The 1995 edition was then further updated by a 2007 version.[22]

The contribution of three of the most significant international human rights conventions to the refugee law framework, the 1966 International Covenant on Civil and Political Rights,[23] the 1984 Convention against Torture and other Cruel,

---

16 UNHCR, Guidelines on Applicable Criteria and Standards relating to the Detention of Asylum Seekers, 3–6 (February 1999). Available at http://www.unhcr.org/refworld/docid/3c2b3f844.html (accessed 27 October 2011).

17 See for example EXCOM Conclusion 101 (LV), 3rd preambular ¶, 2004; EXCOM Conclusion 100 (LV), 4th preambular ¶, 2004; EXCOM Conclusion 93 (LIII), ¶ b.i., 2002; EXCOM Conclusion 84 (XLVIII), 4th preambular ¶, 1997, which references the 1989 Convention on the Rights of the Child in the preamble, and EXCOM Conclusion 71 (XLIV), ¶ u, 1993. EXCOM Conclusion 101 is particularly notable as it specifically mentions the Universal Declaration of Human Rights, the 1966 International Covenant on Civil and Political Rights, the 1966 International Covenant on Economic, Social and Cultural Rights, the 1965 International Convention on the Elimination of All Forms of Racial Discrimination, the 1989 Convention on the Rights of the Child and the 1979 Convention on the Elimination of All Forms of Discrimination against Women. Also see the following General Assembly resolutions: G.A. Res. 61/137, ¶ 10, U.N. Doc. A/RES/61/137 (19 December 2006); G.A. Res. 52/103, ¶ 3, 5, 14, 16, U.N. Doc. A/RES/52/103 (12 December 1997); G.A. Res. 48/116, ¶ 5, 16, 18, U.N. Doc. A/RES/48/116 (20 December 1993).

18 UNHCR, Human Rights and Refugee Protection, Training Module RLD 5 (October 1995).

19 UNHCR, Human Rights and Refugee Protection, Self-Study Module 5, vols 1 and 2 (15 December 2006).

20 UNHCR, Collection of International Instruments and Other Legal Texts Concerning Refugees and Displaced Persons (December 1995).

21 UNHCR, Collection of International Instruments Concerning Refugees (1979).

22 See UNHCR, Collection of International Instruments and Legal Texts Concerning Refugees and Others of Concern to UNHCR (June 2007).

23 International Covenant on Civil and Political Rights, 16 December 1966, 999 U.N.T.S. 171 (hereinafter ICCPR).

Inhuman or Degrading Treatment or Punishment,[24] and the 1989 Convention on the Rights of the Child,[25] illustrates how such instruments assist in filling gaps and clarifying ambiguities in the standards of the 1951 Refugee Convention.

The International Covenant on Civil and Political Rights applies to 'individuals within its territory' and contains a number of protections not found in the 1951 Refugee Convention.[26] These include the right not to be subjected to arbitrary arrest, detention or exile and the right to a fair and public hearing in connection with any criminal charge.[27] The ICCPR therefore extends the protection of refugees and asylum seekers through its expanded list of civil and political rights. Although many of these rights are stated in broad terms, the comments on the ICCPR's articles, furnished by the Human Rights Committee, provide further clarification of the content of such rights, including with respect to the protection afforded asylum seekers and refugees. For example, the Human Rights Committee has noted that pursuant to article 7, States cannot expose 'individuals to the danger of torture or cruel, inhuman or degrading treatment or punishment upon return to another country by way of their extradition, expulsion or *refoulement*'.[28] In addition, the Human Rights Committee found that article 9 of the ICCPR is applicable not only to detention in criminal cases but also to others, including 'immigration control'.[29]

The 1984 Convention against Torture and Other Cruel, Inhuman or Degrading Treatment or Punishment has gained increasing importance in recent years in protecting refugees from return to a country where they fear persecution because it has been interpreted as enhancing the protection against *non-refoulement* contained in article 33 of the 1951 Refugee Convention. The 1984 Convention against Torture prohibits the expulsion, return or extradition of a 'person to another State where there are substantial grounds for believing that he would be in danger of being subjected to torture' and therefore presents an absolute bar against return if the 'substantial grounds' standard of proof can be met and the torture would be committed by a State or the State's agent.[30] In contrast, article 33 of the 1951 Refugee Convention permits an exception to a refugee's return when 'there are reasonable grounds for regarding as a danger to security of the country in which he [the refugee] is, or who, having been convicted by a final judgment of a particularly serious crime, constitutes a danger to the community of that country'. As a result, the 1984 Convention against Torture ensures broader

---

24 Convention against Torture and Other Cruel, Inhuman or Degrading Treatment or Punishment, 10 December 1984, 1465 U.N.T.S. 85 (hereinafter 1984 Convention against Torture).

25 Convention on the Rights of the Child, ¶ 22, 20 November 1989, 1577 U.N.T.S. 3.

26 ICCPR, *supra* note 23, at art. 2.

27 Ibid., at arts. 9, 14.

28 Compilation of General Comments and General Recommendations Adopted by Human Rights Treaty Bodies, (General Comment 20 to Art. 7 of ICCPR, 1992), U.N. Doc. HRI/GEN/1/Rev.7, 152 (2004).

29 Ibid., (General Comment 8 to Art. 9 of ICCPR, 1982) at 130.

30 1984 Convention against Torture, *supra* note 24, at art. 3.

protection against return than article 33 of the 1951 Convention. On the basis of article 33 in the 1984 Convention against Torture and article 7 of the ICCPR, UNHCR has asserted the position that 'international human rights law has established *non-refoulement* as a fundamental component of the absolute prohibition of torture and cruel, inhuman or degrading treatment or punishment.'[31]

The 1989 Convention on the Rights of the Child also is a key instrument for the protection of refugees and asylum seekers. As noted in section 2.2.3.1, UNHCR contributed to the drafting of the 1989 CRC, and as a result, it includes a specific provision, article 22, pertaining to refugee children.[32] Whereas nearly all of the other provisions address the rights of children in general, this article is an exceptional one as it focuses on refugee children. UNHCR now extensively references the provisions in the 1989 CRC in its work to protect refugees, both in internal documents for UNHCR staff as well as in doctrinal positions submitted to governments, non-governmental organizations, academics, and others.

The provisions of the 1989 CRC restate many of the rights that adults have under the Universal Declaration of Human Rights,[33] and therefore, tend to be more broadly worded than the obligations States have toward refugees in the 1951 Refugee Convention. The 1989 CRC also includes rights particular to children, such as the right to a primary education.[34] The purpose of the 1989 CRC is to ensure that all children, including refugee children and children seeking refugee status, have their childhood protected and that children can develop within 'a family environment, in an atmosphere of happiness, love and understanding'.[35]

---

31 UNHCR, Note on International Protection, ¶ 16, U.N. Doc. A/AC.96/951 (13 September 2001).

32 1989 Convention on the Rights of the Child, *supra* note 25, art. 22. Article 22 provides that:'States Parties shall take appropriate measures to ensure that a child who is seeking refugee status or who is considered a refugee in accordance with applicable international or domestic law and procedures shall, whether unaccompanied or accompanied by his or her parents or by any other person, receive appropriate protection and humanitarian assistance in the enjoyment of applicable rights set forth in the present Convention and in other international human rights or humanitarian instruments to which the said States are Parties.'

'For this purpose, States Parties shall provide, as they consider appropriate, co-operation in any efforts by the United Nations and other competent intergovernmental organizations or non-governmental organizations co-operating with the United Nations to protect and assist such a child and to trace the parents or other members of the family of any refugee child in order to obtain information necessary for reunification with his or her family. In cases where no parents or other members of the family can be found, the child shall be accorded the same protection as any other child permanently or temporarily deprived of his or her family environment for any reason, as set forth in the present Convention.'

33 For example, rights in the 1989 Convention on the Rights of the Child that are similar to those in the Universal Declaration of Human Rights, include the right to life, freedom of association, and the right to privacy, those that are particular to the 1989 Convention on the Rights of the Child include that States should disseminate children's books and that they should ensure recognition of the principle that 'both parents have common responsibilities for the upbringing and development of the child'. See 1989 Convention on the Rights of the Child, *supra* note 25, at arts. 6, 15(1), 16, 17(c) and 18(a).

34 Ibid., at art. 28.

35 Ibid., at 5th–6th preambular ¶.

Of particular note among the various provisions of the 1989 CRC is article 3 that contains the principle of the 'best interests of the child'.[36] The 1989 CRC amplifies the protection obligations States have toward children under the 1951 Refugee Convention, since the 1951 Refugee Convention does not contain any specific articles related to children.[37]

These three international human rights instruments, along with many others,[38] extend the content of the refugee law framework beyond the protections offered by the 1951 Refugee Convention and provide standards that should apply to all States, thereby ameliorating the problem of disparate standards. They also can provide protection to asylum seekers and refugees who are located in countries that are not parties to the 1951 Refugee Convention or the 1967 Protocol. For example, the ICCPR's provisions are applicable to over 20 States that have ratified the ICCPR but not the 1967 Protocol. Most significantly, the 1989 CRC, which has been ratified by almost all UN Member States, applies to all States that have not acceded to the 1967 Protocol.

In sum, with the onset of the crisis in States' respect for refugee law standards, UNHCR finally overcame concerns about the political nature of human rights, in light of UNHCR's humanitarian mandate,[39] and began to more actively refer to international human rights standards. Not only did UNHCR use these standards more extensively, but it also increasingly referred to such standards in its own doctrinal positions and thereby provided such positions with a stronger legal foundation. While it is unfortunate that UNHCR did not incorporate human rights into the refugee law framework earlier, as these principles could have served as compelling legal support in countering States' actions and in buttressing the rights of refugees in the early 1990s, at the beginning of the crisis in international refugee law, UNHCR has increasingly utilized these principles to fulfil its protection function.

UNHCR's employment of human rights standards in the protection of refugees was taken by UNHCR at its own initiative and thus, demonstrates UNHCR's organizational autonomy in shaping the content of refugee law. Only after the agency had created a substantial basis for the application of such principles to

---

36 Ibid., at art. 3.¶1. Specifically, this paragraph provides that: 'In all actions concerning children, whether undertaken by public or private social welfare institutions, courts of law, administrative authorities or legislative bodies, the best interest of the child shall be a primary consideration.'

37 The lack of specific provisions related to refugee children in the 1951 Refugee Convention is not surprising given that the refugee definition and the various articles containing the obligations of States in the 1951 Refugee Convention were drafted with adults in mind. Children would generally have been considered as merely part of the refugee's family.

38 For example, see the International Covenant on Economic, Social and Cultural Rights, 16 December 1966, 993 U.N.T.S. 3; the Convention on the Elimination of All Forms of Racial Discrimination, 21 December 1965, 660 U.N.T.S. 195; and the Convention on the Elimination of All Forms of Discrimination against Women, 18 December 1979, 1249 U.N.T.S. 13.

39 UNHCR, Human Rights and Refugee Protection, Training Module RLD 5, *supra* note 18, at 4.

refugees, did it encourage EXCOM to adopt a conclusion endorsing UNHCR's promotion of human rights law.[40]

5.2.2 Other sources of international refugee law

International human rights instruments are not the only agreements used by UNHCR since the 1980s to extend the refugee law framework. As UNHCR's 2007 'Collection of International Instruments and Legal Texts Concerning Refugees and Others of Concern to UNHCR' suggests, international protection can be found in a wide array of instruments. This 2007 edition, which has become quite voluminous at four volumes, demonstrates an even broader incorporation by UNHCR of standards from other instruments to protect refugees, as it includes regional human rights and other instruments, international criminal law, maritime, and aviation law instruments, among others. It is as though once UNHCR decided not to limit itself to specific instruments for the protection of refugees, the organization realized that the whole range of regional and international instruments could be applied to refugees in order to strengthen refugee protection. Among these instruments, two additional treaty areas deserve special attention: international humanitarian law and international criminal law.

With the end of the Cold War, UNHCR became more frequently involved in protecting and assisting refugees who flee their homes because of an armed conflict, including internal conflict, or general violence, as well as refugees in areas where such conflict is occurring. This work has posed new challenges to UNHCR as it seeks to protect not only those persons under its mandate, but also its staff members. Despite the 'humanitarian nature of the problem of refugees', as stated in the preamble to UNHCR's Statute,[41] UNHCR's assistance and protection activities have been interpreted by parties to a conflict as partial and an impediment to their military success. For example, UNHCR convoys were attacked during the conflict in the former Yugoslavia and camps for refugees and internally displaced persons have been subjected to armed incursions in many countries.

To bolster the security of the refugees, UNHCR has increasingly relied on international humanitarian law instruments and their provisions. UNHCR has noted in its training manual for its staff that refugees fall within the category of 'protected persons' under the Fourth Geneva Convention on Humanitarian Law and Protocol 1 to the Geneva Conventions.[42] In addition, UNHCR has encouraged EXCOM to make reference to the civilian and humanitarian character

---

40 See EXCOM Conclusion 68 (XLIII), ¶ p, 1992 that supports UNHCR's activities related to the promotion of human rights law.
41 See the 2nd paragraph of UNHCR's Statute. UNHCR Statute, *supra* note 1.
42 UNHCR, Human Rights and Refugee Protection, Self-Study Module 5, *supra* note 19, at 25. Also see UNHCR, *Handbook for the Protection of Women and Girls* 346–347 (January 2008). Available athttp://www.unhcr.org/refworld/docid/47cfc2962.html (accessed 27 October 2011).

of refugee camps; in this way, UNHCR has asserted the position that attacks should not be targeted at refugee camps, and that refugees are prohibited from undertaking armed activities.[43] As a result of encouragement by UNHCR, General Assembly resolutions and EXCOM conclusions have included specific references to humanitarian law in connection with the protection of refugees.[44]

With respect to international criminal law, the Rome Statute of the International Criminal Court[45] contains provisions that have been incorporated into international refugee law by UNHCR. For example, the Rome Statute's definitions of a 'crime against humanity' and 'war crimes' provide additional clarification to the use of the terms in the exclusion clauses of the refugee definition in the 1951 Refugee Convention.[46] However, UNHCR has not fully articulated the way in which international criminal law supplements refugee law standards and consequently, has not permitted principles from this area of law to be used more actively in the protection of refugees. In recognition that the inter-linkages between refugee law and international criminal law need to be further developed, an Expert Meeting on Complementarities between International Refugee Law, International Criminal Law and International Humanitarian Law was held in Arusha, in April 2011, which was jointly sponsored by UNHCR and the International Criminal Tribunal for Rwanda.[47] However, further work remains to be done in this area by refugee law scholars and UNHCR.

5.2.3 The 1951 Refugee Convention as the central agreement

When UNHCR incorporated human rights law into the refugee law framework, there was a risk that refugee law might be subsumed into human rights law such that human rights agreements would become the dominant treaties for the determination of refugees' rights and States' obligations and eclipse the 1951 Refugee Convention. This risk was particularly acute since States had not adopted any new universal treaties based on or expanding the 1951 Refugee Convention since the late 1960s. In addition, refugee law is a subsidiary area within human rights law.

---

43 For example, see EXCOM Conclusion 48 (XXXVIII), ¶ 1–2, 1987, and EXCOM Conclusion 94 (LIII), ¶ a–c, 2002.
44 For example, see: G.A. Res. 65/194, ¶ 15, U.N. Doc. A/RES/65/194 (21 December 2010); G.A. Res. 64/127, ¶ 15, U.N. Doc. A/RES/64/127 (18 December 2009); G.A. Res. 61/137, ¶ 10, U.N. Doc. A/RES/61/137 (19 December 2006); EXCOM Conclusion 101 (LV), ¶ g, 2004; and EXCOM Conclusion 71 (XLIV), ¶ u, 1993.
45 Rome Statute of the International Criminal Court, 17 July 1998, 2187 U.N.T.S. 90.
46 Ibid., at arts. 7, 8. 1951 Refugee Convention, *supra* note 2, at art. 1(F)(a). Also see UNHCR, Guidelines on International Protection No. 5, Application of the Exclusion Clauses: Article 1F of the 1951 Convention Relating to the Status of Refugees, UNHCR Doc. HCR/GIP/03/05 (4 September 2003).
47 UNHCR and International Criminal Tribunal for Rwanda, Expert Meeting on Complementarities between International Refugee Law, International Criminal Law and International Humanitarian Law, Arusha, Tanzania, 11–13 April 2011. Available at http://www.unhcr.org/refworld/docid/4e1729d52.html (accessed 27 October 2011).

Consequently, while human rights law expands the protections for refugees, its application also raises the question as to why refugees should continue to receive a distinct and special status from other persons who require protection of their rights, such as persons subjected to environmental and man-made disasters, persons displaced as a result of development, and migrants. Thus, the question, of how to ensure that the 1951 Refugee Convention and refugee law in general remain at the forefront of protection for refugees, posed a serious challenge to UNHCR. The same concern did not exist with respect to international humanitarian law and international criminal law since they marginally supplement international refugee law and are distinctly different areas of law from refugee law.

This was not the first time that the universality and centrality of the 1951 Refugee Convention had been challenged. From the earliest days of its work, UNHCR had maintained the 1951 Refugee Convention as the foundation and guidepost for the further development of the refugee law framework. An initial challenge had occurred with the drafting of the 1969 OAU Refugee Convention. However, as UNHCR became substantially involved in the drafting of this regional convention, the agency was able to ensure that the OAU Refugee Convention complemented the 1951 Refugee Convention and that a provision was included in the 1969 OAU Refugee Convention that acknowledges the centrality of the 1951 Refugee Convention.[48] As other regional agreements and instruments were drafted, as noted in Chapter 2,[49] UNHCR attempted to ensure that those instruments were consistent with and upheld the standards in the 1951 Refugee Convention/1967 Protocol. UNHCR wanted regional agreements to supplement, rather than replace, the provisions of the 1951 Refugee Convention. Therefore, UNHCR obtained the inclusion of express provisions in regional instruments that affirmed the fundamental role of the 1951 Refugee Convention both prior to and following the onset of the crisis in refugee law and protection.

Prior to the crisis, the 1969 OAU Refugee Convention recognized the centrality of the 1951 Refugee Convention, due to UNHCR involvement in the drafting process, as noted earlier. Even during the crisis, UNHCR helped ensure that the 1984 Cartagena Declaration on Refugees specifically requested States to accede to the 1951 Refugee Convention and the 1967 Protocol and to adopt national laws implementing these agreements.[50] Moreover, in Europe, the conclusions of the

---

48 The preamble of the 1969 OAU Refugee Convention recognizes that the 1951 Refugee Convention, as supplemented by the 1967 Protocol, 'constitutes the basic and universal instrument relating to the status of refugees' and calls on Member States of the OAU who have not already done so, to accede to these agreements and in the meantime to apply their provisions. OAU Convention Governing the Specific Aspects of Refugee Problems in Africa, ¶ 9–10, *supra* note 9.

49 For UNHCR's involvement in the formulation of other regional agreements see section 2.2.3.3.

50 Cartagena Declaration on Refugees, §III.2, 8, OAS/Ser.L/V.II.66, doc. 10, rev.1, at 190–193, (1984). Available at http://www.unhcr.org/basics/BASICS/45dc19084.pdf (accessed 27 October 2011). While the Declaration is not legally binding on States, numerous resolutions have been

Tampere Summit in 1999, which established the agenda for European harmoniza-tion of asylum policy, recognize the 'full and inclusive application of the Geneva Convention'.[51] Moreover, UNHCR stimulated EXCOM to adopt a conclusion that provided that 'regional standards which are developed conform fully with universally recognized standards'.[52]

Unlike the individual regional agreements concerning refugees, human rights law was an entire body of law and therefore, posed a substantial challenge to the 1951 Refugee Convention as the centrepiece for international refugee law for States. Therefore, UNHCR stimulated EXCOM to adopt conclusions recognizing the importance and the centrality of the 1951 Refugee Convention and the 1967 Protocol.[53] Moreover starting in the mid-1990s, UNHCR encouraged the UN General Assembly to adopt resolutions that reaffirmed that the 1951 Refugee Convention with the 1967 Protocol remain the foundation of the international refugee regime.[54] UNHCR's emphasis on the 1951 Refugee Convention as the key international agreement for the protection of refugees ensured that refugee law was not subsumed into human rights law. This distinction bolstered UNHCR's position that refugees held a special status under human rights law in contrast to other persons who had human rights protections, such as migrants seeking job opportunities in other countries.

UNHCR's success in ensuring that the 1951 Refugee Convention remained the centrepiece for the refugee law framework is evidenced by the Declaration of States Parties during the Global Consultations process, in which States recog-nized 'the enduring importance of the 1951 Convention, as the primary refugee protection instrument'.[55] States' endorsement of the 1951 Refugee Convention in

adopted by the Organization of American States endorsing the Declaration's principles. See Guy Goodwin-Gill and Jane McAdam, *The Refugee in International Law* 38 (3rd edn, 2007).

51 UNHCR, UNHCR Tool Boxes on EU Asylum Matters: Tool Box 2: The Instruments 47 (September 2002). Available at http://www.unhcr.org/publ/PUBL/406a8c432.pdf (accessed 27 October 2011).

52 EXCOM Conclusion 81 (XLVIII), ¶ k, 1997 endorsed by G.A. Res. 52/103, ¶ 1, U.N. Doc. A/RES/52/103 (12 December 1997).

53 See for example EXCOM Conclusion 90 (LII), ¶ a, 2001; EXCOM Conclusion 89 (LI), 10th preambular ¶, 2000; EXCOM Conclusion 87 (L), ¶ f, 1999; EXCOM Conclusion 79 (XLVII), ¶ c, 1996; EXCOM Conclusion 77 (XLVI), ¶ c, 1995; EXCOM Conclusion 74 (XLV), ¶ c, 1994; EXCOM Conclusion 71 (XLIV), ¶ b, 1993; EXCOM Conclusion 61 (XLI) ¶ b, (1990).

54 See for example: G.A. Res. 65/194, ¶ 4, U.N. Doc. A/RES/65/194 (21 December 2010); G.A. Res. 64/127, ¶ 3, U.N. Doc. A/RES/64/127 (18 December 2009); G.A. Res. 57/187, ¶ 4, U.N. Doc. A/RES/57/187 (18 December 2002); G.A. Res. 56/137, ¶ 3, U.N. Doc. A/RES/56/137 (19 December 2001); G.A. Res. 55/74, ¶ 4, U.N. Doc. A/RES/55/74 (4 December 2000); G.A. Res. 54/146, ¶ 3, U.N. Doc. A/RES/54/146 (17 December 1999); G.A. Res. 53/125, ¶ 3, U.N. Doc. A/RES/53/125 (9 December 1998); G.A. Res. 52/103, 3rd preambular ¶, U.N. Doc. A/RES/52/103 (12 December 1997); G.A. Res. 51/75, 3rd preambular ¶, U.N. Doc. A/RES/51/175 (12 December 1996); G.A. Res. 50/152, 3rd preambular ¶, U.N. Doc. A/RES/50/152 (21 December 1995); and G.A. Res. 49/169, 4th preambular ¶, U.N. Doc. A/RES/49/169 (23 December 1994.)

55 UNHCR, Agenda for Protection 23 (2003). States also acknowledged the 'continuing relevance and resilience of this international regime of rights and principles'. Ibid., at 24.

the Declaration of States Parties also served to counter criticism from academics[56] and even governments[57] and bolstered the view that the Convention remains relevant, significant, and the principal agreement for the protection of refugees.

5.3 UNHCR doctrine

UNHCR doctrine, the organization's view of what the law is or should be, is another approach that was adopted by UNHCR to address the weaknesses in the refugee law framework. As shown in Chapter 3, UNHCR had issued doctrinal positions since shortly after its creation. However, following the onset of the crisis in refugee protection in the early 1980s, UNHCR began issuing an increasing number of positions and then in the 1990s, UNHCR began making the doctrinal positions much more publicly available and used them not only to elaborate principles but also to expressly criticize States. Thus, UNHCR's doctrinal positions evolved from a primarily internal form of guidance for UNHCR staff members to a tool that was actively utilized by UNHCR, following the onset of the crisis in refugee protection and law, to ensure the continued development of refugee law in a manner that strengthened and enhanced the protection afforded to refugees.

5.3.1 Filling gaps

UNHCR doctrine was particularly useful in addressing the significant gaps in the protections afforded refugees under the refugee law framework, comprised of the 1951 Refugee Convention, other refugee agreements, and regional refugee instruments. While no legal framework ever provides perfect legal coverage, when States ceased to co-operate with UNHCR in the 1980s, the gaps in the refugee law framework became glaringly apparent. UNHCR then utilized its doctrinal positions as a means to provide non-binding, yet authoritative principles to fill important gaps.

One substantive area in which UNHCR doctrine was particularly useful in this manner was that of voluntary repatriation. The 1951 Refugee Convention does not contain any provisions regarding voluntary repatriation. However, voluntary repatriation is one of three solutions traditionally foreseen to what is supposed to be a temporary situation of 'refugee status' for refugees, with the other two solutions being local integration and resettlement. UNHCR's Statute establishes the organization's role related to voluntary repatriation by stating that as part of its

---

56 See for example, Joan Fitzpatrick, 'Revitalizing the 1951 Refugee Convention', 9 *Harvard Human Rights Journal* 229, 229–31 (1996) which summarizes the various criticisms of the 1951 Refugee Convention.

57 See footnote 37 in Chapter 4.

international protection function, UNHCR is to assist 'governmental and private efforts to promote voluntary repatriation'.[58]

During the Cold War, UNHCR had emphasized the solutions of local integration and resettlement since most refugees from Eastern European countries and the Soviet Union did not want to return to their home countries and Western countries were not interested, due to the politicized nature of the refugee issue, in encouraging refugees to return to such countries. However, with the end of the Cold War and the depolitization of the refugee issue, States became more interested in returning asylum seekers to their home countries and in reducing the number of persons seeking asylum in their countries. UNHCR then began to emphasize the solution of repatriation in the 1980s.[59] UNHCR had no difficulty obtaining the agreement of EXCOM Member States to the inclusion of a paragraph in EXCOM conclusions that voluntary repatriation was the ideal and preferred solution[60] since such statements coincided with the interest of asylum States in the return of the refugees they were hosting.

The issues on which UNHCR and States did not agree, with respect to voluntary repatriation, were the meaning and content of 'voluntary' and the principles to be observed in effectuating the return of refugees. In order to deter States from forcing refugees to return to their countries of origin, UNHCR emphasized the voluntariness of the refugee's choice to return and that the physical safety of refugees was to be ensured and their rights respected throughout the return process.[61] UNHCR then utilized these principles in its advice to States on the advisability of return in certain cases, such as with Iraqi refugees.[62] In addition, UNHCR incorporated specific articles on the voluntary nature of the return and return in safety and dignity in the sample voluntary repatriation agreement in UNHCR's Handbook on Voluntary Repatriation.[63] The sample agreement then served as the basis for trilateral voluntary repatriation agreements, among the

58 UNHCR Statute, *supra* note 1, at ¶ 8(c). UNHCR is to assist 'governmental and private efforts to promote voluntary repatriation'.
59 See for example UNHCR, Note on International Protection, ¶ 16, U.N. Doc. A/AC.96/609/Rev.1 (26 August 1982), which stresses voluntary repatriation as 'both the optimum and also the only workable solution'.
60 See for example, EXCOM Conclusion 41 (XXXVII), ¶ d, 1986; EXCOM Conclusion 46 (XXXVIII), ¶ l, 1987; EXCOM Conclusion 62 (XLI), ¶ a(iv), 1990; EXCOM Conclusion 68 (XLIII), ¶ s, 1992; EXCOM Conclusion 74 (XLV), ¶ v, 1994; EXCOM Conclusion 79 (XLVII), ¶ q, 1996; EXCOM Conclusion 81 (XLVIII), ¶ q, 1997; EXCOM Conclusion 85 (XLIX), ¶ gg, 1998; EXCOM Conclusion 87 (L), ¶ r, 1999.
61 See UNHCR, *Handbook: Voluntary Repatriation: International Protection*, §2 (1996). Available at http://www.unhcr.org/pub/PUBL/3bfe68d32.pdf (accessed 27 October 2011). See also EXCOM Conclusion 40 (XXXVI), ¶ b, 1985.
62 See for example, UNHCR, UNHCR Advisory Regarding the Return of Iraqis (September 2005). Available at http://www.unhcr.org/cgi-bin/texis/vtx/refworld/rwmain?docid=432a89d54 (accessed 27 October 2011).
63 UNHCR, *Handbook: Voluntary Repatriation: International Protection*, Annex 5, arts. 7, 9 (1996). Available at http://www.unhcr.org/pub/PUBL/3bfe68d32.pdf (accessed 27 October 2011).

country of asylum, the country of origin of the refugees, and UNHCR, as well as bilateral voluntary repatriation agreements between UNHCR and the country of asylum and country of origin, respectively.[64]

These multilateral and bilateral voluntary repatriation agreements are treaties that are considered to be 'special agreements' under UNHCR's Statute.[65] Since they are treaties, they are binding on the State parties that have signed and ratified them. Moreover, as an increasing number of States enter into such agreements and are bound by provisions on the voluntary nature of repatriation and the return of refugees in safety and dignity, these treaties will evidence States' *opinio juris* on such principles and thereby contribute to the development of such principles into customary international law.

UNHCR doctrinal positions not only assisted in filling gaps on substantive protection issues, such as voluntary repatriation, but also on procedural standards for the determination of refugee status, that is, who shall receive the full range of protections under refugee law. The 1951 Refugee Convention does not explicitly provide whom, whether States or UNHCR, is to make the determination as to whether a person qualifies as a refugee under the Convention. Initially, UNHCR conducted refugee status determination in many countries, like its predecessor the International Refugee Organization,[66] but this function has become increasingly vested in States, although UNHCR continues to play an advisory or consultative role in many countries.

Prior to the beginning of the crisis, UNHCR's primary concern in this area was to ensure consistent, harmonized procedures among States for the determination of whether an asylum seeker was a refugee.[67] Following the onset of the crisis in

---

64 See for example, Tripartite Agreement between The Government of the Republic of Mozambique, The Government of Zimbabwe and the United Nations High Commissioner for Refugees for the Voluntary Repatriation of Mozambican Refugees from Zimbabwe, 22 March 1993. Available at http://www.unhcr.org/refworld/docid/3ee884a74.html (accessed 27 October 2011). Tripartite agreements adopted within the past decade have included these principles and others and are increasingly being made public by UNHCR. For example, see Tripartite Agreement between the Government of the Central African Republic and the Government of the Republic of the Sudan and the United Nations High Commissioner for Refugees for the Voluntary Repatriation of Sudanese Refugees in the Central African Republic back to the Sudan, 1 February 2006. Available at http://www.unhcr.org/refworld/docid/44044a274.html (accessed 27 October 2011).

65 Marjoleine Zieck, 'Voluntary Repatriation: Paradigm, Pitfalls, Progress', 23 *Refugee Surv. Q.* 33, 37 (2004).

66 Report of the Secretary-General, ¶ 12, U.N. Doc. A/C.3/527 and Corr.1 (26 October 1949). The IRO, like UNHCR, wanted to ensure uniformity in the application of the refugee definition. Thus, the IRO, to assure that its officers were consistent in their evaluation of who qualified as a refugee, issued a *Manual for Eligibility Officers*. More recently, in 2005, UNHCR issued a position related to its own determination of refugee status under its mandate. See UNHCR, Procedural Standards for Refugee Status Determination under UNHCR's Mandate (1 September 2005). Available at http://www.unhcr.org/pub/PUBL/4317223c9.pdf (accessed 27 October 2011).

67 It should also be noted that UNHCR's Statute and the 1951 Refugee Convention establish similar, but not identical, criteria for determining who qualifies as a refugee, in particular, the refugee definition in UNHCR's Statute does not contain 'particular social group' as a grounds for persecution

the 1980s, UNHCR shifted its focus to doctrinal positions that would curb the adoption and use by States of restrictive procedural practices. For example, UNHCR suggested to EXCOM that it adopt a conclusion that would ensure that States' determination of whether an asylum application is 'manifestly unfounded or abusive' would be made by the authority competent to determine refugee status and that a negative determination would be subject to an appeal or review.[68] UNHCR succeeded in obtaining part of its suggested doctrinal position. The resulting EXCOM conclusion provided that such decision was made by a qualified official, but States only agreed to a simplified review of such decision before the asylum seeker would be rejected at the frontier or forcibly removed.[69]

States also attempted to channel asylum applications through the use of the 'safe country of origin' concept into an expedited procedure. In doing so, they tried to avoid having to give full consideration to the claims of asylum seekers from countries that they considered had a low risk of persecution. UNHCR then had to formulate a response to this new mechanism. Thus, UNHCR established the doctrinal position that the 'safe country of origin' concept can be utilized to channel certain asylum applications into expedited or accelerated procedures, but not to completely deny access to asylum procedures.[70] UNHCR also provided guidance to ensure that States utilize an appropriate standard of proof and permit a right of appeal for rejected asylum applicants[71] to counter States' tendencies to lower the standard of proof and limit the right to appeal of the asylum seeker.

5.3.2 Clarifying ambiguities

UNHCR also crafted doctrinal positions to clarify certain provisions in the 1951 Refugee Convention in order to counter restrictive interpretations of both the refugee definition and the rights to be accorded refugees under the 1951 Refugee Convention. Two topics related to the refugee definition, asylum claims by refugee women and the exclusion clauses, and a third topic in the area of substantive obligations of States toward refugees, detention, illustrate the role of UNHCR doctrine in providing further content to provisions in the 1951 Refugee Convention.

---

and the grounds for exclusion from refugee status on the basis of the commission of a crime are much less detailed than those contained in Article 1F of the refugee definition in the 1951 Refugee Convention.

68 UNHCR, Follow-up on Earlier Conclusions of the Sub-Committee on the Determination of Refugee Status, *inter alia*, with Reference to the Role of UNHCR in National Refugee Status Determination Procedure, ¶ 31, EC/SCP/22/Rev.1 (3 September 1982).

69 EXCOM Conclusion 28 (XXXIII), ¶ d, 1982. EXCOM Conclusion 30 (XXXIV), ¶ e, 1983.

70 See UNHCR, Background Note on the Safe Country Concept and Refugee Status, UNHCR Doc. EC/SCP/68, 26 July 1991. On safe country of origin also see EXCOM Conclusion 85 (XLIX), ¶ aa, 1998.

71 See UNHCR, Note on Burden and Standard of Proof in Refugee Claims (16 December 1998). Available at http://www.unhcr.org/refworld/docid/3ae6b3338.html (accessed 27 October 2011).

UNHCR utilized doctrinal positions to significantly clarify the applicability of the refugee definition to asylum claims by women. The refugee definition had traditionally been interpreted by States based on the types of persecution experienced by men, despite the fact that women often experience persecution differently from men.[72] A greater awareness of women's issues in the international community coincided with UNHCR's interest in the topic. The World Conferences on Women, held in Mexico in 1975, in Copenhagen in 1980, and in Nairobi in 1985, had progressively helped to raise the awareness of the rights of women. The 4th World Conference on Women in 1995 in Beijing, in which UNHCR actively participated, was particularly important in calling attention to women's issues. Thus, UNHCR capitalized on the growing recognition of the need to fully implement women's rights as it developed doctrinal positions on the meaning of 'particular social group' in the refugee definition and on gender-related persecution in order to create a more expansive interpretation of a 'refugee' under the 1951 Refugee Convention.

UNHCR began to clarify the applicability of the refugee definition to asylum claims by women with doctrinal positions that elaborated the meaning of 'membership of a particular social group' in the refugee definition. This clarification was relevant not only to women asylum claimants, but also to persons who constitute part of groups such as families, tribes, and homosexuals.[73]

UNHCR prompted EXCOM to adopt a conclusion in 1985 suggesting that States take the view that 'women asylum-seekers who face harsh or inhuman treatment due to their having transgressed the social mores of the society' should be considered as a 'particular social group'.[74] Then in 2002, UNHCR issued guidelines that essentially combined two dominant approaches, the 'protected characteristics' and the 'social perception' approaches, into a single standard for the meaning of 'particular social group' following the discussion of the topic during the Global Consultations process.[75]

---

72 EXCOM Conclusion 73 (XLIV), ¶ e, 1993.

73 UNHCR, Guidelines on International Protection: 'Membership of a Particular Social Group' within the Context of Article 1A(2) of the 1951 Convention and/or its 1967 Protocol Relating to the Status of Refugees, ¶ 1, HCR/GIP/02/02 (7 May 2002).

74 EXCOM Conclusion 39 (XXXVI), ¶ k, 1985. Also see UNHCR, Guidelines on International Protection: The Application of Article 1A(2) of the 1951 Convention/1967 Protocol Relating to the Status of Refugees to Victims of Trafficking and Persons at Risk of Being Trafficked, ¶ 32, 37–9, HCR/GIP/06/07 (7 April 2006), which notes, in paragraph 32, that 'women may be especially vulnerable to being trafficked and constitute a social group within the terms of the refugee definition.'

75 UNHCR, Guidelines on International Protection: 'Membership of a Particular Social Group' within the Context of Article 1A(2) of the 1951 Convention and/or its 1967 Protocol Relating to the Status of Refugees, *supra* note 73, at ¶ 6, 7. The standard adopted by UNHCR, in combining these two approaches is that 'a particular social group is a group of persons who share a common characteristic other than their risk of being persecuted, or who are perceived as a group by society. The characteristic will often be one which is innate, unchangeable, or which is otherwise fundamental to identity, conscience or the exercise of one's human rights.' Ibid., at 11.

On the subject of the type of persecution encountered by women refugees, UNHCR initially worked through the General Assembly and EXCOM to promote the position that women, whose claims are based on a well-founded fear derived from sexual violence or other gender-related persecution, should be recognized as refugees. In 1993, UNHCR addressed a Note to EXCOM concerning sexual violence against refugee women[76] and encouraged the body to adopt a conclusion that expresses support for States' recognition of persons as refugees who claim a well-founded fear of persecution due to sexual violence, for one of the reasons in the refugee definition.[77] Numerous General Assembly resolutions and EXCOM conclusions in the mid- to late 1990s reiterated this UNHCR position.[78] EXCOM also requested UNHCR, in 1995, to assist States in developing guidelines that contain this principle.[79]

UNHCR also included the topic of gender-related persecution in the Global Consultations process. Following the discussions, UNHCR drafted guidelines that acknowledged that gender-related reasons, such as rape and dowry-related violence, a pattern of discrimination or less favourable treatment, and being trafficked for the purposes of prostitution or sexual exploitation, could be considered as forms of persecution.[80] Moreover, UNHCR's guidelines assert that these types of persecution can be committed by State and non-State actors and provide insight into how the various grounds of persecution can apply to gender-related claims.[81]

In the area of exclusion, UNHCR used doctrinal positions to counter States' attempts to interpret the definition of a refugee more narrowly. The exclusion clauses, contained in article 1(F) of the 1951 Refugee Convention, establish certain categories of acts for which a person may be excluded from refugee status recognition, despite fulfilment of the inclusion clauses in part 1(A) of the definition. Civil conflicts in the former Yugoslavia, beginning with the war in Croatia in 1991, and the mass killings in Rwanda in 1994, which led to the subsequent establishment of international criminal tribunals to prosecute perpetrators of 'serious violations of international humanitarian law',[82] gave rise to an increased

---

76 UNHCR, Note on Certain Aspects of Sexual Violence against Refugee Women, A/AC.96/822 (12 October 1993).

77 EXCOM Conclusion 73 (XLIV), ¶ d, 1993.

78 See for example, EXCOM Conclusion 81 (XLVIII), ¶ t, 1997 and G.A. Res. 52/103, ¶ 15, U.N. Doc. A/RES/52/103 (12 December 1997).

79 EXCOM Conclusion 77 (XLVI), ¶ g, 1995.

80 UNHCR, Guidelines on International Protection: Gender-Related Persecution within the Context of Article 1A(2) of the 1951 Convention and/or its 1967 Protocol Relating to the Status of Refugees, ¶14-18, HCR/GIP/02/01 (7 May 2002). Also see UNHCR, Guidelines on International Protection: the Application of Article 1A(2) of the 1951 Convention/1967 Protocol Relating to the Status of Refugees to Victims of Trafficking and Persons at Risk of being Trafficked, *supra* note 74, at ¶ 14–20.

81 Ibid., at ¶ 19, 22–34.

82 See S.C. Res. 827, U.N. Doc. S/RES/827 (25 May 1993) Concerning the Establishment of the International Tribunal for the Prosecution of Persons Responsible for Serious Violations of

focus on the use of the exclusion clauses to deny refugee status to persons who were suspected, alleged, or accused of having committed crimes in connection with the conflicts.[83] UNHCR then responded by issuing guidelines on the exclusion clauses, which provide information on the category of crimes for which a refugee can be excluded as well as other crimes that were emerging as excludable crimes under 1(F), and a background paper that addresses procedural issues relating to the exclusion clause.[84]

In addition, the increased interest of States in applying the exclusion clauses to limit refugee status[85] prompted UNHCR to include them as a topic in the Global Consultations process launched in late 2000. The timing was propitious. Following the terrorist attacks on the World Trade Center towers in New York in 2001, States became exceedingly concerned about security, and thus, persons that threaten a nation's security. UNHCR utilized the Global Consultations process to further develop its doctrinal positions on the application of the exclusion clauses and then in 2003 issued guidelines on the issue. These guidelines set forth detailed advice on the content of the grounds on which a person may be excluded, as well as guidance on procedural issues, such as whether exclusion clauses should be examined prior to the evaluation of the inclusion clauses of the refugee definition.[86]

At the same time that UNHCR employed doctrinal positions to extend the definition of a 'refugee' under the 1951 Refugee Convention, as shown earlier, it also used such positions to clarify standards in the 1951 Refugee Convention. As noted in Chapter 4, one of the restrictive measures adopted by States was the detention of asylum seekers. States detained asylum seekers for a number of reasons: to restrict access to the State's territory, to discourage others from seeking asylum, to impede movement within the territory, and to keep an asylum

International Humanitarian Law Committed in the Territory of the Former Yugoslavia since 1991 and S.C. Res. 955, U.N. Doc. S/RES/955 (8 November 1994) Concerning the Establishment of an International Criminal Tribunal for Rwanda.

83 UNHCR, Note on the Exclusion Clauses, ¶ 2, UNHCR Doc. EC/47/SC/CRP.29 (30 May 1997).

84 See UNHCR, The Exclusion Clauses: Guidelines on Their Application (2 Dec. 1996). Available at http://www.unhcr.org/refworld/docid/3ae6b31d9f.html (accessed 27 October 2011) and UNHCR, Background Paper on the Article 1F Exclusion Clauses (June 1998) (on file with author).

85 Geoff Gilbert, 'Current Issues in the Application of the Exclusion Clauses' in *Refugee Protection In International Law: UNHCR's Global Consultations on International Protection* 425, 429 (Erika Feller, Volker Türk & Frances Nicholson eds, 2003). This paper was prepared as a background paper for the expert roundtable discussion on exclusion as part of the Global consultations process. Also see UNHCR, Background Note on the Application of the Exclusion Clauses: Article 1F of the 1951 Convention relating to the Status of Refugees, ¶ 2 (4 Sept. 2003). Available at http://www.unhcr.org/refworld/docid/3f5857d24.html (accessed 27 October 2011).

86 UNHCR, Guidelines on International Protection No. 5, Application of the Exclusion Clauses: Article 1F of the 1951 Convention Relating to the Status of Refugees, *supra* note 46. Surprisingly, the guidelines, while providing that inclusion should generally be considered before exclusion, do not, as had been the case in the 1996 guidelines, categorically exclude the possibility of considering exclusion before inclusion.

seeker under control in case the asylum claim was rejected and the person needed
to be returned to their country of origin or first asylum country. Therefore,
UNHCR found it necessary to clarify the interpretation of article 31 of the
1951 Refugee Convention, one of only three provisions therein that establishes
a prohibition on States' treatment of refugees.[87] Under this article:

> 1   The Contracting States shall not impose penalties, on account of their
> illegal entry or presence, on refugees who, coming directly from a territory
> where their life or freedom was threatened in the sense of Article 1, enter or
> are present in their territory without authorization, provided they present
> themselves without delay to the authorities and show good cause for their
> illegal entry or presence.
> 2   The Contracting States shall not apply to the movements of such refu-
> gees restrictions other than those which are necessary and such restrictions
> shall only be applied until their status in the country is regularized or they
> obtain admission into another country.[88]

Throughout the 1980s and 1990s, UNHCR pursued the adoption of General
Assembly resolutions and EXCOM conclusions expressing concern about arbitrary and unjustified detention.[89] UNHCR also encouraged EXCOM to adopt the
1986 conclusion that sets forth principles concerning detention. The conclusion
states that detention should normally be avoided, and establishes stringent criteria
for when it can be exceptionally used.[90] In addition, UNHCR issued, in 1995, a
publication on the detention of asylum seekers in Europe and guidelines on the
detention of asylum seekers that established minimum standards for States' use
of detention.[91] These guidelines were updated in 1999 to further clarify the exceptional grounds for detention; they also specify alternatives to detention.[92] UNHCR
then addressed the topic in a report to the Standing Committee of EXCOM,

87 The other two articles of the 1951 Refugee Convention which establish prohibitions on States'
    conduct are article 32, prohibiting States from expelling refugees lawfully on their territory except
    on grounds of national security or public order and article 33, which prohibits the expulsion or
    return of refugees.
88 1951 Refugee Convention, *supra* note 2, at art. 31.
89 See for example: G.A. Res. 36/125 ¶ 9, U.N. Doc. A/RES/36/125 (14 December 1981); G.A. Res.
    49/169 ¶ 11, U.N. Doc. A/RES/49/169 (23 December 1994); EXCOM Conclusion 36 (XXXVI),
    ¶ f, 1985; and EXCOM Conclusion 85 (XLIX), ¶ cc, 1998.
90 EXCOM Conclusion 44 (XXXVII), ¶ b, 1986. This followed UNHCR's articulation of such
    standards in its 1984 Note on International Protection. UNHCR, Note on International Protection,
    ¶ 26–30, U.N. Doc. A/AC.96/643 (9 August 1984).
91 UNHCR, Detention of Asylum-Seekers and Refugees: The Framework, the Problem and
    Recommended Practice, UNHCR Doc. EC/49/SC/CRP.13, ¶ 12, 3 (4 June 1999).
92 UNHCR, Guidelines on Applicable Criteria and Standards relating to the Detention of Asylum
    Seekers, 3–6 (February 1999). Available at http://www.unhcr.org/refworld/docid/3c2b3f844.html
    (accessed 27 October 2011).

which suggested a minimum set of recommended practices that were to form the basis for an EXCOM Conclusion.[93] However, States and UNHCR failed to reach a consensus on the content of an EXCOM conclusion and consequently, no EXCOM conclusion was adopted on detention.[94] Despite such failure, UNHCR's doctrinal work clearly established principles that furnish more precise content to the 1951 Refugee Convention's article 31 and States' use of detention of asylum seekers.

5.3.3 *Influencing the development of refugee law*

UNHCR doctrine not only assisted in filling in gaps and clarifying ambiguities in the refugee law framework following the onset of the crisis in refugee law and protection, but also served, and continues to serve, another very important function; it contributes to the development of the three primary sources of international law, which are articulated in article 38 of the Statute of the International Court of Justice: international conventions, international customary rules, and general principles of law.[95] UNHCR's work to influence these three primary sources, through its doctrinal positions, can be said to have received the implicit support from EXCOM, since several EXCOM conclusions adopted during the early years of the crisis in refugee law encourage UNHCR to promote the development of international refugee law.[96]

93 UNHCR, Detention of Asylum-Seekers and Refugees: The Framework, the Problem and Recommended Practice, *supra* note 91.

94 Also, note that Professor Goodwin-Gill prepared a paper for the Global Consultations Process concerning article 31 of the 1951 Refugee Convention. See Guy Goodwin-Gill, 'Article 31 of the 1951 Convention Relating to the Status of Refugees: Non-penalization, Detention and Protection', in Refugee Protection in International Law: UNHCR's Global Consultations on International Protection 185 (Erika Feller, Volker Türk and Frances Nicholson, eds, 2003). However, the Agenda for Protection only provides that 'States [are] more concertedly to explore appropriate alternatives to the detention of asylum-seekers and refugees, and to abstain, in principles, from detaining children.' UNHCR, Agenda for Protection 38 (2003). This limited reference in the Agenda for Protection attests to the fact that detention remains a difficult topic for States.

95 I.C.J. Statute, art. 38. Article 38 of the ICJ's Statute also provides for consideration of 'judicial decisions and the teachings of the most highly qualified publicists of the various nations, as subsidiary means for the determination of the rules of law'. These sources are sometimes termed 'secondary sources' due to the fact that States do not create them. Only UNHCR's contribution to the primary sources will be considered in this chapter, since international legal scholars and practitioners hold them to be the only true sources of international law between States. UNHCR's influence on the subsidiary sources will be discussed in Chapter 6, in connection with UNHCR's promotion of international refugee law.

96 EXCOM Conclusion 41 (XXXVII), ¶ h, 1986; EXCOM Conclusion 36 (XXXVI), ¶ m, 1985.

5.3.3.1 Treaty law[97]

As shown in Chapter 2, UNHCR contributed to the drafting of provisions of not only international and regional treaties specifically for the protection of refugees, but also human rights instruments and other agreements that affect their rights. UNHCR's suggested additions and/or modifications to draft treaties have not always been further developments in the law. In some cases, UNHCR's proposed provision for inclusion in a treaty was merely a reiteration of a 1951 Refugee Convention standard. In others, UNHCR had to formulate new doctrinal positions and thus, these positions actively contributed to furthering the development of refugee law. For example, UNHCR's positions on the European Union directives, in connection with the EU harmonization process on asylum, often required UNHCR to formulate new principles and to refine existing 1951 Refugee Convention standards.

However, for the moment, UNHCR doctrinal positions appear to be of less importance in the formulation of new treaties affecting refugees, since most of UNHCR's contributions ensure that such treaties complement the 1951 Refugee Convention and do not affect the current rights of refugees protected under the Convention, rather than constituting formulations of new rights for refugees. Recent examples include the Protocol to Prevent, Suppress and Punish Trafficking in Persons, especially Women and Children, supplementing the United Nations Convention against Transnational Organized Crime, and the Protocol against the Smuggling of Migrants by Land, Air and Sea, supplementing the United Nations Convention against Transnational Organized Crime.[98]

In theory, in the future, States may incorporate doctrinal principles, articulated by UNHCR during the past several decades, into a new treaty that affects the rights of refugees. However, the recent practice of the European Union suggests that even States that have traditionally been at the forefront of refugee protection are reluctant to expand refugee rights in a manner suggested by UNHCR doctrinal positions. Therefore, realistically, there will need to be a change in States' humanitarian approach to refugees before States are ready to draft a new universal refugee law instrument that expands, rather than contracts, the obligations States owe to refugees.

97 Although directives, drafted by the European Commission and approved by the Council of Ministers of the European Union, are not treaties, EU Member States are obliged to implement such directives through their national laws, and therefore, such directives also are included within the scope of this section.

98 See the Saving clause in article 14 of the Protocol to Prevent, Suppress and Punish Trafficking in Persons, especially Women and Children, supplementing the United Nations Convention against Transnational Organized Crime, G.A. Res. 55/25, Annex II, U.N. Doc. A/RES/55/25 (15 November 2000) and a similar provision in article 19 of the Protocol against the Smuggling of Migrants by Land, Air and Sea, supplementing the United Nations Convention against Transnational Organized Crime, G.A. Res. 55/25, Annex III, U.N. Doc. A/RES/55/25 (15 November 2000).

5.3.3.2 Customary international refugee law

UNHCR doctrinal positions also have influenced the development of customary international law.[99] From a theoretical perspective, UNHCR doctrine can articulate an existing customary international law standard (*lex lata*), identify a standard that is emerging as law (*in statu nascendi*), and state what the law should be (*de lege ferenda*).[100] However, in practice, it is not always easy to differentiate which of these three applies to a particular doctrinal position as the doctrinal positions present the legal principles without a statement as to whether the principles are recognized as law, are emerging standards, or are 'hoped for' standards. In order accurately to assess whether a particular doctrinal position is *lex lata*, *in statu nascendi* or *de lege ferenda*, one must consider each doctrinal position individually. The key is to evaluate States' actions and views to determine to what extent there is state practice and *opinio juris* in support of a particular principle. However, it must be noted that this approach, in itself, involves a subjective process of assessment that is influenced by the person who undertakes the evaluation.[101]

General Assembly resolutions and EXCOM conclusions, particularly those endorsed by the General Assembly that contain UNHCR doctrine, may serve as evidence of the elements of customary international law, either of state practice or of *opinio juris*. Specifically, a doctrinal position may constitute State practice in support of a customary international law norm where States in the General Assembly or EXCOM assert that the position is existing law and provided that other States do not challenge this assertion.[102] However, with respect to EXCOM, as not all States are members, unlike in the UN General Assembly, it is also necessary to consider the practice of non-Member States. Where there is no practice, by non-Member States to EXCOM, which conflicts with the doctrinal position, then the State practice by EXCOM members would be sufficient.[103] EXCOM or General Assembly resolutions may also evidence *opinio juris* where States have the belief that the practice is required by law.[104]

Even where EXCOM conclusions and General Assembly resolutions, which contain UNHCR doctrinal principles, do not create customary international law, they may still entail certain obligations for States. While there is no legal obligation for States to act consistently with such conclusions or resolutions, States

---

99 For a consideration of the basis for UNHCR's activities to influence the development of customary international law, see Corinne Lewis, 'UNHCR's Contribution to the Development of International Refugee Law: Its Foundations and Evolution', 17 *Int'l. J. Refugee L.* 67, 85–6 (2005).

100 This analysis is based on the influence of General Assembly resolutions on the development of customary international law. Blaine Sloan, 'General Assembly Resolutions Revisited (Forty Years Later)', 58 *Brit. Y.B. Int'l. L.* 39, 68 (1987).

101 Jorge Casteñeda, *Legal Effects of United Nations Resolutions* 171 (1969).

102 Michael Akehurst, 'Custom as a Source of International Law', 47 *Brit. Y.B. Int'l.* 1, 5 (1975).

103 Ibid., at 18.

104 Sloan, *supra* note 100, at 75.

could be said to have, at a minimum, an obligation to consider the recommend-ations by the General Assembly, and at least EXCOM conclusions endorsed by the General Assembly, if not all EXCOM conclusions, in good faith.[105] Moreover, it is possible to posit that States, which have voted in favour of a resolution or a conclusion, are estopped, under an obligation of good faith, from acting in a manner that contradicts such standards.[106]

The most prominent example of a customary international law standard to whose development UNHCR doctrinal positions have contributed is that of *non-refoulement. Non-refoulement* 'is a concept which prohibits States from returning a refugee or asylum-seeker to territories where there is a risk that his or her life or freedom would be threatened on account of race, religion, nationality, membership of a particular social group or political opinion'.[107] UNHCR doctri-nal positions contributed to both the *opinio juris* and state practice elements of the formation of the customary rule.

UNHCR has repeatedly affirmed the *non-refoulement* obligation of States in its Notes on International Protection and its Annual Reports. UNHCR, often simply referred to it as a 'principle' in documents in the 1970s, but when States began to adopt more restrictive approaches toward refugees in the 1980s, UNHCR became more assertive and began to characterize it in stronger language, as 'an internationally accepted principle',[108] a 'peremptory norm',[109] a 'fundamental principle',[110] and a 'mandatory principle'.[111] In addition, UNHCR pursued the

105 Paul Szasz, 'General Law-Making Processes', in *The United Nations and International Law* 27, 41–42 (Christopher Joyner, ed., 1997).
106 Oscar Schachter, *International Law in Theory and Practice* 92–93 (1991).
107 Elihu Lauterpacht and Daniel Bethlehem, 'The Scope and Content of the Principle of Non-Refoulement', in *Refugee Protection in International Law: UNHCR's Global Consultations on International Protection* 89, 91 (Erika Feller, Volker Türk and Frances Nicholson, eds, 2003). Some scholars have asserted that temporary refuge, for aliens in their territory who have fled for humanitarian reasons, has become a customary international law rule. For the advocacy of the norm of temporary refuge, see Deborah Perluss and Joan Hartman, 'Temporary Refuge: Emergence of a Customary Norm', 26 *Va. J. Int'l. L.* 551, 624 (1986), Greig also supports the notion of temporary refuge as a customary rule. D.W. Greig, 'The Protection of Refugees and Customary International Law', 8 *Australian Y.B. Int'l. L.* 108, 141 (1983). Hailbronner, however, contends that no such customary right exists. Kay Hailbronner, 'Non-refoulement and 'Humanitarian' Refugees: Customary International Law or Wishful Legal Thinking?', in *The New Asylum Seekers: Refugee Law in the 1980s* 123, 132–136 (David Martin, ed., 1988).
108 UNHCR, Note on International Protection, ¶ 9, U.N. Doc. A/AC.96/579 (11 August 1980).
109 UNHCR, Note on International Protection, ¶ 5, U.N. Doc. A/AC.96/609 (26 August 1982) and UNHCR, Note on International Protection, ¶ 15, U.N. Doc. A/AC.96/643 (9 August 1984). EXCOM Conclusion 25 (XXXIII), ¶ b, 1982 noted that the principle 'was progressively acquiring the character of a peremptory rule of international law.' Also see Jean Allain, 'The Jus Cogens Nature of Non-Refoulement', 13 *Int'l. J. Refugee L.* 533 (2001). Allain finds that *non-refoument* has acquired *jus cogens* status.
110 UNHCR, Note on International Protection, ¶ 3, U.N. Doc. A/AC.96/660 (23 July 1985).
111 UNHCR, Note on International Protection, ¶ 8, U.N. Doc. A/AC.96/694 (3 August 1987).

formulation of EXCOM conclusions and General Assembly resolutions that reiterated the fundamental importance of the principle.

UNHCR's objections to occurrences of *refoulement* in its Annual Protection Reports and its Notes on International Protection,[112] as well as its expression of disapproval of violations of this principle to States, both formally and informally, have served to reinforce the principle and affect state practice. UNHCR also spurred EXCOM to express concern about violations of the *non-refoulement* principle nearly every year following the creation of the Standing Committee in 1975 through the year 2000[113] and has provided expert legal opinions in cases involving *non-refoulement*.[114]

UNHCR's efforts were crowned with success when States' recognized, in the Declaration of States Parties, an important outcome to the Global Consultations process, that the principle of *non-refoulement* is 'embedded in customary international law.'[115] As a result, even States that have not acceded to the 1951 Refugee Convention, with its article 33 prohibition on *refoulement*, are bound by the rule.[116]

5.3.3.3 General principles of law

Before embarking on a discussion of how UNHCR has contributed to the development of the third category of international law created by States, 'general principles of law', the term must be clarified in light of the varied meanings ascribed by different scholars. One view is that it refers to legal rules extracted from natural law, while another interpretation finds that it means general international legal principles.[117] Cassese notes two different types of international legal principles. First, those which can be 'inferred or extracted by way of induction and generalization from conventional and customary rules of international law'

---

112 UNHCR regularly reports the occurrence of violations of the principle in its Notes on International Protection and its Annual Reports, without mentioning the specific country. For example, see UNHCR, Note on International Protection, ¶ 10–11, U.N.Doc. A/AC.96/1038 (29 June 2007) and UNHCR, Report of the UNHCR, ¶ 23, U.N. Doc. A/62/12 (2007).

113 See UNHCR, Thematic Compilation of Executive Committee Conclusions 355–358 (6th edn, June 2011). Available at http://www.unhcr.org/3d4ab3ff2.html (accessed 27 October 2011).

114 Chahal v. United Kindgom, 23 Eur. Ct. H.R. 413 (1996) and Sale v. Haitian Centers Council, 113 U.S. Sup. Ct. 2549 (21 June 1983).

115 UNHCR, Agenda for Protection, *supra* note 55, at 24. However, note Hathaway's opposing views summarized in Guy Goodwin-Gill and Jane McAdam, *supra* note 50, at 351–354.

116 The difficulty is in establishing the exact content and the parameters of this right. The text of Goodwin-Gill and McAdam posits that it covers not only *non-refoulement* to persecution, but also to torture or cruel, inhuman or degrading treatment or punishment. Guy Goodwin-Gill and Jane McAdam, *supra* note 55, at 354. Zoller and Hailbronner, for example, find that there is no right to *non-refoulement* with respect to refugees fleeing for humanitarian reasons, such as a civil war. Elisabeth Zoller, 'Bilan de Recherches de la Section de Langue Française du Centre d'Etude et de Recherche de L'Académie', in *The Right of Asylum* 1989, Hague Academy of International Law 15, 27 (1990). Kay Hailbronner, *supra* note 107, at 130–132.

117 Malcolm Shaw, *International Law* 99 (6th edn, 2008).

and second, those that relate to a certain area of international law, such as humanitarian law and overarch the whole body of law in that area.[118] General principles of law, while much less significant as a source of international law than the two sources of law created by States, international conventions and international custom, can nevertheless make an important contribution. In particular, general principles of law can provide guidance where there are voids in the rules of law and new laws need to be formulated, as in international refugee law.[119]

With respect to the meaning of general principles that holds that they are extracted from national law, UNHCR doctrinal positions may influence States' national rules thus leading to greater uniformity among States and eventually resulting in the emergence of a general principle of law. The adoption of status determination procedures to evaluate individuals' claims for refugee status could be said to be in the process of developing as a general principle. Regarding the second meaning ascribed to the term, that of general international legal principles, UNHCR doctrinal positions that advocate consistent and fair procedures may support the general international legal principle of the 'good administration of justice'[120] and the principle of *non-refoulement* could be considered to be a general principle that overarches the body of international refugee law.[121]

5.4 The Convention Plus initiative

The Convention Plus initiative is a third approach that was adopted by UNHCR to counter the weaknesses in the refugee law framework. Unlike the other two approaches, discussed earlier in this chapter, namely UNHCR's use of other instruments to extend the refugee law framework and its articulation of doctrinal positions, the Convention Plus initiative had a much broader purpose. The initiative was intended to improve refugee protection and to resolve refugee problems, which are UNHCR's two primary mandated functions under its Statute.[122] Thus, while UNHCR's other two approaches were primarily oriented toward the protection of rights of refugees, the Convention Plus initiative was intended not only to contribute to the protection of refugees but also, simultaneously, to have a positive benefit for States.

---

118 Antonio Cassese, *International Law* 188–189 (2nd edn, 2005).

119 Shaw, *supra* note 117, at 98.

120 This principle has been recognized by the International Court of Justice. See Richard Plender, 'The Present State of Research Carried Out By the English-Speaking Section of the Centre for Studies and Research', in *The Right of Asylum*, Hague Academy of International Law 63, 83 (1990).

121 While States, in the Declaration of States Parties during the Global Consultations Process, concurred that the concept of *non-refoulement* is embedded in international customary law, UNHCR has asserted that it has become a peremptory rule of international law. See for example, EXCOM Conclusion 25 (XXXIII), ¶ b, 1982.

122 UNHCR, *Convention Plus At a Glance*, ¶ 1 (1 June 2005). Available at http://www.unhcr.org/cgi-bin/texis/vtx/search?page=search&docid=403b30684&query=Convention%20Plus%20at%20a%20Glance (accessed 27 October 2011).

The initiative, undertaken from October 2002 when it was proposed to EXCOM by former High Commissioner Ruud Lubbers, to November 2005,[123] was a means for UNHCR to address the theme of burden sharing, also referred to as 'responsibility sharing'. The 'sharing [of] burdens and responsibilities' was established as one of the six goals requiring further action by States and UNHCR in the outcome document, the Agenda for Protection, to the Global Consultations process.[124] Special and multilateral agreements were to be drafted to improve burden sharing and to identify durable solutions to specific refugee situations.[125] UNHCR specified that the agreements were to focus on three areas: i) resettlement, ii) targeting of development assistance, and iii) irregular secondary movements.[126]

Burden sharing has been a subject of EXCOM conclusions since as early as 1981,[127] but the Convention Plus initiative attempted to create a normative framework on burden sharing,[128] that is, to provide the concept with a legal basis. While asylum and burden sharing could be said to be the two key principles that guide the obligations of States to provide refugee protection, only asylum is well established in law; burden sharing lacks a legal framework for its implementation.[129] Thus, through the creation of agreements with States, it was hoped that the agreements would have soft law status.[130]

The Convention Plus initiative was the most innovative attempt, among the three approaches adopted by UNHCR, to address the weaknesses in the refugee law framework and to contribute to the development of international refugee law. The initiative attempted to balance additional protection for refugees with the resolution of States' problem of refugees at the same time. As UNHCR is statutorily mandated to promote 'special agreements', as part of its responsibilities related to international protection, UNHCR's use of special and multilateral agreements among States to create mutual and reciprocal obligations provided a strong treaty basis for States' obligations. UNHCR had clear authority to encourage and facilitate States' entry into special and multilateral treaties to accomplish the objectives of the Convention Plus initiative. The initiative is particularly laudable for its attempt to address through law the political problem of the disparate burdens borne by States relative to refugee populations.

However, enticing States to enter into agreements to share the responsibilities and burdens of refugees was difficult in practice. UNHCR had acquired experience with special agreements, primarily in connection with voluntary

---

123 Alexander Betts and Jean-Francois Durieux, 'Convention Plus as a Norm-Setting Exercise', 20 *J. Refugee Stud.*, 509, 512 (2007).
124 Agenda for Protection, *supra* note 55, at 10, 29.
125 Betts and Durieux, *supra* note 123, at 512.
126 UNHCR, *Convention Plus at a Glance, supra* note 122.
127 See EXCOM Conclusion 22 (XXXII), ¶ II.B.2.c (1981).
128 Betts and Durieux, *supra* note 123, at 511.
129 Ibid., at 517.
130 Ibid., at 525.

repatriation situations.[131] However, agreements on resettlement, targeting of development assistance and irregular secondary movements dealt with significantly more complex relationships and interests among States.

In addition, the concept was weakened by its failure not to be linked to an existing legal principle. The 1951 Refugee Convention, while referring to the need for 'international co-operation' in its preamble[132] nowhere refers to burden or responsibility sharing. While refugee protection principles derive from the rights of refugees, based on the 1951 Refugee Convention and the extended legal framework, including human rights principles, the elaboration of burden sharing lacked links to existing legal principles that would provide legitimacy and recognition to the principles. Even worse, the lack of a legal basis left the process subject to criticism that it was a 'European-led containment agenda' and thus, southern States viewed the initiative as oriented toward 'burden shifting' not 'burden sharing'.[133] As has happened before, UNHCR lost credibility with southern States, which bear the primary burden for the reception of refugees, when UNHCR undertook an initiative that was perceived by southern States as a validation of their fear that UNHCR is an instrument of northern States and in particular, of its main financial contributors.

5.5 Conclusion

The onset of the crisis in international refugee law and protection, coupled with States' unwillingness to create new universally applicable treaties for the protection of refugees, led UNHCR to undertake substantial work to extend and refine the international refugee law framework. Two key approaches have been essential to UNHCR's efforts.

First, while maintaining the centrality of the 1951 Refugee Convention, within the refugee law framework, to ensure that refugees maintain their distinct status, UNHCR has woven relevant provisions from other agreements into the framework. UNHCR's use of other legal instruments to extend international refugee law has permitted UNHCR to use law that has already been agreed to by States to supplement the refugee law framework at a time when it was clear that States did not wish to create new law extending the rights of refugees. UNHCR's use of international human rights instruments has been of particular importance in expanding States' obligations to refugees.

Human rights agreements supplement and expand the protection provided under the provisions in the 1951 Refugee Convention, such as in the case of the 1984 Convention against Torture's article 3, which is a broader protection against *non-refoulement* than the 1951 Refugee Convention's article 33. Human rights

131 Marjoleine Zieck, 'Doomed to Fail From the Outset? UNHCR's Convention Plus Initiative Revisited', 21 *Int'l. J. Refugee L.* 387, 390 (2009).
132 1951 Refugee Convention, *supra* note 2, at preambular ¶ 4.
133 Betts and Durieux, *supra* note 123, at 527.

agreements also add new rights for refugees, which are not contained in the 1951 Refugee Convention, such as in the case of the 1989 Convention on the Rights of the Child, which provides children with a right to a primary education. International humanitarian law standards as well as international criminal law provisions of the Rome Statute also have been incorporated into international refugee law. In effect, the extended legal framework provide additional standards and supplements the standards of the 1951 Refugee Convention.

Second, UNHCR doctrine has permitted, and continues to permit, UNHCR to provide additional content to existing provisions of the 1951 Refugee Convention, where other instruments do not provide the necessary clarification. Examples of provisions in the 1951 Refugee Convention to which doctrinal positions have contributed include the refugee definition and article 31. Doctrinal positions also provide guidance to States where the 1951 Refugee Convention does not address the issue and thereby fill gaps in the refugee law framework, such as with respect to voluntary repatriation and the procedural standards for the determination of refugee status.

At the same time, UNHCR has used its doctrine to establish criteria for the use of concepts created by States, and in this way to attempt to limit States' use of such practices. As a result, UNHCR doctrine is crucial to not only the creation of principles, but also to UNHCR's supervisory responsibility. As will be discussed in Chapter 6, with doctrinal principles in hand, UNHCR is more easily able to counter negative trends and policies by States and thus, to attempt to reorient States' actions toward the protection of refugees.

Moreover, UNHCR doctrine can contribute to the further development of the traditional sources of international refugee law: treaty law standards; customary international law principles, as has been done with *non-refoulement*; and general principles of law. The time is not ripe for the further development of international treaties that extend the protection afforded refugees, but UNHCR could still strive to further develop customary international law and general principles of law through its doctrine.

The two approaches adopted by UNHCR were new but founded on previously established approaches that were already accepted by States. UNHCR's initiative, related to human rights, humanitarian and criminal law, extended its prior work of incorporating regional agreements for the protection of refugees and other international agreements, discussed in Chapter 2, but in this case, UNHCR did not just incorporate provisions from other treaties but a significant portion of a *corpus* of law, human rights law, and relevant portions of international humanitarian and criminal law. Similarly, UNHCR's issuance and use of doctrine was a continuation of its prior work, but in a significantly more utilitarian, public, and active manner to maintain the initiative in developing legal standards for the protection of refugees.

Thus, UNHCR chose not to seek formal prior approval from the General Assembly or EXCOM for its efforts to amplify the refugee law framework, through its incorporation of human rights, humanitarian and international criminal law standards and to further develop its doctrinal positions. Thus, UNHCR exhibited its organizational independence in formulating approaches to the development of refugee law.

Although UNHCR's efforts to develop international refugee law, since the onset of the refugee law crisis, are laudable, when they are compared to the magnitude of the problem of insufficient protection of refugees by States, they nevertheless appear to be insufficiently creative, daring, and extensive. Even bearing in mind that UNHCR is an organization that improvises in small measures to avoid condemnation or rejection of its actions by States and to ensure that it maintains consistency with its mandate and prior actions, UNHCR can be criticized for not maintaining a sufficient commitment to refugee law principles. Instead of reinforcing the principles, UNHCR has accorded too much deference to States' political needs. The Convention Plus initiative serves as guidance as to the dangers inherent in attempting to accommodate States' political concerns about refugees when the approach is not firmly based on legal principles. Not only does UNHCR endanger its credibility as an organization responsible for refugee protection based on law, but it also alienates those States that bear the primary burden for receiving and hosting refugees.

In the face of States' continued unwillingness to develop new standards for the protection of refugees and their inclination to try to limit and diminish their refugee law obligations, UNHCR should try to adopt a more proactive approach to refugee law. Since UNHCR's continuing contribution to the development of international refugee law has been implicitly endorsed, with EXCOM's approval of the Agenda for Protection, which provides a range of activities for UNHCR to carry out to further the development of international refugee law and thereby reinforce refugee protection,[134] UNHCR should actively pursue the further clarification of refugee law standards. UNHCR should strategically consider the crucial rights that it would like to see developed into norms and principles and then conceptually formulate how to further this process.

There are numerous concepts that merit additional elaboration by UNHCR. Specifically, topics such as the rights of individual asylum seekers as well as asylum seekers in mass influxes, when and how group determination of refugee status should be used, the content and parameters of temporary protection, and the employment of complementary protection have not been fully addressed by UNHCR and deserve further exploration. Also, a greater attempt needs to be made by the organization to consider clarification of legal principles related to burden sharing as this is a topic that is frequently addressed from a policy standpoint, but would benefit from legal support. In seeking a way forward in this area, UNHCR and scholars should further examine the intersection of international relations and international refugee law in order to devise appropriate means for the development of the refugee law framework.

---

134 For example, UNHCR is to produce complementary guidelines to the UNHCR *Handbook on Procedures and Criteria for Determining Refugee Status* and explore areas that would benefit from further standard setting. See UNHCR, Agenda for Protection, *supra* note 55, at 36.

In the past, UNHCR has not always grounded its doctrinal positions on legal principles, thereby lessening the significance of the position from a legal standpoint and weakening the general legal framework for the protection of refugees. The integrity and acceptability of UNHCR's positions reside in their legal nature. Thus, all further developments of refugee law principles should be firmly based on current legal standards and principles.

UNHCR also has not been as clear about the relationship between human rights law and refugee law as it needs to be. The organization still appears to be hesitant to fully utilize human rights principles, given the criticisms of the 1951 Refugee Convention as outdated, and the extensive nature of human rights law as compared to refugee law. However, UNHCR should reaffirm the applicability of human rights principles and in so doing, must confront several difficult issues with States, such as the restrictions on the freedom of movement of refugees who reside in camps and the applicability of economic, social and cultural rights to refugees.

6 UNHCR's approaches to improve the effectiveness of international refugee law

6.1 Introduction

When the crisis in refugee protection began in the 1980s, UNHCR was faced with States' attempts to disregard, diminish and alter the protections of the refugee law framework as it stood at the time, as shown in Chapter 4. In essence, the crisis posed a continual threat to the effectiveness of the international refugee law framework of protection. UNHCR not only needed to, and did, further develop the refugee law framework, as discussed in the previous chapter, but also was compelled to reinforce the effectiveness of refugee law.

Initially, at the onset of the crisis in international refugee law and refugee protection in the 1980s, UNHCR appeared to think that it could maintain its traditional approach, which consisted of i) promotion of ratifications/accessions to international conventions for the protection of refugees, ii) promotion of implementation of standards from these agreements into national law, and iii) advice to States on the application of such standards. In essence, UNHCR attempted to rely on the relationship it had with States to render the refugee law standards effective. UNHCR encouraged the General Assembly to adopt resolutions that repeatedly emphasized the necessity of States' co-operation with UNHCR, through accession, full implementation, and observance of their refugee law obligations.[1] Yet, these were insufficient to bring States' actions into closer alignment with UNHCR's views. Hence, UNHCR turned to other approaches, which are considered in the next sections by area of effectiveness: first, accessions to conventions for the protection of refugees; second, implementation of such conventions; and finally, application of the provisions of these conventions.

6.2 Accessions to conventions for the protection of refugees

When UNHCR incorporated new approaches into its work, in the area of accession to conventions for the protection of refugees, it did not relinquish its traditional

---

1 See for example, G.A. Res. 40/118, ¶ 2, U.N. Doc. A/RES/40/118 (13 December 1985).

role of promoting States' universal accession to the 1951 Refugee Convention[2] and the 1967 Protocol. The organization continued to encourage States to accede to these instruments and prompted the General Assembly to adopt resolutions and EXCOM to adopt conclusions that encouraged accessions. UNHCR's new approaches in this area built on the existing approaches. For example, during the Global Accession Campaign, undertaken by UNHCR in 1998, the organization provided information packages and held workshops on the 1951 Refugee Convention and the 1967 Protocol.[3] Means to improve the number of accessions to the two key refugee law instruments also was a subject of the Agenda for Protection, the concluding document for the Global Consultations process. The Agenda for Protection provides that States are to promote accessions in their contacts with other governments and in international fora and that UNHCR is to carry out a survey of the difficulties States have in acceding to the 1951 Refugee Convention and the 1967 Protocol with a view to assisting States to overcome such difficulties.[4] UNHCR also obtained the inclusion of the 1951 Refugee Convention and the 1967 Protocol in the United Nations' annual treaty event, in which States are encouraged to ratify and/or accede to instruments deposited with the United Nations.[5]

As reservations to the 1951 Refugee Convention and 1967 Protocol hinder full State application, UNHCR undertook formal initiatives to encourage States to remove reservations, which initiatives complemented the informal requests UNHCR has traditionally made. UNHCR had EXCOM conclusions encourage States to remove reservations made to these instruments.[6] In addition, in the Agenda for Protection, the concluding document to the Global Consultations process, UNHCR provided that States parties to these two key refugee agreements are to consider withdrawing reservations and lifting any geographic reservation they have maintained.[7]

When UNHCR incorporated other agreements into the refugee law framework, most notably international human rights, international humanitarian law, and criminal law instruments to complement the 1951 Refugee Convention and the 1967 Protocol, as seen in Chapter 5, UNHCR began to advocate for accession to these instruments as well. Specifically, UNHCR spurred the General Assembly to

---

2 As noted in section 4.4.1, all original signatories to the 1951 Refugee Convention have ratified the convention.

3 UNHCR, Global Report 2000, 48 (June 2001).

4 UNHCR, Agenda for Protection 32 (October 2003).

5 The 1951 Refugee Convention and the 1967 Protocol have been included in the UN's annual treaty event from 2004 through 2006 and in 2011. Other treaties that provide protection to refugees, such as international human rights instruments, are also included in the treaty event. For example, at the 2006 treaty event, Bahrain and the Maldives acceded to the 1966 Covenant on Civil and Political Rights, while Bulgaria ratified the 1979 Convention on the Elimination of All Forms of Discrimination against Women.

6 See EXCOM Conclusion 99 (LV), ¶ c, 2004; EXCOM Conclusion 79 (XLVII), ¶ e, 1996; and EXCOM Conclusion 42 (XXXVII), ¶ g, 1986.

7 Agenda for Protection, *supra* note 4, at 26, 32.

adopt resolutions and EXCOM to adopt conclusions that encourage States to accede to relevant international human rights and humanitarian law agreements[8] as well as to regional agreements.[9] Moreover, UNHCR provided in the Agenda for Protection, that the organization is to encourage accessions to the 1979 Convention on the Elimination of All Forms of Discrimination against Women, its 1999 Optional Protocol, and the 1989 Convention on the Rights of the Child.[10] The Agenda for Protection encourages States to accede to not only human rights agreements, but also certain international criminal law instruments, namely, the 2000 United Nations Convention against Transnational Organized Crime and its Protocols, as well as specific migration law instruments, the 1990 United Nations Convention on the Protection of the Rights of all Migrant Workers and Members of their Families and relevant ILO Conventions.[11]

UNHCR also has become increasingly involved in encouraging accessions to the conventions concerning statelessness in light of its additional responsibilities in this area.[12] The organization actively promotes accessions to the two conventions relating to statelessness, the 1954 Convention relating to the Status of Stateless Persons and the 1961 Convention on the Reduction of Statelessness. For example, UNHCR prompted the General Assembly and EXCOM to encourage UNHCR to promote accessions to both stateless conventions[13] and to encourage States to ratify the two statelessness conventions.[14] In addition, UNHCR prepared an information and accession package on the statelessness conventions[15] and

---

8 See for example, G.A. Res. 56/166, ¶ 5, U.N. Doc. A/RES/56/166 (19 December 2001) and G.A. Res. 54/180, ¶ 11, U.N. Doc. A/RES/54/180 (17 December 1999). Also see EXCOM Conclusion 25 (XXXIII), ¶ g, 1982, and EXCOM Conclusion 42 (XXXVII), ¶ h, 1986.

9 See, for example, G.A. Res. 50/182, ¶ 5, U.N. Doc. A/RES/50/182 (22 December 1995) and G.A. Res. 54/180, ¶ 11, U.N. Doc. A/RES/54/180 (17 December 1999). Also see EXCOM Conclusion 79 (XLVII), ¶ d, 1996 and EXCOM Conclusion 81 (XLVIII), ¶ m, 1997.

10 Agenda for Protection, *supra* note 4, at 18.

11 Ibid., at 13, 47.

12 UNHCR's responsibility for activities on behalf of stateless persons is considered part of UNHCR's statutory function of providing international protection. See G.A. Res. 50/152 ¶ 14, U.N. Doc. A/RES/50/152 (21 December 1995). UNHCR was originally requested to carry out such responsibilities on a temporary basis. G.A. Res. 3274 (XXIX) ¶ 1 (10 December 1974). The General Assembly then requested UNHCR to continue to carry out such functions without establishing an end date. G.A. Res. 31/36, U.N. Doc. A/RES/31/36 (30 November 1976).

13 See G.A. Res. 60/129 ¶ 4, U.N. Doc. 60/129 (16 December 2005); G.A. Res. 59/170 ¶ 3, U.N. Doc. A/RES/59/170 (20 December 2004); G.A. Res. 58/151 ¶ 4, U.N. Doc. A/RES/58/151 (22 December 2003); and G.A. Res. 57/187 ¶ 5, U.N. Doc. A/RES/57/187 (18 December 2002). Also see EXCOM Conclusion 99 (LV), ¶ z, 2004.

14 See EXCOM Conclusion 106 (LVII), ¶ n, s, 2006 endorsed by G.A. Res. 60/129, ¶ 1, U.N. Doc. A/RES/60/129 (16 December 2005). EXCOM also has acknowledged States' accessions to the conventions. See for example, the 2005 EXCOM Conclusion acknowledging Senegal's accession to the 1961 Convention on the Reduction of Statelessness. EXCOM Conclusion 102 (LVI), ¶ y, 2005.

15 UNHCR, Information and Accession Package: the 1954 Convention Relating to the Status of Stateless Persons and the 1961 Convention on the Reduction of Statelessness (2nd edn, 1999).

recently inveighed the UN to include the two statelessness conventions in its annual treaty event.[16]

The additional approaches, adopted by UNHCR, which concern accession to the 1951 Refugee Convention and 1967 Protocol, clearly fall within UNHCR's mandatory responsibility to 'promot[e]...the ratification of international conventions for the protection of refugees'. Arguably, the wording of this responsibility is sufficiently broad so as to include UNHCR's work to promote ratifications and accessions to other agreements, such as international human rights and humanitarian law instruments, as well as to regional instruments. In case of any doubt, such work could be considered as an implied power derived from either its responsibility to promote the ratification of international conventions for the protection of refugees or its international protection function.

6.3 Implementation of conventions for the protection of refugees

In the area of States' implementation of their international refugee law obligations, the drafters of UNHCR's statute assigned UNHCR an extremely limited statutory responsibility: to obtain information about States' laws and regulations concerning refugees.[17] However, from UNHCR's earliest days, the agency utilized this responsibility as an important wedge into States' sovereign control of implementation of international refugee law standards into national law. Even before the crisis in refugee protection, UNHCR carried out work that extended beyond its statutory responsibility and promoted the implementation of the 1951 Refugee Convention, as seen in section 2.4.2. UNHCR even had EXCOM encourage the organization to continue to follow up on the implementation of the provisions of the 1951 Refugee Convention and the 1967 Protocol by States, in 1976.[18] However, it was not until 1999 that the General Assembly provided formal approval of UNHCR's promotional work in this area.[19]

Thus, prior to 1999, the organization's work related to States' implementation of the 1951 Refugee Convention and the 1967 Protocol could be considered legally authorized as an implied power derived either from UNHCR's general

Available at http://www.unhcr.org/protect/PROTECTION/3dc69f1d4.pdf (accessed 27 October 2011).

16 The two statelessness conventions were included in the United Nation's 2006, 2009, 2010 and 2011 treaty events. During the UN Treaty Event held in September 2011, Nigeria acceded to the 1954 Convention relating to the Status of Stateless Persons and the 1961 Convention on the Reduction of Statelessness.

17 Statute of the Office of the United Nations High Commissioner for Refugees, contained in the Annex to UN General Assembly Resolution 428(V) of 14 December 1950. G.A. Res. 428(V) ¶ 8(f), (14 December 1950) (hereinafter UNHCR Statute). See section 2.3.3 for a review of UNHCR's responsibilities related to States' implementation of international refugee law standards into national law.

18 EXCOM Conclusion 2 (XXVII), ¶ c, 1976.

19 See G.A. Res. 54/146, ¶ 3, U.N. Doc. A/RES/54/146 (17 December 1999).

international protection function, which, as discussed in section 3.3, permits UNHCR a great deal of flexibility, or its responsibility to supervise the application of international conventions for the protection of refugees.

6.3.1 *Promotion of implementation of the 1951 Refugee Convention/1967 Protocol*

With the onset of the divergence in views between States and UNHCR in the 1980s, as discussed in Chapter 4, UNHCR staff continued the agency's traditional approach of encouraging governmental officials to implement the provisions of the 1951 Refugee Convention and the 1967 Protocol at the national level. UNHCR fostered the adoption of resolutions by the General Assembly that promote the implementation of the 1951 Refugee Convention/1967 Protocol[20] and stimulated EXCOM to adopt conclusions that exhorted States to implement their obligations under these two agreements. For example, EXCOM suggested that States adopt 'appropriate legislative and/or administrative measures for the effective implementation' of the 1951 Refugee Convention and 1967 Protocol[21] and take 'whatever steps are necessary to identify and remove possible legal or administrative obstacles to full implementation'.[22]

During the past decade, UNHCR has added some new means to its array of traditional approaches in order to promote States' implementation of the 1951 Refugee Convention and 1967 Protocol. For example, UNHCR prepared, in co-operation with the Inter-Parliamentary Union,[23] a guide for parliamentarians on international refugee law.[24] This guide serves as an invitation and inducement to parliamentarians to draft and adopt national legislation that implements States' obligations under the 1951 Refugee Convention and 1967 Protocol. It is also a reference tool that assists States' Parliaments to understand the standards contained in the articles of the 1951 Convention and how they can be formulated into national legislative provisions.[25] In addition, when UNHCR initiated the Global Consultations process, the agency included a more complete implementation of the 1951 Refugee Convention and the 1967 Protocol as one of its

20 See G.A. Res. 51/75 3rd preambular ¶, U.N. Doc. A/RES/51/75 (12 December 1996) and G.A. Res. 44/137, ¶ 2, U.N. Doc. A/RES/44/137 (15 November 1989) which endorses EXCOM Conclusion 57 (XL) 1989 concerning the implementation of the 1951 Refugee Convention and the 1967 Protocol.
21 See EXCOM Conclusion 42 (XXXVII), ¶ j, 1986 and EXCOM Conclusion 57 (XL), ¶ b, 1989.
22 See EXCOM Conclusion 57 (XL), ¶ c, 1989.
23 The Inter-Parliamentary Union, which is located in Geneva, is an international organization of parliaments of over 140 States.
24 Inter-Parliamentary Union and UNHCR, Refugee Protection: a Guide to International Refugee Law (2001). Available at http://www.unhcr.org/publ/PUBL/3d4aba564.pdf (accessed 27 October 2011).
25 Ibid., at 102, 106–111.

primary objectives.[26] Pursuant to the Agenda for Protection, the concluding document of the Global Consultations process, UNHCR is to carry out a survey of the difficulties States have in implementing the 1951 Refugee Convention/1967 Protocol with a view to assisting States to overcome such difficulties.[27]

6.3.2 Promotion of implementation of other agreements

Since other international agreements, international human rights, humanitarian law and regional agreements have been incorporated into the refugee law framework through UNHCR doctrinal positions (see Chapter 5), these agreements need to be implemented at the national level to facilitate States' application of their treaty obligations. Thus, UNHCR encouraged the General Assembly to adopt resolutions requesting States to implement statelessness conventions,[28] regional refugee agreements and international human rights and humanitarian law conventions.[29] UNHCR also had the General Assembly articulate that the implementation of international human rights conventions is important in averting new massive flows of refugees and displaced persons.[30] Moreover, UNHCR formulated conclusions adopted by EXCOM, which encourage States to implement human rights and humanitarian law instruments[31] and statelessness conventions.[32]

6.3.3 Capacity building

A frank assessment of the problems States have in fully implementing the provisions of the 1951 Refugee Convention into national law was provided by UNHCR to EXCOM's Standing Committee in 1989 and then again in 1992. UNHCR identified three types of obstacle to full implementation: first, socioeconomic

---

26 See UNHCR, Ministerial Meeting of States Parties to the 1951 Convention Relating to the Status of Refugees and UNHCR's Global Consultations on International Protection: Background, 2 (11 December 2001). Available at http://www.unhcr.org/protect/PROTECTION/3c1622ab4.pdf (accessed 27 October 2011).

27 Agenda for Protection, *supra* note 4, at 32.

28 See for example G.A. Res. 50/152, ¶ 16, U.N. Doc. A/RES/50/152 (21 December 1995) and G.A. Res. 49/169 ¶ 20, U.N. Doc. A/RES/49/169 (23 December 1994).

29 See G.A. Res. 56/166 ¶ 5, U.N. Doc. A/RES/56/166 (19 December 2001) and G.A. Res. 54/180 ¶ 11, U.N. Doc. A/RES/54/180 (17 December 1999).

30 As examples, see: G.A. Res. 46/127, ¶ 3, U.N. Doc. A/RES/46/127 (17 December 1991); G.A. Res. 45/153, ¶ 3, U.N. Doc. A/RES/45/153 (18 Dec. 1990); G.A. Res. 44/164, ¶ 3, U.N. Doc. A/RES/44/164 (15 Dec. 1989); G.A. Res. 43/154, ¶ 3, U.N. Doc. A/RES/43/154 (8 December 1988); and G.A. Res. 42/144, ¶ 4, U.N. Doc. A/RES/42/144 (7 December 1987). However, there is some ambiguity as to whether the use of the term 'implementation' in these resolutions might not mean 'application' of human rights instruments.

31 EXCOM Conclusion 81 (XLVIII), ¶ e, 1997 and EXCOM Conclusion 79 (XLVII) ¶ w, 1996.

32 See for example, EXCOM Conclusion 78 (XLVI), ¶ b, 1995 and EXCOM Conclusion 85 (XLIX), ¶ m, 1998.

factors, such as: 'economic difficulties, high unemployment, declining living standards, and shortages in housing and land' which are compounded by man-made and natural disasters; second, legal impediments, such as inconsistencies between international law obligations and national law provisions or a lack of implementing legislation; and, third, practical obstacles, such as the lack of administrative, legal and other structures.[33] These reports constituted a significant step toward understanding the reasons why States had not fully implemented their obligations under the 1951 Refugee Convention. This understanding then led to greater involvement by UNHCR in States' adoption of national legislation that implements their legal obligations toward refugees as well as in activities that shape and influence such national implementation. UNHCR assigned the term 'capacity building' to these various activities.

UNHCR considered capacity-building activities to be an integral part of its international protection mandate [34] and thus, activities that it has been authorized to carry out since the inception of its Statute. Although UNHCR had been undertaking 'capacity-building activities' for decades,[35] it was not until the 1990s that UNHCR began to label particular activities as 'capacity-building activities' and to obtain explicit endorsement from the General Assembly for such activities.[36] The underlying purpose of capacity-building activities, according to UNHCR, is to 'enhanc[e] the capabilities of States to meet international legal obligations in the refugee protection area. Such activities also contribute to strengthening the rule of law by creating national protection structures.'[37] However, the term 'capacity-building activities' has never been clearly or consistently formulated. In a guide on capacity building, UNHCR stated:

33 See UNHCR, Implementation of the 1951 Convention and the 1967 Protocol Relating to the Status of Refugees, ¶ 10–22, UNHCR Doc. EC/SCP/54 (7 July 1989). Also see UNHCR, Implementation of the 1951 Convention and the 1967 Protocol Relating to the Status of Refugees – Some Basic Questions, ¶ 9–10, UNHCR Doc. EC/1992/SC.2/CRP.10 (15 June 1992). While the 1989 report appears to subsume implementation and application difficulties under the term 'implementation', the 1992 report distinguishes between the two. Moreover, UNHCR noted that the legislation of some countries tends to define the powers of refugee officials rather than the rights of refugees. UNHCR, Implementation of the 1951 Convention and the 1967 Protocol Relating to the Status of Refugees, *supra* note 33, at 16.

34 As UNHCR has noted, '[s]trengthening protection capacities is a function inherent in UNHCR's international protection mandate.' UNHCR, Strengthening Protection Capacities in Host Countries, ¶ 11, UNHCR Doc. EC/GC/01/19 (19 April 2002).

35 UNHCR provided assistance to countries in their creation of appropriate legal and administrative arrangements even during the 1960s. See UNHCR, Report of the UNHCR, ¶ 18, U.N. Doc. A/5211/Rev. 1 (1962).

36 However, note that as early as 1980, the General Assembly was referring to a 'universal collective responsibility ... to strengthen the capacity of countries of asylum to provide adequately for the refugees' G.A. Res. 35/42, 9th preambular ¶, U.N. Doc. A/RES/35/42 (25 November 1980).

37 UNHCR, Strengthening Protection Capacities in Host Countries, *supra* note 34, at ¶ 2. UNHCR has also noted that another important component of these efforts is the fostering of international cooperation to ensure a fair sharing of the burden and responsibility of receiving and hosting refugees. Ibid.

[The concept I]mplies the reinforcement of human, institutional or community performance, skill, knowledge and attitudes on a sustainable basis. It is both an approach and a set of activities, intimately linked to nationally driven reform processes.

As an approach, it focuses on existing initiatives, commitments and potential as distinct from relief, which addresses needs and problems. It aims to build a network of partners at various levels, is highly participatory by nature and requires shared commitments and objectives on the part of external and domestic actors.

As a set of activities, it implies provision of technical support, including training, advisory services and specialised expertise in favour of national/local institutions or structures, aimed, in UNHCR's case, at fulfilling the Office's primary objectives of Protection and Solutions, in both countries of asylum and origin.[38]

More recently, a more succinct definition was provided by the General Assembly in a 2002 resolution with UNHCR's guidance, noting that 'capacity-building' activities include:

[T]raining of relevant officers, disseminating information about refugee instruments and principles and providing financial, technical and advisory services to accelerate the enactment or amendment and implementation of legislation relating to refugees, strengthening emergency response and enhancing capacities for the coordination of humanitarian activities.[39]

Despite the lack of a clear articulation of activities,[40] UNHCR's identification of capacity-building activities can be said to primarily include work related

---

38 UNHCR, A Practical Guide to Capacity Building as a Feature of UNHCR's Humanitarian Programmes 3 (September 1999). Available at http://www.unhcr.org/3bbd64845.pdf (accessed 27 October 2011). Another elaboration of the concept can be found in UNHCR, Strengthening Protection Capacities in Host Countries, *supra* note 34. An earlier formulation of the concept states that it is 'providing assistance and support to States in their efforts to develop the structures and operational systems which will enable refugees, returnees and others of concern to benefit from effective national protection. It also aims at strengthening the skills, knowledge and sustained ability of Governments, other local entities and non-governmental partners in this area.' UNHCR, UNHCR's Role in National Legal and Judicial Capacity-Building, ¶ 1, UNHCR Doc. EC/46/SC/CRP.31 (28 May 1996).

39 G.A. Res. 57/183, ¶ 21, U.N. Doc. A/RES/ 57/183 (18 December 2002).

40 Maria Stavropoulou provides a cogent four part division of the purposes of capacity building: (i) development of a legal framework; (ii) development of an institutional framework; (iii) networking and empowerment of local NGO and civil society actors; and (iv) provision of training to both government officials and NGO staff. Maria Stavropoulou, 'Protection: The Office of the United Nations High Commissioner for Refugees Experience', in *The Human Rights Field Operation: Law, Theory and Practice* 207, 215–217 (Michael O'Flaherty, ed., 2007).

to States' implementation of international refugee law standards.[41] However, the organization also has designated its promotional work related to States' accession to 'international refugee instruments and other relevant human rights instruments' as a capacity-building activity.[42]

In 1995, UNHCR stimulated the General Assembly to make its first request to UNHCR to undertake capacity-building activities; UNHCR was to 'intensify its protection activities by, *inter alia*, supporting the efforts of African Governments through appropriate training of relevant officers and other capacity-building activities'.[43] Many African countries did not have refugee status determination procedures in place and had not implemented international refugee law standards at the national level. With the dissolution of the former Soviet Union, Eastern European countries and former Soviet republics by and large did not have national legislation implementing the 1951 Refugee Convention. Therefore UNHCR worked closely with many of the countries to help draft legislation and assisted them with the creation of the necessary judicial and administrative structures to protect and care for refugees and asylum seekers.[44]

UNHCR's performance of capacity-building activities also received a significant boost as a result of the European Union accession process. Candidate countries, which included Turkey, Cyprus, Malta and the 10 Central European and Baltic States, were required, as part of the pre-accession requirements, to transpose what are often termed the 'European acquis', which includes not only European Community legislation but also relevant international agreements, into their national laws. Thus, candidate Member States were required to ensure that the provisions of the 1951 Refugee Convention and the 1967 Protocol were incorporated into national legislation.[45]

41 UNHCR also has carried out certain capacity-building activities with respect to the statelessness conventions. EXCOM has requested UNHCR to improve the training of its staff and that of other UN agencies on statelessness 'to enable UNHCR to provide technical advice to States Parties on the implementation of the 1954 Convention'. EXCOM Conclusion 106 (LVII), ¶ x, 2006. And the General Assembly 'encouraged the High Commissioner to continue his activities on behalf of stateless persons'. G.A. Res. 60/129, ¶ 4, U.N. Doc. A/RES/60/129 (16 December 2005). In 2004, for example, UNHCR reported that it had provided advice to more than 60 States on modifications to nationality laws to prevent and reduce cases of statelessness. UNHCR, Final Report Concerning the Questionnaire on Statelessness Pursuant to the Agenda for Protection: Steps Taken by States to Reduce Statelessness and to Meet the Protection Needs of Stateless Persons, ¶ 108 (March 2004). Available at http://www.unhcr.org/protect/PROTECTION/4047002e4.pdf (accessed 27 October 2011).
42 UNHCR, A Practical Guide to Capacity Building as a Feature of UNHCR's Humanitarian Programmes, *supra* note 38, at 7.
43 G.A. Res. 50/149, ¶ 10, U.N. Doc. A/RES/50/149 (21 December 1995).
44 UNHCR, A Review of Capacity Building in Central and Eastern Europe (August 1996). Available at http://www.unhcr.org/research/RESEARCH/3ae6bcf44.html (accessed 27 October 2011).
45 See UNHCR, UNHCR Tool Boxes on EU Asylum Matters: Tool Box 1: the Fundamentals 141–142 (November 2003). Available at http://www.unhcr.org/publ/PUBL/406a8aa11.pdf (accessed 27 October 2011) and UNHCR, UNHCR Tool Boxes on EU Asylum Matters: Tool Box 2: the

As part of its capacity-building activities, UNHCR offices have provided comments on draft legislation to countless governments and even assisted in the drafting of amendments, provided training to government officials, and judicial and administrative officers, and advised on the creation, structure, and functions of asylum bodies to ensure the better protection of refugees. Such advice has been particularly pertinent to countries creating national refugee laws for the first time.

When UNHCR carries out capacity-building activities, the standards advocated by UNHCR not only reflect the provisions of the 1951 Refugee Convention but also other standards incorporated into the refugee law framework, such as international and regional human rights standards and international humanitarian law and criminal law standards. In addition, UNHCR doctrine permeates UNHCR's capacity-building activities. For example, when UNHCR provided advice on the content of European Union directives to harmonize States' asylum legislation and policies, UNHCR produced doctrinal positions on issues, such as reception and asylum procedures, which are not addressed in the 1951 Refugee Convention.[46] UNHCR doctrinal positions also are a crucial component in UNHCR's advice to States on their creation or modification of institutional structures that handle refugees and refugee claims. Since the 1951 Refugee Convention does not contain any standards related to such national institutions or the procedures used for evaluating claims for asylum, UNHCR doctrine serves as fundamental guidance for UNHCR's advice to States.

States demonstrated their support for building the capacity of countries, particularly developing countries and those with economies that are in transition, to receive and protect refugees in the 2001 Declaration of State Parties in connection with the Global Consultations Process.[47] Pursuant to the Agenda for Protection, UNHCR is to extend its activities in this area and further develop the guiding principles and framework on capacity building that it presented in a note prepared for the Global Consultations process, develop a Handbook on Strengthening Capacities in Host Countries for the Protection of Refugees and maintain an 'updated catalogue of initiatives and activities in this area'.[48]

Instruments 9–10 (September 2002). Available at http://www.unhcr.org/publ/PUBL/406a8c432.pdf (accessed 27 October 2011).

46 See UNHCR's Comments on the European Commission Proposal for a Council Directive laying down Minimum Standards on the Reception of Applicants for Asylum in Member States (COM (2001) 181 final) and UNHCR's Summary Observations on the Amended Proposal by the European Commission for a Council Directive on Minimum Standards on Procedures in Member States for Granting and Withdrawing Refugee Status (COM (2000) 326 final/2, 18 June 2002) in UNHCR, UNHCR Tool Boxes on EU Asylum Matters: Tool Box 2: the Instruments 203–210, 319–330 (September 2002). Available at http://www.unhcr.org/publ/PUBL/406a8c432.pdf (accessed 27 October 2011).

47 UNHCR, Agenda for Protection, *supra* note 4, at 28. States were urged by the General Assembly to enhance the capacity of countries that have received large numbers of asylum seekers in G.A. Res. 57/187, ¶ 9, U.N. Doc. A/RES/57/187 (18 December 2002).

48 UNHCR, Agenda for Protection, *supra* note 4, at 58. The document on capacity building that was prepared for the Global Consultations process is UNHCR, Strengthening Protection

While capacity-building activities have become a significant component of UNHCR's tools to help ensure that States fully implement the 1951 Refugee Convention and the 1967 Protocol, their design and implementation are frequently quite complex and affect a multitude of aspects in a country's social fabric, ranging from economic and societal issues to cultural and political ones.[49] UNHCR has evidenced sensitivity to a number of problems related to capacity building; such problems include that governments may be too political or non-governmental organizations too weak.[50]

6.4 Application of conventions for the protection of refugees

States' adoption, in the 1980s, of restrictive measures that violated the provisions of the 1951 Refugee Convention or its humanitarian spirit, highlighted the insufficiency of the structures for ensuring States' application of international refugee law standards (see Chapter 4). UNHCR's supervisory responsibility remained the key method for furthering States' compliance with their international refugee law obligations. However, States' lack of co-operation with UNHCR resulted in a decline in its ability to affect States' actions and meant that when UNHCR raised concerns about such restrictive measures to States they were less likely to modify their actions.

Fortunately, the flexibility in UNHCR's determination of the content of its supervisory responsibility, as noted in section 2.3.4, has meant that UNHCR has had wide latitude in adjusting its work to counter the decline in States' protection. Thus, UNHCR supplemented its traditional supervisory work, which ranges from monitoring and gathering information on States' policies, legislation, and actions, to raising concerns about inconsistencies with international law informally and through more formal channels, such as the General Assembly, with a number of measures to bolster the effectiveness of international law for the protection of refugees. At the same time, from an internal standpoint, the organization began requiring field offices to produce an Annual Protection report, which evaluated States' compliance with international refugee law standards. UNHCR also increased the training provided to staff members on protection matters, including human rights standards. Therefore, UNHCR staff not only became

Capacities in Host Countries, *supra* note 37 (19 Apr. 2002). This has been supplemented by UNHCR with UNHCR, Protection Gaps Framework for Analysis: Enhancing Protection of Refugees: Strengthening Protection Capacity Project (SPCP) (2008). Available at http://www.unhcr.org/41fe3ab92.pdf (accessed 27 October 2011). Also see EXCOM conclusion 108, which 'Welcomes the development of asylum legislation and the establishment of processes for status determination and admission in a number of countries often with the help and advice of UNHCR, ... and welcomes in this regard the technical and financial support of other States and UNHCR as appropriate.' EXCOM Conclusion 108 (LIX), ¶ c, 2008.

49 UNHCR, A Practical Guide to Capacity-Building as a Feature of UNHCR's Humanitarian Programmes, *supra* note 38, at ¶ 5, page 4.

50 Ibid., At ¶ 6 page 11.

aware of deficiencies in States' compliance with legal standards through the Annual Protection reports, but also from their training and communications with other offices and could proactively formulate strategies to strengthen States' application of such standards.

Prior to detailing the various approaches utilized by UNHCR, it is important to note the function of doctrine throughout UNHCR's efforts to ensure the effectiveness of international refugee law for the protection of asylum seekers and refugees. UNHCR doctrinal positions, which filled gaps and clarified ambiguities in international refugee law, as discussed in Chapter 5, constituted clear and authoritative statements by UNHCR of its understanding, interpretation, and view of international refugee law. Thus, when UNHCR undertook actions to influence States' application of international refugee law, whether it was UNHCR's creation of operational responses to meet protection needs of asylum seekers or refugees, its articulation of concerns about States' policies toward refugees, or its submission of its views to national refugee status determination bodies, these actions were based on and incorporated UNHCR's doctrinal positions. With the incorporation of other instruments into the international refugee law framework, as discussed in section 5.2, UNHCR's doctrinal positions included international human rights, humanitarian law, and criminal law standards. Doctrinal positions were particularly beneficial in situations where a specific international refugee law standard did not cover a State's conduct as UNHCR could then evaluate the State's conduct against a principle. Moreover, when UNHCR issued a new doctrinal position, States were effectively placed on notice by UNHCR of the conduct that was expected of them.[51]

6.4.1 Support for UNHCR's supervisory responsibility

Appreciating the need for additional recognition and support from States for its supervisory work, one approach employed by UNHCR to enhance States' application of international refugee law was to obtain States' express affirmation of the organization's supervisory role. Therefore, UNHCR had States members of EXCOM adopt resolutions that reiterated the importance of UNHCR's supervisory role.[52] UNHCR also garnered additional support for its supervisory role during the Global Consultations process. UNHCR placed the topic of its supervisory

---

51 See Antonio Cassese, *International Law in a Divided World* 150 (1986) who finds that 'UN organs are authorized to call upon Member States to intensify their co-operation by indicating the policy to be followed, by suggesting guidelines and goals, and by propounding possible methods for attaining the purposes set out in Article 55.'

52 See for example, EXCOM Conclusion 79 (XLVII), ¶ f, 1996; EXCOM Conclusion 77 (XLVI), ¶ e, 1995; EXCOM Conclusion 74 (XLV), ¶ c, 1994; EXCOM Conclusion 57 (XL), 5th preambular ¶, 1989 and EXCOM Conclusion 43 (XXXVII), ¶ 3, 1986. The General Assembly also has reiterated UNHCR's supervisory responsibility. G.A. Res. 52/103, ¶ 1, U.N. Doc. A/RES52/103 (12 December 1997) which endorses EXCOM Conclusion 81 (XLVIII), ¶ e, 1997 contained in the report of EXCOM.

responsibility, under the 1951 Refugee Convention, on the agenda of the Global Consultations process and requested Walter Kälin to prepare a paper on the topic.[53] This paper then formed the basis for discussions and led to summary conclusions that identify the following activities as part of UNHCR's statutory supervisory responsibility:

(a)   working with States to design operational responses which are sensitive to and meet protection needs, including of the most vulnerable;

(b)   making representations to governments and other relevant actors on protection concerns and monitoring, reporting on and following up these interventions with governments regarding the situation of refugees (e.g. on admission, reception, treatment of asylum seekers and refugees);

(c)   advising and being consulted on national asylum or refugee status determination procedures;

(d)   intervening and making submissions to quasi-judicial institutions or courts in the form of *amicus curiae* briefs, statements or letters;

(e)   having access to asylum applicants and refugees, either as recognized in law or in administrative practice;

(f)   advising governments and parliaments on legislation and administrative decrees affecting asylum seekers and refugees at all stages of the process, and providing comments on and technical input into draft refugee legislation and related administrative decrees;

(g)   fulfilling an advocacy role, including through public statements, as an essential tool of international protection and the Office's supervisory responsibility;

(h)   strengthening capacity, for example, through promotional and training activities;

(i)   receiving and gathering data and information concerning asylum seekers and refugees as set out in Article 35(2) of the 1951 Convention.[54]

53   See Walter Kälin, 'Supervising the 1951 Convention on the Status of Refugees: Article 35 and Beyond', in *Refugee Protection in International Law: UNHCR's Global Consultations on International Protection* 613–666 (Erika Feller, Volker Türk and Frances Nicholson, eds, 2003). Also see seven working papers on the topic of 'Overseeing the Refugee Convention', prepared for a meeting of the International Council of Voluntary Agencies and the University of Michigan. Available at http://www.icva.ch/doc00000505.html (accessed 27 October 2011) as well as James Hathaway, 'Who Should Watch Over Refugee Law', 14 *Forced Migration Rev.* 23 (2002). Volker Türk, the Chief of the Protection Policy and Legal Advice Section of UNHCR's Department of International Protection at the time, also contributed a valuable article to the discussion. See Volker Türk, 'UNHCR's Supervisory Responsibility', 14 *Revue Québécoise de Droit International* 135 (2001). Intricately intertwined into this debate is the issue of the extent to which UNHCR should carry out any type of enforcement mechanism.

54   'Summary Conclusions: Supervisory Responsibility: Expert roundtable organized by the United Nations High Commissioner for Refugees and the Lauterpacht Research Centre for International Law, University of Cambridge, UK, 9–10 July 2001', in *Refugee Protection in International Law: UNHCR's Global Consultations on International Protection* 667, 668–669 (Erika Feller, Volker Türk and Frances Nicholson, eds, 2003).

These activities are drawn from UNHCR's supervisory activities agreed to by States[55] and EXCOM conclusions. They are not only wide ranging but also overlap with UNHCR's activities in the area of implementation and the promotion of international refugee law (this is discussed later). By compiling these activities and defining them as the components of UNHCR's supervisory work, in the context of the Global Consultations process, UNHCR succeeded in drawing States' attention to and acknowledgement of them and thereby strengthened their importance. As the International Court of Justice has noted, '[a] system of supervision devoid of an element of legal obligation and legal sanction can nevertheless provide a powerful degree of supervision because of the moral force inherent in its findings and recommendations.'[56] UNHCR has therefore worked to obtain greater respect by States for its supervisory responsibility in order to render UNHCR's advice to States on their policies and actions more authoritative. The Declaration of States Parties during the Global Consultations Process, in which States pledge to consider ways to 'facilitate UNHCR's duty of supervising the application' of the 1951 Refugee Convention and the 1967 Protocol[57] constitutes a reinforcement of UNHCR's observation, guidance, and direction of States' application of international refugee law and thus, a step toward the heightened authority of UNHCR's statements.

6.4.2 *UNHCR's enhanced co-operation with international and regional human rights bodies*

Another means employed by UNHCR to counter the decline in States' application of international standards for the protection of refugees is the reinforcement and extension of its co-operation with various regional and international bodies that can render decisions on and evaluate States' treatment of refugees.[58]

In the international sphere, UNHCR monitors, more closely than ever, the work of the treaty bodies to international human rights conventions.[59] These treaty bodies are the Human Rights Committee, under the 1976 Covenant on Civil and Political Rights,[60] the Committee on Economic, Social and Cultural Rights under the 1976 Covenant on Economic, Social and Cultural Rights,[61]

---

55 Ibid., at 669.
56 Voting Procedure on Questions relating to Reports and Petitions concerning the Territory of South West Africa, Advisory Opinion, 1955 I.C.J. 67, 120–121 (7 June) (separate opinion of Judge Lauterpacht).
57 Agenda for Protection, *supra* note 4, at 23.
58 UNHCR has always maintained contacts of various sorts with both regional and international bodies. For example, see UNHCR, Report of the UNHCR, ¶ 53–60, U.N. Doc. A/2394 (1953).
59 Türk, *supra* note 53, at 145. In addition to the six noted by Türk, UNHCR has now added the Committee on Migrant Workers.
60 International Covenant on Civil and Political Rights, 16 December 1966, 999 U.N.T.S. 171.
61 International Covenant on Economic, Social and Cultural Rights, 16 December 1966, 993 U.N.T.S. 3.

the Committee against Torture under the 1984 United Nations Convention against Torture and the Sub-Committee on the Prevention of Torture under the Optional Protocol to the Convention against Torture,[62] the Committee on the Elimination of Racial Discrimination under the 1965 Convention on the Elimination of Racial Discrimination,[63] the Committee on the Elimination of Discrimination against Women under the 1979 Convention on Elimination of Discrimination against Women,[64] the Committee on the Rights of the Child, under the 1989 Convention on the Rights of the Child,[65] the Committee on the Rights of Persons with Disabilities under the 2006 Convention on the Rights of Persons with Disabilities,[66] and the Committee on Migrant Workers under the 1990 International Convention on the Protection of the Rights of All Migrant Workers and Members of Their Families.[67]

Interpretative decisions rendered by these committees on treaty provisions can significantly affect refugees. For example, the Human Rights Committee has issued a decision that concludes that the general obligations imposed on States under the ICCPR apply not only to citizens, but also to aliens within their territory, and thus, to refugees.[68] Decisions on individual claims made by persons, other than asylum seekers and refugees, also may affect the rights of asylum seekers and refugees.[69] Finally, some international human rights treaties, such as the ICCPR, the 1965 Convention on Elimination of Racial Discrimination and the 1984 Convention Against Torture provide for interstate complaints and thus, decisions rendered by treaty bodies in such cases also may bear on the rights of

---

62 Convention Against Torture and Other Cruel, Inhuman or Degrading Treatment or Punishment, 1465 U.N.T.S. 85 and Optional Protocol to the Convention against Torture and Other Cruel, Inhuman or Degrading Treatment or Punishment, 18 December 2002, UN Doc. A/RES/57/199 (2003), 42 ILM 26 (2003).

63 International Convention on the Elimination of All Forms of Racial Discrimination, 21 December 1965, 600 U.N.T.S. 195 (hereinafter 1965 Convention on the Elimination of Racial Discrimination).

64 Convention on the Elimination of All Forms of Discrimination against Women, 18 December 1979, 1249 U.N.T.S. 13 (hereinafter 1979 Convention on Elimination of Discrimination Against Women).

65 Convention on the Rights of the Child, 20 November 1989, 1577 U.N.T.S. 3.

66 International Convention on the Protection and Promotion of the Rights and Dignity of Persons with Disabilities, G.A. Res. 61/106, Annex I, U.N. Doc. A/61/49 (13 December 2006). The Convention entered into force on 3 May 2008. See EXCOM Conclusion 108 (LIX), ¶ i, (2008), which welcomes the entry into force of this Convention.

67 International Convention on the Protection of the Rights of All Migrant Workers and Members of their Families, G.A. Res. 45/158, U.N. Doc. A/RES/45/158 (Annex) (18 December 1990) (hereinafter 1990 Convention on the Protection of Migrant Workers). This Convention explicitly excludes refugees unless the State has agreed otherwise.

68 Compilation of General Comments and General Recommendations Adopted by Human Rights Treaty Bodies, (General Comment 15 to Art. 2 of ICCPR, 1986), U.N. Doc. HRI/GEN/1/Rev.7, 140 (2004).

69 See for example, the decision by the Human Rights Committee in Charles E. Stewart v. Canada, Commun. No. 538/1993, U.N. Doc. CCPR/C/58/D/538/1993 (16 December 1996), which concerns the expulsion of an alien.

asylum seekers and refugees. Therefore, UNHCR co-operates closely with treaty bodies drafting general comments to ensure they further refugee protection,[70] as UNHCR did in the case of the Committee on the Rights of the Child's drafting of comment 6 to the 1989 Convention on the Rights of the Child.[71]

Many of the treaty bodies can render decisions on individual claims by asylum seekers and refugees, which not only affect the individual(s) concerned but also establish a valuable precedent for the treatment of similar cases by States.[72] UNHCR therefore provides information on the situation of refugees as well as doctrinal positions on legal issues concerning refugees to these bodies. UNHCR's doctrinal positions may be implicitly or sometimes even explicitly reflected in the decisions of the treaty bodies. For example, the Committee against Torture cited the UNHCR Handbook as an international standard, noting that it provides that the 'asylum-seeker has an obligation to make an effort to support his/her statements by any available evidence and to give a satisfactory explanation for any lack of evidence'.[73] In another case, it referred to EXCOM Conclusion 12 concerning the extraterritorial effect of the determination of refugee status.[74] Treaty bodies also may make comments on refugee issues raised, or avoided, in States' periodic reports.[75] UNHCR provides information and its views on the situation of refugees, which may then be reflected in the committees' comments on such reports.

At the regional level, UNHCR also has reinforced its co-operation with treaty bodies to regional human rights conventions. The treaty bodies for the main regional human rights conventions in Africa, Central America, and Europe have all rendered decisions of relevance to refugees. These bodies include: the African Commission on Human and People's Rights under the African Charter

---

70 UNHCR, Human Rights and Refugee Protection, Self-Study Module 5, 17 (15 December 2006).
71 Ibid., at 82.
72 Treaty bodies that can hear individual claims include those under the ICCPR, the 1979 Convention on Elimination of Discrimination Against Women, 1965 Convention on Elimination of Racial Discrimination, 1984 Convention Against Torture, the 2006 International Convention on the Protection and Promotion of the Rights and Dignity of Persons with Disabilities, and the 1990 Convention on the Protection of Migrant Workers. For an example of an important decision by the Committee against Torture concerning whether return to the country of origin would constitute a violation of article 3 of the 1984 Convention Against Torture and Other Cruel, Inhuman or Degrading Treatment or Punishment, see Mutombo v. Switzerland, Commun. No. 13/1993, U.N. Doc. A/RES/49/44 at 45 (27 April 1994). An example of an important decision made by the Human Rights Committee is A v. Australia, Commun. No. 560/1993, U.N. Doc. CCPR/C/59/D/560/1993 (30 April 1997) with respect to detention of an asylum seeker.
73 A.S. v. Sweden, ¶ 8.5, Commun. No. 149/1999, U.N. Doc. CAT/C/25/D/149/1999 (15 February 2001).
74 Ms. Elif Pelit v. Azerbaijan, ¶ 11, Commun. No. 281/2005, U.N. Doc. CAT/C/38/D/281/2005 (5 June 2007).
75 For some examples, see See Brian Gorlick, 'Human Rights and Refugees: Enhancing Protection Through International Human Rights Law', 69 *Nordic J. of Int'l. L.* 117, 161–164, 166–170, 172–174 (2000).

on Human Rights and People's Rights with its two protocols,[76] the Inter-American
Commission and Court for Human Rights, for the American Convention on
Human Rights with its Additional Protocol,[77] and the European Court of Human
Rights under the Convention for the Protection of Human Rights and Fundamental
Freedoms, with its numerous protocols.[78] The Organization of the Islamic
Conference also has recently created the Independent Permanent Human Rights
Commission, which is to 'promote the civil, political, social and economic rights
enshrined in the organization's covenants and declarations and in universally
recognized human rights instruments, in conformity with Islamic values'.[79] In
addition, there are treaty bodies for regional conventions on specific human rights
topics, such as torture, women and children.[80]

76 The African Charter on Human and Peoples' Rights, June 27, 1981, 21 I.L.M. 58 (1982). For
example, see Organization Mondiale Contre la Torture et al. v. Rwanda, Commun. Nos. 27/89,
46/91, 49/91, 99/93, African Commission of Human and Peoples' Rights (1996) concerning
the right of refugees to a fair trial in cases of expulsion. The Commission also has decided
cases related to detention, collective expulsion, protection of the family, and freedom of expression, among others. An African Court on Human and Peoples' Rights was established by a 1998
protocol, which entered into force on 1 January 2004. Judges for the court were elected in 2006
and the court began functioning the same year. However, in 2008, the Court was merged with the
African Court of Justice and the new court was named the African Court of Justice and Human
Rights.
77 American Convention on Human Rights, 22 Nov. 1969, 1144 U.N.T.S. 123. For example, see
The Haitian Centre for Human Rights et al. v. U.S., Case 10.675, Inter-Am. C.H.R., Report
No. 51/96, OEA/Ser.L/VII.95, doc. 7 rev. (1997) concerning the right to seek and receive asylum
and *non-refoulement*. The Inter-American Commission on Human Rights also has issued other
decisions relevant to the right to asylum and with respect to women and children. The Inter-
American Court also has issued decisions of relevance to refugees, such as that of the Juridical
Status and Human Rights of the Child, Advisory Opinion, 2002 Inter-Am. Ct. H.R. (Ser. A)
No. 17 (28 August 2002). In addition, the Court has heard cases related to a fair trial, family,
and the right to education that impact on refugees' rights.
78 Convention for the Protection of Human Rights and Fundamental Freedoms, 4 Nov. 1950, 213
U.N.T.S. 222. The European Court has heard numerous cases related to refugees' rights, which
have covered issues of expulsion, *non-refoulement*, rape as torture, the right to personal security,
detention, due process, right to property, and the protection of the family. One of the key decisions of the European Court of Human Rights on the scope of *non-refoulement*, for example, was
Chahal v. United Kingdom, 23 Eur. Ct. H.R. 413 (1996). The European Commission on Human
Rights also heard cases until 1999, but is no longer in existence.
79 Charter of the Organization of the Islamic Conference, art. 15, 4 March 1972, 914 U.N.T.S.103.
The draft statute for the Independent Permanent Human Rights Commission was adopted in
June 2010 at the 38th Session of Council of Foreign Ministers of the Organization of the Islamic
Conference, OIC/CFM-38/2011/LEG/RES/FINAL (28–30 June 2011).
80 In addition to the regional bodies described earlier, in Africa, there is the African Committee
of Experts on the Rights and Welfare of the Child for the African Charter on the Rights and
Welfare of the Child, 11 July 1990, OAU doc. CAB/LEG/24.9/49. In Latin America there is the
Inter-American Commission of Women for the Inter-American Convention on the Prevention,
Punishment and Eradication of Violence against Women, 9 June 1994 33 I.L.M 1534. In Europe,
there are also supervisory bodies to the European Social Charter, 18 October 1961, 529 U.N.T.S.
89, the European Convention for the Prevention of Torture and Inhuman or Degrading Treatment

Furthermore, States' application of international refugee law standards may be affected by the work of special *rapporteurs*, members of working groups, representatives, and independent experts, who are part of the 'special procedures' established by the Commission on Human Rights, now the Human Rights Council. In particular, these persons often follow up their examination and monitoring with public reports, which are read by States, non-governmental organizations and others.

Therefore, UNHCR provides information about the situation of refugees and applicable international laws, as well as its doctrinal views, to these persons and groups. International refugee law standards as well as UNHCR doctrinal positions may then be reflected in their findings. For example, a study by the Special Rapporteur on Housing and Property Restitution, Paulo Sérgio Pinheiro, pursuant to a request by the Sub-Commission on Protection and Promotion of Human Rights,[81] entitled 'The return of refugees or displaced persons property' cites the UNHCR Handbook on Voluntary Repatriation as well as EXCOM conclusions in its discussion of voluntary repatriation as a durable solution.[82]

Moreover, UNHCR has strengthened its co-operation with the United Nations Human Rights Commission and its successor the Human Rights Council. In 1998, the Commission on Human Rights expressed appreciation for UNHCR's contributions to the body and other 'international human rights bodies and mechanisms' and invited the High Commissioner to address the Commission on Human Rights at each future session.[83] In the same resolution, the Commission requested:

> [A]ll United Nations bodies, including the human rights treaty bodies, acting within their mandates, and the specialized agencies, as well as governmental, intergovernmental and non-governmental organizations and the special rapporteurs, special representatives and working groups of the Commission to provide the High Commissioner for Human Rights with all relevant information in their possession on human rights situations that create or affect refugees and displaced persons for appropriate action in fulfilment of her mandate in consultation with the United Nations High Commissioner for Refugees.[84]

---

or Punishment, 26 November 1987, 27 I.L.M. 1152 and the Framework Convention for the Protection of National Minorities, 1 February 1995, Europ.T.S. No. 157.

81 Sub-Comm. on Promotion and Prot. of Human Rights, 2001/122 (16 August 2001). When the Commission on Human Rights was replaced by the Human Rights Council, the Sub-Commission was replaced by the Advisory Committee.

82 Special Rapporteur on Housing and Property Restitution, The Return of Refugees or Displaced Persons' Property, ¶ 20, U.N. Doc. E/CN.4/Sub.2/2002/17 (12 June 2002).

83 Comm. on Human Rights Res. 1998/49, ¶ 12, U.N. Doc. E/CN.4/RES/1998/49 (17 April 1998).

84 Ibid., at ¶ 11.

The increased involvement of UNHCR in the work and meetings of the Commission, and now the Human Rights Council, has been reflected in the resolutions of the Commission on Human Rights that refer to specific UNHCR doctrinal principles.[85]

Finally, UNHCR has encouraged the use of the work of such human rights bodies through its training materials for staff, through the availability of human rights materials on its websites, and training provided to not only governmental officials, but also non-governmental organizations, lawyers, and others concerned with the protection of refugees.

6.4.3 *Amicus curiae*

A third approach adopted by UNHCR to enhance States' application of international refugee law standards, and thus, the effectiveness of international refugee law, is the submission of *amicus curiae* by UNHCR, to both national and regional courts and administrative or quasi-judicial institutions, on issues related to the 1951 Refugee Convention, the 1967 Protocol and other legislative provisions concerning international protection.[86] As noted in section 6.4.1, States have generally accepted this activity as part of UNHCR's supervisory role.[87] The refugee law issues, in cases brought before these bodies, generally concern the parameters and content of refugee law, in connection with the actions of the governmental authority.

UNHCR's briefs, on issues such as *non-refoulement*, well-founded fear, and the exclusion and cessation clauses, are a key means for UNHCR to bring its doctrinal positions to the attention of judicial and administrative institutions and in so doing, to have such positions incorporated into the decisions of such bodies and thus, binding in the country/countries concerned. UNHCR has recently broadened its submission of such briefs from primarily developed countries, such as the USA, Canada, Western European countries, and Japan, among others, to also include the regional institution, the Court of Justice of the European Communities. Admittedly, the submission of such briefs is primarily a tool that is used in individual cases and in countries with developed asylum systems, but despite the limited fora, these decisions can affect the consideration of similar issues by courts and administrative bodies in other countries.

---

85 See for example Comm. on Human Rights Res. 2005/48, ¶ 7, U.N. Doc. E/CN.4/RES/2005/48 (19 April 2005), which requests States to respect the right to seek and enjoy asylum under the Universal Declaration of Human Rights and the principle of *non-refoulement*.

86 UNHCR, R (Saeedi) v. Secretary of State for the Home Department – Submissions by UNHCR, ¶ 2 (15 February 2010). Available at http://www.unhcr.org/refworld/docid/4b83fceb2.html (accessed 27 October 2011).

87 Walter Kälin, 'Supervising the 1951 Convention on the Status of Refugees: Article 35 and Beyond', in *Refugee Protection in International Law: UNHCR's Global Consultations on International Protection* 613; 624 (Erika Feller, Volker Türk and Frances Nicholson, eds, 2003).

Additionally, UNHCR is increasingly utilizng human rights instruments, as well as decisions of human rights treaty bodies,[88] in its *amicus curiae*, to support its positions in light of UNHCR's incorporation of human rights agreements into the refugee law framework. Moreover, UNHCR has even recently addressed the issue of the relationship of refugee status to diplomatic protection concepts.[89]

The significance of UNHCR's submissions to national courts is attested to by a decision of the highest court in Ireland. Ireland's Supreme Court found that despite the lack of statutory provisions or rules of the court for the appointment of an *amicus curiae*, except in Human Rights Commission cases, 'the court is satisfied that it does have an inherent jurisdiction to appoint an amicus curiae where it appears that this might be of assistance in determining an issue before the court.'[90] Thus, even though there is no provision for *amicus curiae* in asylum and refugee law cases in Ireland, the Court found UNHCR's views of such significant import to the Court that it granted a right of *amicus curiae* in the case to UNHCR.

6.4.4 *Promotion of international refugee law*

UNHCR has countered States' unwillingness to assure the necessary protection to refugees by a fourth key approach, namely, the promotion of international refugee law. UNHCR's promotion of the importance of and standards for international protection can contribute to a State's decision to accede to instruments for the protection of refugees and to implement the standards contained in such instruments into national law. Most importantly, such promotional activities affect States' application of their international refugee law obligations and are therefore considered in relation to this latter crucial aspect of the effectiveness of international refugee law.

88 See for example UNHCR, UNHCR Statement on the Right to an Effective Remedy in Relation to Accelerated Asylum Procedures. (Issued in the Context of the Preliminary Ruling Reference to the Court of Justice of the European Union from the Luxembourg Administrative Tribunal Regarding the Interpretation of Article 39, Asylum Procedures Directive (APD); and Articles 6 and 13 ECHR), ¶ 23–25, 30–32, 42–49 (21 May 2010). Available at http://www.unhcr.org/refworld/docid/4bf67fa12.html (accessed 27 October 2011).

89 UNHCR, The Queen on the Application of Al Rawi and Others (Appellants) and (1) the Secretary of State for Foreign and Commonwealth Affairs and (2) the Secretary of State for the Home Department (Respondents) and the Office of the United Nations High Commissioner for Refugees (Intervener). Written Submissions on Behalf of Intervener (UNHCR), (12 July 2006). Available at http://www.unhcr.org/refworld/docid/ 45c350974.html (accessed 27 October 2011). In this case, two people recognized as refugees by the United Kingdom were detained in Guantanamo Bay under the authority of the USA and the issue considered was whether the diplomatic protection of the UK applied to refugees recognized by the UK, not just citizens.

90 See I. v. The Minister for Justice, Equality and Law Reform, On the Application of the United Nations High Commissioner for Refugees, 1 ILRM 27, Ireland: Supreme Court (14 July 2003). Available at http://www.unhcr.org/refworld/docid/42cb9ac34.html (accessed 27 October 2011).

Like capacity building, the promotion of refugee law can be said to be an inherent part of UNHCR's international protection mandate. Yet, it was not until the late 1980s, with the need for additional measures to ensure a more widespread and consistent application of international refugee law standards, that UNHCR had its work explicitly acknowledged by EXCOM and endorsed by the General Assembly.[91] As a result of UNHCR's initiative, EXCOM resolutions have encouraged UNHCR to broadly disseminate refugee law and its principles, including through training,[92] through co-operation with States, non-governmental organizations, academic institutions, and others,[93] as well as the International Institute of Humanitarian Law in San Remo,[94] and through the organization of roundtables, seminars and discussion groups in different areas of the world.[95] EXCOM also has requested UNHCR to promote greater knowledge and understanding of international refugee law[96] and recognized the value of UNHCR's continuing activities that 'encourag[e] the teaching ... of international refugee law'.[97]

Therefore, UNHCR has expanded its training activities so as to provide extensive training on law applicable to refugees to government officials, judges and administrative law officers, non-governmental organization staff, lawyers and others and is involved in the teaching of refugee law courses at universities. In addition, UNHCR staff members attend national, regional, and international conferences, roundtables and seminars of relevance to UNHCR's work. Non-governmental organizations and academic institutions, governments or other organizations may organize these fora. UNHCR also initiates such conferences itself.

The Global Consultations process is UNHCR's most significant organizational undertaking to date to promote international refugee law through discussions with persons from a range of organizations. This process, begun in 2000, provided 'an important forum for open discussion on complex legal and operational

---

91 See the key 1988 Conclusion, EXCOM Conclusion 51 (XXXIX), 1st preambular ¶, 1988. EXCOM reiterated UNHCR's responsibility in this area in a number of subsequent conclusions. For example, see EXCOM Conclusion 71 (XLIV), ¶ aa, 1993; EXCOM Conclusion 74 (XLV), ¶ kk, 1994; and EXCOM Conclusion 79 (XLVII), ¶ n, 1996. Also see the following General Assembly resolutions: G.A. Res. 43/117, ¶ 18, U.N. Doc. A/RES/43/117 (8 December 1988) and G.A. Res. 48/116, ¶ 16, U.N. Doc. A/RES/48/116 (20 December 1993).

92 See for example, EXCOM Conclusion 81 (XLVIII), ¶ u, 1997 endorsed by G.A. Res. 52/103, ¶ 1, U.N. Doc. A/RES/52/103 (12 December 1997) and EXCOM Conclusion 65 (XLII), ¶ s, 1991 endorsed by G.A. Res. 46/106, ¶ 6, U.N. Doc. A/RES/46/106 (16 December 1991).

93 EXCOM Conclusion 77 (XLVI), ¶ m, 1995.

94 EXCOM Conclusion 36 (XXXVI), ¶ m, 1985.

95 EXCOM Conclusion 41 (XXXVII), ¶ h, 1986.

96 EXCOM Conclusion 46 (XXXVIII), ¶ o, 1987; EXCOM Conclusion 33 (XXV), ¶ j, 1984; EXCOM Conclusion 25 (XXXIII), ¶ i, 1982; EXCOM Conclusion 21 (XXXII), ¶ j, 1981; and EXCOM Conclusion 16 (XXXI), ¶ k, 1980.

97 EXCOM Conclusion 29 (XXXIV), ¶ k, 1983. See also EXCOM Conclusion 25 (XXXIII), ¶ j, 1982 concerning the High Commissioner's 'initiative to organize courses of lectures on refugee law in cooperation with the International Institute of Humanitarian Law (San Remo)'.

protection issues', as stated in an EXCOM conclusion endorsed by the General Assembly.[98] UNHCR's creation of the process, identification of topics to be addressed, and its substantive positions on various issues helped create a unique forum through which UNHCR could promote international refugee law.

With its promotional activities, UNHCR works to enhance awareness and understanding of international refugee law and thereby ensures greater application of such principles in practice by States. Such promotion also encourages States to implement their international obligations into national law, as noted earlier, and thereby overlaps with UNHCR's definition of its capacity-building activities. UNHCR's promotional efforts are directed not only toward national, regional and international bodies and their officials, but also toward other groups of persons that can influence the views of governments and citizens. Three special groups: academics, non-governmental organizations, and the media, merit particular attention given the important, but often undervalued, role they play in influencing governments' legislation, policies and practices related to refugees.

The views of academics, disseminated through articles and books, seminar papers, and their teachings, among other means, can have a significant impact on national bodies determining refugee status, the rights accorded by governments to refugees, as well as the regional and international bodies discussed earlier. From a legal standpoint, the views of the most highly qualified publicists constitute a subsidiary source of law under article 38 of the Statute of the International Court of Justice. Although the influence of such academics has decreased significantly since the drafting of the Statute of the International Court of Justice,[99] their views remain influential in the refugee law field given the absence of international treaty standards on many refugee issues. Given the influence of academics, UNHCR not only obtains their input on refugee law questions, but, in connection with UNHCR's promotional role, provides them with UNHCR information and doctrinal positions on issues undergoing research and development, posts their papers in the 'New Issues in Refugee Research' on its website,[100] and co-operates with them in providing seminars and courses on refugee law.

Non-governmental organizations affect the drafting or amendment of legislation concerning refugees as well as governments' policies through their advocacy work. Many are in the frontline of ensuring the protection of refugees through their interactions with refugees. In refugee camps, such organizations may be

---

98 EXCOM Conclusion 90 (LII), ¶ g, 2001 endorsed by G.A. Res. 56/137, ¶ 1, U.N. Doc. A/RES/56/137 (19 December 2001).

99 Schwarzenberger found, even in 1967, that the writings of the most highly qualified publicists in the various nations, as stated in article 38 of the ICJ Statute, have 'considerably decreased in significance'. Georg Schwarzenberger, *A Manual of International Law* 40 (5th edn, 1967). Van Hoof correctly notes, in this author's view, that '[t]here are no hard and fast criteria to decide what part of doctrine is highly qualified and what is not'. G.J.H. van Hoof, *Rethinking the Sources of International Law* 177 (1983).

100 Available at http://www.unhcr.org/pages/4a1d28526.html (accessed 27 October 2011).

involved in assistance activities, such as health care and educational services for refugees, and therefore are well placed to monitor the refugees' day-to-day protection situation. In urban areas, they may provide advice, counselling and assistance to refugees. Since in many cases, refugees, while the subject of States' conduct, are not able to effectively advocate their own rights, non-governmental organizations serve as important representatives for these essentially voiceless refugees. UNHCR has developed close working relationships with non-governmental organizations, throughout the world, that are involved with refugees and refugee law issues.

The media are undeniably one of the most powerful sources of influence on the perceptions, attitudes, and values of the public and national officials in the field of refugee protection. The media can aggravate misunderstandings, such as the confusion about the distinction between migrants, sometimes termed 'economic refugees' in the press, and 'refugees'. By the same token, to the extent that the media understand and appreciate the special protection needs of refugees, then this can lead to more sympathetic stories and coverage of the plight and problems of refugees as well as questions about governments' treatment of refugees. UNHCR has a public information office in its headquarters and officers responsible for dealing with the media in offices around the globe in order to ensure a direct link to the media. Through these contacts, UNHCR provides background information as well as its doctrinal positions.[101]

6.5 Conclusion

Following the appearance of the international refugee law crisis in the 1980s, UNHCR supplemented the work it had been carrying out pursuant to its statutory responsibilities of: '[p]romoting ... the ratification of international conventions for the protection of refugees', 'supervising their application' and '[o]btaining from Governments information concerning ... the laws and regulations concerning' refugees.[102] With respect to accessions to conventions for the protection of refugees, UNHCR has i) launched the Global Accession Campaign in 1998, ii) included the topic of accessions in the Agenda for Protection, iii) had the primary refugee instruments included in the UN's annual treaty event, iv) encouraged removal of reservations to the 1951 Refugee Convention and the 1967 Protocol, and v) widened the scope of its promotion of accessions to other relevant agreements.

101 Schachter has noted that 'public opinion as an element in achieving compliance ... is an amorphous factor, but it may be given more concrete form through the activities of nongovernmental organizations that are dedicated to achieving implementation of one or more specific international norms.' Oscar Schachter, 'The UN Legal Order: An Overview', in *The United Nations and International Law* 3, 19 (Christopher Joyner, ed., 1997).
102 UNHCR Statute, *supra* note 17, at ¶ 8(a), (f).

In the area of implementation, UNHCR has i) co-operated with another international organization to produce a guide on implementation, ii) included implementation in the Agenda for Protection, iii) widened the scope of its promotion to implementation of other relevant agreements, and iv) instituted capacity-building activities. Finally, in the area of application, UNHCR has i) obtained expressions of support from States for its supervisory work, ii) enhanced its co-operation with international and regional bodies, iii) increasingly utilized *amicus curiae* submissions and iv) actively promoted international refugee law.

UNHCR added new activities and enhanced activities that it had been carrying out prior to the crisis in refugee law and protection through an extension of the parameters of its refugee law related responsibilities, under paragraph 8(a) of its mandate. While the General Assembly formally added capacity building and the promotion of international refugee law to UNHCR's mandatory responsibilities, this was done only after UNHCR had instituted such activities and at UNHCR's request. Moreover, policy guidance related to UNHCR's activities was provided at UNHCR's initiative through EXCOM conclusions that were then endorsed by the General Assembly. Thus, UNHCR continued to demonstrate its organizational autonomy with respect to its role related to international refugee law and international protection in the area of effectiveness of international refugee law.

Generally speaking, UNHCR manifested a rather incremental approach to improving the effectiveness of refugee protection. However, these approaches did expand the organization's work beyond the traditional refugee law agreements. Specifically, as UNHCR had extended the scope of the refugee law framework, including through its doctrinal positions, to a wide range of human rights, humanitarian law and regional agreements, as seen in Chapter 5, UNHCR also extended its promotional work to include accessions and implementation of such agreements, as well as the application of provisions relevant to refugees, in particular in its doctrinal positions. Moreover, UNHCR's *amicus curiae* positions have recently begun to cite international and regional human rights instruments.

Through the process of preparing Annual Protection reports and obtaining extended training on refugee law, including relevant human rights standards, UNHCR staff became more knowledgeable about States' application of legal standards and principles and the ways in which they could employ international law and UNHCR doctrinal positions to ensure States' protection of refugees. Thus, laws and principles related to refugees became not just ideals that UNHCR wished governments to aspire to reach, but also a basis for dialogue between UNHCR and governmental staff persons. An extended dialogue complemented this greater institutional awareness and understanding with States related to effectiveness. UNHCR's inclusion of the topics of accession to and implementation of refugee law agreements as well as UNHCR's supervisory role, within the discussions with States during the Global Consultations process, has made States greater stakeholders in ensuring that UNHCR carries out its mandated responsibilities related to international refugee law. The enumeration of specific follow-up action in the Agenda for Protection further established a basis for UNHCR to understand the obstacles that States encounter in making refugee law effective and to work with States to remove them.

Capacity-building activities were greatly expanded by UNHCR and provided the means for greater involvement in States' policy structures and processes related to asylum seekers and refugees. This greater involvement has led to a closer working relationship with States and a more pronounced influence by UNHCR on their decisions and policies concerning asylum seekers and refugees. The key components of UNHCR's capacity-building work include assisting States with drafting legislation that affects refugees as well as the creation of the necessary structures, administrative, legal, and judicial, to recognize refugees and ensure respect for their rights.

Through its direct involvement with States in creating legislation and structures to ensure protection of refugees, UNHCR worked toward having States incorporate into their national legislation and policies, not only the 1951 Refugee Convention standards, but also relevant legal standards from human rights, humanitarian law, criminal law, and regional instruments, as well as UNHCR's doctrinal positions. UNHCR doctrine has permeated UNHCR's work in this area; whether UNHCR provides training to adjudicators of asylum claims, assists States with the creation of asylum bodies, or supports States' efforts to draft national legislation for the protection of refugees, UNHCR relies on its doctrinal positions to supplement the refugee law framework. UNHCR doctrinal positions also serve as the basis for UNHCR's work related to the application of international refugee law by States.

However, the experience of economic agencies, such as the World Trade Organization, suggests that UNHCR must be sensitive to how it defines the objectives of the capacity-building activities and the input provided by donors. Activities that are donor driven may serve donor interests[103] rather than those of UNHCR and the countries in which such activities are being carried out. Capacity-building activities in a given country also may draw financial and personnel resources in that country away from other areas, thereby creating deficiencies in areas that deserve greater priority.[104] If the activities incorporate values that are significantly different from those in the country in which the capacity building is taking place and rely on structures and practices from developed countries with very different economic, social and political sub-structures, then there is a risk that the country receiving capacity-building assistance will view such assistance as an intrusion, thus increasing the likelihood that such assistance will be ineffectual in the long term.

While capacity building is viewed as a crucial means for the transfer of humanitarian values and the importance of legal standards concerning refugees, it must

---

103 Gregory Shaffer, 'Can WTO Technical Assistance and Capacity-Building Serve Developing Countries', 23 *Wis. Int'l. L.J.* 643, 650 (2005).
104 Ibid., at 651.

be undertaken with reflection on the precise means and their implications for the country in which such activities occur. Thus, UNHCR must be sensitive to how it carries out capacity building. In particular, UNHCR should ensure that these activities are devised with a thorough understanding and sensitivity to the needs of the countries in which capacity building is being undertaken and that they are not driven by the desire of donors to keep refugees in the regions of origin and deny them access to asylum in donor countries.

In addition to furthering its direct involvement with States, UNHCR also intensified its submission of *amicus curiae* to national and regional courts and administrative or quasi-judicial institutions, but also enhanced its co-operation with other organizations. UNHCR had the UN include the 1951 Refugee Convention and the 1967 Protocol in several Annual Treaty Events and prepared a brochure on implementation in co-operation with the Inter-Parliamentary Union. UNHCR more actively provided information to and utilized the work of international and regional human rights bodies. The organization's co-operation with such bodies not only assisted in helping to ensure more effective protection of refugees' rights, but also facilitated the development of regional and international refugee law standards since decisions of these bodies further the articulation and clarification of legal standards.

UNHCR also enhanced its promotional role with respect to the application of refugee law, with extensive training activities, attendance and participation in conferences, roundtables and seminars, among others, in an effort to further the knowledge and understanding of such law. This work was directed toward and affected not only persons in national, regional and international bodies concerned with refugees, but also other groups of persons that influence the perception and understanding of refugee law, such as academics, non-governmental organizations and the media. Moreover, such promotional work affected not only States' application of international and regional standards for the protection of refugees, but also their accessions to conventions containing such standards as well as the implementation of such standards into national law. As part of this promotional work, UNHCR has encouraged States, both formally and informally, to remove reservations.

While many of these measures have led to a more in-depth collaboration with States and thus, a more active understanding of the needs, motivations, and difficulties of States with respect to the protection of refugees, more remains to be done in the prevailing climate of States' continued reluctance to permit asylum seekers to enter onto their territories, to recognize refugees, and to accord them effective protection. In the area of accessions, approximately 45 countries have still not acceded to the 1951 Refugee Convention or the 1967 Protocol and, thus, these agreements still lack universal applicability. Moreover, not all States have enacted national legislation that incorporates the necessary international standards for the protection of refugees and other States continue to maintain national legislation or regulations that violate either express standards for the protection of refugees or the humanitarian spirit of the 1951 Refugee Convention. Finally, States' application of international law standards for the protection of refugees is still woefully inadequate.

UNHCR's approaches to improve effectiveness can be faulted for remaining too tempered in light of States' policies. These approaches were designed by UNHCR based on its work undertaken prior to the 1980s and thus, while innovative, have not sufficiently addressed the problems associated with the effectiveness of refugee law. They establish important bases for the future in terms of working with States and other organizations, but more creativity is required by UNHCR and is possible, given the autonomy that UNHCR has vis-à-vis States.

In addition, UNHCR must be careful to avoid being criticized for failing to respect the standards and principles that it requires States to respect. For example, UNHCR's refugee status determination process, which it performs instead of the State authorities in nearly 60 countries,[105] is not uniformly in compliance with the standards for such procedures that it sets for States.[106] Also, UNHCR has been criticized for not fully complying with human rights standards for the protection of refugees in camps that are under its administration.[107]

From an institutional standpoint, UNHCR should further consider how to utilize its ability to define the activities that it can carry out with respect to international refugee law to enhance its work. UNHCR's attempt to bolster its supervisory responsibility during the Global Consultations was not well received by States and therefore indicates that UNHCR must consider alternative avenues to ensure effectiveness that do not necessarily entail formal recognition by States. Moreover, an exclusive focus on the ability of UNHCR to supervise States' policies and actions is too limited, since it considers only the organization's powers and not the effectiveness of what can and should be done. In this connection, international relations studies have a great deal to offer as to why States provide protection and comply not only with treaty law, but also soft law principles.

UNHCR should develop a more profound understanding of what motivates States to accord refugees protection and to comply with international laws for

---

105 UNHCR, *Note on International Protection*, ¶ 22, U.N. Doc. A/AC.96/1098 (28 June 2011).

106 In 2005, in response to heavy criticism of UNHCR's failure to abide by the same procedural standards for refugee status determination (RSD) that it established for States, UNHCR Issued UNHCR, Procedural Standards for Refugee Status Determination under UNHCR's Mandate (1 September 2005). Available at http://www.unhcr.org/pub/PUBL/4317223c9.pdf (accessed 27 October 2011). However, UNHCR remains vulnerable to criticism for its RSD practices where offices are not in compliance with its internal standards and the standards to which it holds States. For a recent example, see criticisms of UNHCR's RSD procedures in Malaysia, which were highlighted by non-governmental organizations in connection with Australia's arrangement with Malaysia for transfer of asylum seekers to Malaysia for RSD by UNHCR in Malaysia, before the High Court of Australia ruled the arrangement illegal. Refugee Rights Network, APPRN Joint Statement on the Australia–Malaysia Refugee Swap Agreement (17 May 2001). Available at http://refugeerightsasiapacific.org/ 2011/05/17/aprrn-joint-statement-on-the-australia-malaysia-refugee-swap-agreement/ (accessed 27 October 2011).

107 For a detailed criticism of UNHCR's violations of rights of asylum seekers in Kenya and Uganda, see Guglielmo Verdirame and Barbara Harrell-Bond, *Rights in Exile: Janus-Faced Humanitarianism* (2005).

their protection. The Dialogue on Protection Challenges, initiated in 2007 by High Commissioner Guterres and held annually through 2010, has served as a useful event to permit a frank discussion on key protection issues with representatives from States, with the participation of academics, non-governmental organizations and other interested parties. However, the information gleaned from these sessions does not appear to be systemically channelled into the measures utilized by UNHCR to ensure effectiveness.

7   Concluding remarks

Applying lessons from the past to enhance UNHCR's role in the future

States created UNHCR, pursuant to a General Assembly resolution, in order to serve as a means for States collectively to continue to deal with the problem of refugees. States assigned UNHCR two principal statutory functions related to refugees: one, the provision of international protection to refugees and two, to seek permanent solutions to the problem of refugees. States also attributed to UNHCR certain responsibilities related to international refugee law that contribute to UNHCR's fulfilment of its international protection function. These responsibilities are contained in paragraph 8 of its Statute and concern both the development of international refugee law and the effectiveness of such law, that is, whether refugees can enjoy their fundamental rights and freedoms.

With respect to the development of international refugee law, UNHCR's Statute provides the organization with the responsibilities of '[p]romoting the conclusion ... of international conventions for the protection of refugees' and 'proposing amendments thereto'. In the area of effectiveness, the Statute assigns UNHCR responsibilities for 'promoting the ratification of international conventions for the protection of refugees', 'supervising their application', and 'obtaining from Governments information concerning ... the laws and regulations concerning' refugees.

In assigning UNHCR such responsibilities, States maintained their primacy not only in the development of treaty law for the protection of refugees, but also concerning their ratification, implementation and application of such treaties. UNHCR's role related to international refugee law, under the terms of its Statute, is one of assisting and supporting States. UNHCR is to promote and encourage States' creation of a refugee law framework and States' ratification and accession to conventions for the protection of refugees. In the area of States' implementation of conventions for the protection of refugees, UNHCR's task is even more limited; it is merely to seek information from States on their implementation of international refugee law obligations into national law standards. The limited role assigned to UNHCR by the drafters of its Statute is consistent with the view at the time of the drafting of UNHCR's Statute that implementation was a State domain. Finally, in the area of States' application of international refugee law standards in practice, UNHCR was provided with a supervisory role under its Statute, but one that has no enforcement mechanisms and thus, is essentially an advisory role since UNHCR is dependent on the co-operation of States.

UNHCR's statutory responsibilities related to international refugee law are firmly rooted in the mandates and experiences of its predecessors, international organizations which had been assigned responsibilities for refugees, beginning with the first High Commissioner, Fridtjof Nansen, appointed by the League of Nations. Whether or not UNHCR's predecessors were specifically mandated to do so, nearly all these organizations were involved in the creation of instruments for the protection of refugees. New refugee situations required new instruments to establish the obligations of States toward refugees. Therefore, some of these earlier organizations encouraged governments to draft agreements or amendments to agreements; others actually prepared the agreement, while still others provided suggestions on the content of such agreements. These early refugee organizations also were involved in ensuring that the refugee law standards were effective. They encouraged accessions, facilitated States' actual application of the agreements in a practical manner, and supervised States' application of agreements to protect refugees. Underpinning the work undertaken by these early refugee organizations was the notion that States should have binding legal obligations toward refugees and that these obligations should be respected by States in practice.

Throughout UNHCR's existence, its work related to the creation and effectiveness of international refugee law has been based on its statutory responsibilities. In carrying out these responsibilities to promote the conclusion and amendment of international conventions for the protection of refugees, UNHCR has encouraged States to formulate treaties for the protection of refugees and has actively participated in the drafting of such treaties and conventions. In particular, UNHCR played a key part in the creation of the only universal refugee law treaties to follow the 1951 Refugee Convention, namely, the 1957 Agreement relating to Refugee Seamen and also the 1967 Protocol Relating to the Status of Refugees. In addition, UNHCR monitors the formulation of instruments initiated by States or by other regional and international bodies, which might affect the rights of refugees. Specifically, UNHCR works toward ensuring that the instruments do not contradict or abrogate any of the protections afforded to refugees under the 1951 Refugee Convention/1967 Protocol and that such agreements enhance the protections afforded refugees. Consequently, UNHCR has contributed to numerous other agreements that provide protections to refugees, including regional refugee instruments, human rights agreements, and agreements on particular topics, ranging from social security to organized crime.

Similarly, in the area of effectiveness, UNHCR's work since its creation has been grounded in the responsibilities articulated in its Statute. Over the years, UNHCR has consistently encouraged States to undertake international obligations concerning refugees, through the promotion of ratification and accession to the 1951 Refugee Convention and accession to the 1967 Protocol. Moreover, it also encouraged States to become bound by other conventions for the protections of refugees to which UNHCR had contributed. In the area of States' implementation of their international refugee law obligations into national law standards, UNHCR, with its statutory responsibility for obtaining information, attempts to gather information on States' implementation of the 1951 Refugee Convention/1967 Protocol from governments through informal and formal requests. And in the area of States' application of their international refugee law obligations, UNHCR has carried out its supervisory responsibility through a variety of activities. These include monitoring and gathering information on States' policies and legislation, analysing such information, and following up on States' actions, such as by raising concerns, about States' policies, practices, legislation and decisions that are inconsistent with international refugee law, directly with States and in reports to the General Assembly. UNHCR also participates in refugee determination procedures, in various capacities depending on the country concerned.

The traditional work UNHCR has carried out, pursuant to its statutory responsibilities concerning the development and effectiveness of international refugee law, takes as its centre point international treaties for the protection of refugees. UNHCR is to ensure that sufficient treaties exist to protect refugees' rights and that these treaties become binding on States and are respected by them. With the drafting of the 1951 Refugee Convention, the first concrete and practical link between UNHCR and international refugee law was established. The Convention also established States' obligation to co-operate with UNHCR, as article 35 provides: 'in the exercise of [UNHCR's] functions, and shall in particular facilitate [UNHCR's] duty of supervising the application of the provisions of this Convention'. As a result, UNHCR and States became partners in ensuring protection for refugees through the bias of international law.

The international protection crisis, which initially appeared in the 1980s, constituted a true test of UNHCR's ability to adapt and remain relevant. The crisis resulted from States' actions and policies that demonstrated an unwillingness to protect refugees. They included actions and policies to limit the number of refugees reaching their territory, to reduce the number of persons eligible for refugee status, and the provision of lower levels of protection. These actions and the unwillingness of States to modify their actions in response to UNHCR's objections signalled that States were reassuming greater control over refugee matters and were conferring on UNHCR less influence over their actions. Consequently, a degree of strain was introduced into the relationship between UNHCR and States, which relationship was one based on co-operation. UNHCR's relationship with States became more complicated and significant differences in views relating to the content of international refugee law appeared.

States' actions capitalized on the gaps and ambiguities in the provisions of the 1951 Refugee Convention/1967 Protocol. For example, some States adopted overly restrictive interpretations of the refugee definition that took advantage of the ambiguities in the Convention's refugee definition, while others adopted concepts, such as first country of asylum, which do not explicitly violate the Convention's standards, but nevertheless contradict the humanitarian and protection spirit of the 1951 Refugee Convention. Regional standards became increasingly important, but resulted in different standards for different regions. As the weaknesses in the framework permitted States greater latitude in interpreting and applying their obligations towards refugees, they therefore, understandably, did not manifest any intention to remedy these weaknesses through an instrument that would update the 1951 Refugee Convention and the 1967 Protocol.

The crisis also highlighted the weaknesses in the means for ensuring the effectiveness of the protection of refugees. At the time, not all States had acceded to the 1951 Refugee Convention or the 1967 Protocol and some States had made reservations that limited certain protections for refugees. Although some States did not have national legislation in place that reflected their international obligations towards refugees, others adopted legislative provisions that expressly violated the Convention's standards or contradicted the humanitarian spirit of the Convention and the notion of international protection. Moreover, with no multinational mechanism in place to ensure that States applied their international refugee law obligations in practice, UNHCR's supervisory mechanism was the sole means to help ensure the enforcement of such obligations. UNHCR's means for persuading States to respect their refugee law obligations were primarily soft ones, those of encouragement, persuasion and inducement. Although UNHCR could bring violations to the attention of EXCOM or the General Assembly, in order to obtain, respectively, a conclusion or resolution, these were not legally binding on States. Essentially, the responsibility for taking the necessary actions to ensure the effectiveness of international refugee law rested squarely within States' domain.

Faced with a crisis in the protection of refugees, UNHCR has demonstrated that it is an independent organization with a degree of autonomy, rather than just an expression of States' interests. Specifically, UNHCR employed two key techniques so that it could continue to influence both the development and effectiveness of refugee law by States. First, pursuant to its implied powers, UNHCR has adopted a flexible interpretation of its international protection function in order to alter and extend its responsibilities related to international refugee law. Second, independently, based on its implied powers, or following requests by EXCOM, UNHCR has formulated and articulated doctrinal positions on refugee law issues. UNHCR has then frequently employed the more formal means for the modification of its mandate, namely the General Assembly's assignment of additional responsibilities or the General Assembly's or EXCOM's provision of policy guidance, after it has instigated new approaches.

As concerns the development of international refugee law, UNHCR has continued to carry out the activities mentioned earlier and supplemented this work with three approaches, two of which are still in use. First, UNHCR has helped to create a more comprehensive legal framework for the protection of refugees through the incorporation of standards from other international instruments that relate to refugees' rights. International human rights law instruments have been particularly important to UNHCR's effort to expand and supplement the coverage of the 1951 Refugee Convention. International humanitarian law and criminal law standards also have contributed to the development of the international refugee law framework. Thus, these standards assist in filling in the gaps and can extend the protections contained in the 1951 Refugee Convention/1967 Protocol.

Second, UNHCR has further developed its doctrinal positions to counter States' restrictive interpretations of the refugee definition and standards in the 1951 Refugee Convention and to impede their adoption of concepts that restrict refugees' rights but do not explicitly violate provisions in the 1951 Refugee Convention. UNHCR has been formulating its views on refugee law since shortly after its creation. However, following the appearance of the crisis in refugee protection in the 1980s, UNHCR's positions increasingly articulated new principles and became more widely and more publicly disseminated. Such positions have assisted in filling in the gaps and resolving ambiguities in the coverage of the provisions of the 1951 Refugee Convention, in numerous areas, including with respect to voluntary repatriation, the procedural standards for the determination of refugee status, the exclusion clauses related to the refugee definition, the application of the refugee definition in connection with claims by women asylum seekers, and detention.

Moreover, UNHCR doctrinal positions serve as a means to further the development of international refugee law. UNHCR doctrine may influence provisions in future treaties and can impact on the development of customary international law standards, as is amply illustrated by UNHCR's role in the evolution of *non-refoulement* into a customary international law standard. Doctrinal positions may even serve as a catalyst for the development of general principles of international law. If they lead to more consistent State action and therefore greater uniformity among States, a general principle of law could emerge. For example, status determination procedures may be in the process of developing into a general principle.

These two approaches were based on work that UNHCR had carried out and States had accepted prior to the crisis in refugee protection and refugee law, but were innovations in how UNHCR contributes to the development of refugee law. Specifically, UNHCR's incorporation of human rights, humanitarian and criminal law standards extended its previous work of incorporating relevant provisions from regional and international agreements on non-refugee topics. UNHCR's extensive use and public articulation of doctrinal positions on refugee law issues was an evolution from UNHCR's initial primarily internal and infrequent use of such positions.

A third approach adopted by UNHCR but abandoned after three years, the Convention Plus initiative, was UNHCR's most innovative attempt yet to contribute to the development of the refugee law framework. The initiative, which attempted to provide legal content to the concepts of burden sharing and responsibility sharing, in order to address the political problem of disparate refugee burdens borne by States, was admirable for its creativity in utilizing treaties containing standards that would evolve into norms. The initiative was weakened, however, by its failure to be linked to existing refugee law principles and by the perception that it served the interests of northern States, rather than the southern States, which contain the largest refugee populations.

The crisis in refugee protection has also led UNHCR to develop approaches to help ensure the effectiveness of international refugee law. To ensure that as many States as possible are bound by the 1951 Refugee Convention/1967 Protocol, UNHCR has employed some new means for encouraging accessions, such as the Global Accession campaign in 1998, inclusion of the agreements in the UN's annual treaty event, and the expression of additional activities by UNHCR and States to further States' accessions in the Agenda for Protection, the concluding document of the Global Consultations process. UNHCR also has encouraged the removal of reservations to the 1951 Refugee Convention and 1967 Protocol. Moreover, since UNHCR has articulated a refugee law framework that includes international human rights, humanitarian and regional law standards, among others, it also encourages the ratification of such additional instruments.

To ensure that States implement their international obligations towards refugees in the form of national legislation and administrative measures, UNHCR has prompted the General Assembly to authorize it to promote the implementation of the 1951 Refugee Convention and 1967 Protocol. In addition to co-operatively creating a guide on implementation with another organization, UNHCR included the topic of States' implementation of the 1951 Refugee Convention and the 1967 Protocol in the Global Consultations process. Pursuant to the Agenda for Protection, UNHCR is to survey States in order to obtain a better understanding of the problems they have with the implementation of such agreements. Furthermore, since UNHCR considers that the refugee law framework encompasses other instruments, including international human rights, international humanitarian law, and regional agreements, UNHCR promotes States' accession to these instruments as well.

One of the most important developments in UNHCR's responsibilities related to States' implementation of their international refugee law obligations toward refugees is the addition of capacity-building activities. These activities include the provision of comments on draft legislation, training for governmental officials and others concerned with refugees, and advice on the creation, structure and functions of asylum bodies. As part of such capacity-building activities, UNHCR works with States to create the necessary legal structures and national legal framework for the protection of refugees. This work has lead to a closer involvement by UNHCR in States' work related to refugees and has generally enhanced the working relationship that UNHCR has with such States. While capacity-building activities allow UNHCR to more easily shape and influence the actions of States in an area that was traditionally viewed as one solely within the State's discretion and authority, UNHCR must carry out such work in a manner that is sensitive to not only the needs, but also the constraints, of such countries.

In the crucial area of States' application of international refugee law standards for the protection of refugees, UNHCR has pursued several approaches. First, UNHCR has increased the awareness of its own staff of refugee law principles and how they can be utilized to bolster States' protection of refugees and has utilized the Global Consultations process as a means to solidify State support for its supervisory responsibility. UNHCR also reinforced and extended its co-operation with a multitude of regional and international bodies, which can issue decisions and evaluate States' treatment of refugees, and has intensified its use of *amicus curiae* positions, which now use not only 1951 Refugee Convention standards but also human rights law principles. In addition, UNHCR has intensified its promotional activities relating to international refugee law. Thus, UNHCR actively disseminates refugee law principles, conducts training and teaching activities, and attends seminars relevant to refugees. Not only do such promotional activities enhance States' application of international refugee law, but they also serve as an additional incentive to States' implementation of international refugee law standards as well as their accession to not only the 1951 Refugee Convention/1967 Protocol, but also to other agreements that provide protections to refugees.

UNHCR's activities related to the development of international refugee law standards and principles are integrally linked to the organisation's ability to ensure the effectiveness of refugee law, that is, the ability of refugees to enjoy their fundamental rights and freedoms. UNHCR advocates the implementation of not only standards from the 1951 Refugee Convention, but also standards from human rights treaties and other instruments as well as UNHCR doctrinal principles, into national law. Similarly, in carrying out its supervisory responsibility, UNHCR's evaluation of States' legislation, policies, and actions is based on the expanded refugee law framework, which includes standards from international and regional instruments, and principles articulated in its doctrinal positions. Moreover, non-governmental organizations and States also may use such standards and doctrinal positions to assess States' treatment of refugees. Thus, the development of standards enhances the effectiveness of international refugee law.

Throughout the over 60 years of its work, UNHCR has maintained the 1951 Refugee Convention and the 1967 Protocol as the basis for international refugee law standards, even while it extended the refugee law framework to include international human rights law, the area of law that actually overreaches refugee law. Given that it is unlikely that a new refugee instrument will be drafted to supplement the provisions of the 1951 Refugee Convention, UNHCR must continue to incorporate other standards and principles into the refugee law framework.

In general, UNHCR can be said to be moving from a promotional role to one that involves a greater understanding and involvement with States. UNHCR's initiatives, such as the Global Consultations Process and the Dialogue on Protection Challenges, as well as its enhanced training activities and extended capacity-building initiatives signal the need, but also the willingness, to understand the views, difficulties and needs of States. In particular, these approaches strengthen the relationship between States and UNHCR, facilitate greater access by UNHCR to the governmental officials and staff concerned with refugees, and result in enhanced co-operation between States and UNHCR. UNHCR also becomes, through a closer relationship with States, more integrally involved in States' decisions relative to refugees. Furthermore, UNHCR garners support for the principles it considers should apply to refugees through the dissemination of refugee law principles, in legal instruments and its doctrinal positions, to other bodies as well as the public.

As UNHCR has demonstrated since the onset of the crisis in refugee protection and law, the informal means, namely its interpretation of its international protection function and its doctrinal positions, are key to UNHCR's flexibility in carrying out its responsibilities related to international refugee law. UNHCR will have to carefully consider how to balance its flexibility with formal approval from States in the form of EXCOM conclusions and General Assembly resolutions. In particular, as Member States of EXCOM have become increasingly assertive about the choice of EXCOM topics and the content of EXCOM resolutions in recent years, UNHCR will have to more carefully select when it wishes to obtain EXCOM's express support for the new approaches it uses and give more attention to the language used in such conclusions.

UNHCR should also carefully evaluate the areas in which it could undertake significant initiatives. UNHCR's approaches to developing refugee law and enhancing its effectiveness have generally been incremental ones. Certainly, it has to be careful not to undertake activities that would be opposed or significantly criticized by States, but at the same time, in the current context of refugee crises and States' unwillingness to protect refugees, UNHCR must exhibit a forward-looking creativity.

In particular, UNHCR should address the significant gaps and ambiguities that remain in the legal standards applicable to asylum seekers and refugees. Asylum seekers' rights, the parameters and content of temporary protection, the means and approach for determining the status of asylum seekers in mass influxes, to name a few, remain unclear and without the necessary content to permit States to handle these matters in a consistent and harmonized manner. Admittedly, UNHCR is on stronger ground when it clarifies and extends the standards in the 1951 Refugee Convention through the employment of standards from other international instruments, in particular, human rights agreements, rather than articulating new doctrinal principles that complete gaps in this convention or in the refugee law framework in general. Yet, it will need to continue to formulate and promote its doctrinal principles if the organization is to ensure the necessary protection to refugees.

At the same time, a compilation of UNHCR doctrine would assist refugee advocates, governmental officials dealing with refugees as well as UNHCR staff to better understand and employ such doctrine. The use of UNHCR doctrine to create more complete legal frameworks for other groups of persons requiring protection could also be explored. While the Guiding Principles on Internal Displacement[1] are becoming increasingly accepted by States for the protection of internally displaced persons, other groups, such as people fleeing situations of conflict, do not have a clear legal framework. Moreover, an interdisciplinary consideration of the relative influence of political factors and legal standards on

---

1 Guiding Principles on Internal Displacement, U.N. Doc. E/CN.4/1998/53/Add2 (22 July 1998).

the formation of doctrine would assist in clarifying how UNHCR could better formulate and articulate positions.

UNHCR also must consider what additional measures should be taken to ensure the effectiveness of international refugee law, specifically, what further 'soft' steps would be useful to obtain further accessions and better implementation and application by States of their international refugee law obligations. UNHCR should also ensure that, in the midst of its capacity-building activities, the organization does not become unduly influenced by the views of States, but that it maintains its objectivity and continues to base its work on refugee law principles. One area in which UNHCR is perhaps too close to governments is where it is part of refugee status determination bodies. Given the changed relationship between UNHCR and States, UNHCR's involvement in national refugee status determination processes in certain countries can be questioned as to whether it can maintain its principles and role of ensuring protection in such countries when it does not agree with the decision taken or where compromise is necessary in rendering a decision. UNHCR might be better placed outside of such processes. Alternatively, it may wish to consider further intensifying and developing its provision of *amicus curiae* briefs.

To the extent that UNHCR conducts refugee status determination in place of States, it must remedy the deficiencies in its own procedures. UNHCR's inability to respect the very standards and principles that it asks States to observe places the very protection of refugees at risk and denigrates UNHCR's reputation and credibility as an organization that ensures international protection to refugees. UNHCR cannot ask States to respect principles that the organization itself does not observe.

In addition to continuing to strengthen its relationships with international human rights tribunals and treaty bodies for international human rights treaties, UNHCR could further develop its relationship with the international tribunals, the International Criminal Court as well as the International Tribunal for the Prosecution of Persons Responsible for Serious Violations of International Humanitarian Law Committed in the Territory of the Former Yugoslavia and the International Criminal Tribunal for Rwanda, since the decisions of these bodies may impact on the content and parameters of refugee law principles.[2] In particular, their decisions can affect the general meaning of the term 'persecution' in the refugee definition and their recognition of enslavement and rape as crimes against humanity, bolster the legal status of these crimes as persecution and clarify forms of gender persecution. As UNHCR cites the courts' decisions in support of its

---

2   As Chaloka Beyani has noted, the International Criminal Tribunals for the former Yugoslavia and Rwanda 'provide a wind of opportunity for determining the existence of persecution as a crime against humanity on essentially the same grounds as those covered by the Refugee Convention'. Chaloka Beyani, 'The Role of Human Rights Bodies in Protecting Refugees', in *Human Rights and Refugees, Internally Displaced Persons and Migrant Workers: Essays in Memory of Joan Fitzpatrick and Arthur Helton* 269, 276 (Anne Bayefsky, ed., 2006).

doctrinal positions,[3] UNHCR could also contribute to and facilitate the tribunals' understanding of persecution by providing its doctrinal views to them.

UNHCR doctrinal documents, which contain legal principles related to the concept of persecution and gender-related persecution, and documents produced by UNHCR on the background for such principles could assist the tribunals in obtaining a broader understanding and thus, the necessary context for its consideration of relevant legal issues. UNHCR's doctrinal views might then be reflected in the courts' rulings thereby strengthening the legal status of its doctrine and creating increasingly normative standards with which States must comply.

UNHCR's continued influence on the development and effectiveness of international refugee law is closely linked to two key factors. First, UNHCR must be able to operate with the necessary financial resources in order to hire sufficient staff and to maintain its worldwide operations. This ability is heavily dependent on the willingness of States to adequately fund UNHCR. One area where UNHCR is in need of additional staff is in its Policy Development and Evaluation Service unit. While UNHCR is an operational agency, it must also have sufficient time to reflect on developments and assess current needs and operations as well as to formulate new policies and approaches. Second, UNHCR should formulate its doctrinal positions and perform its activities related to effectiveness in a manner that builds on existing legal standards and encapsulates a strong commitment by UNHCR to the protection of refugees. Thus, UNHCR also must have sufficient staff to research and develop such legal principles and should actively call on academics and other experts in the area.

Numerous issues related to UNHCR's role in international refugee law would benefit from additional research. First, it is of crucial importance to consider how UNHCR's effectiveness in ensuring international protection can be strengthened. In addition, while UNHCR has been mandated to protect other groups, such as asylum seekers, returnees, internally displaced people and people fleeing generalized violence or internal conflict, its supervisory functions are not necessarily delineated to cover these persons to the same extent as they cover refugees. Thus, even though UNHCR encountered difficulties during the Global Consultations process with clarifying and expanding its supervisory role, it should give further thought to how to ensure international refugee law effectiveness. There is room for the continued development of States' obligation to co-operate with UNHCR, including the principle of good faith.

UNHCR should look beyond refugee law to the law of international organizations and international relations studies. These areas can provide insights into the interaction between States and UNHCR as well as new perspectives on States' compliance with refugee law. An interdisciplinary consideration of the relative influence of political factors and legal standards on the formation of doctrine would assist UNHCR in determining how it could better formulate and articulate

---

3 See for example, UNHCR, Human Rights and Refugee Protection: Self-Study Module 5, at 27–28 (15 December 2006).

positions that further the protection of refugees but are accepted by States and would therefore be more readily applied by States.

As a final note, it must be remembered that UNHCR remains uniquely situated to influence both the development and the effectiveness of international refugee law. Yet, UNHCR must be viewed through a realistic lens in order to assure the enhancement of its capacities. UNHCR's authority is based on international law, but it operates in a political environment. With continuing changes in the political, economic and social situations within States as well as their relationships with other States, the approach of States to refugees continues to fluctuate and evolve. Thus, while taking into account the political currents of the time, UNHCR's actions must be soundly based in law and framed by the overall objective of its primary function, international protection.

Bibliography

Books, monographs, articles and working papers

Akehurst, Michael, 'Custom as a Source of International Law', 47 *British Yearbook of International Law* 1 (1975).

Allain, Jean, 'The Jus Cogens Nature of Non-Refoulement', 13 *International Journal of Refugee Law* 533 (2001).

Allande, Denis and Rials, Stéphane, *Dictionnaire de la Culture Juridique*, Paris: Presses Universitaires de France, 2003.

Alvarez, José, *International Organizations as Law-Makers*, Oxford: Oxford University Press, 2005.

Arboleda, Eduardo, 'Refugee Definition in Africa and Latin America: The Lessons of Pragmatism', 3 *International Journal of Refugee Law* 185 (1991).

Asian–African Legal Consultative Committee, *The Rights of Refugees: Report of the Committee and Background Materials*, New Delhi: Asian–African Legal Consultative Committee, 1966.

Barnett, Laura, 'Global Governance and the Evolution`of the International Refugee Regime', 14 *International Journal of Refugee Law* 238 (2002).

Bayefsky, Anne, ed., *Human Rights and Refugees, Internally Displaced Persons and Migrant Workers: Essays in Memory of Joan Fitzpatrick and Arthur Helton*, The Hague: Martinus Nijhoff Publishers, 2006.

Bem, Kazimierz, 'The Coming of a "Blank Cheque"' – Europe, the 1951 Convention and the 1967 Protocol', 16 *International Journal of Refugee Law* 609 (2004).

Betts, Alexander and Durieux, Jean-François, 'Convention Plus as a Norm-Setting Exercise', 20 *Journal of Refugee Studies* 509 (2007).

Blokker, Neils and Muller, Sam, eds, *Towards More Effective Supervision by International Organizations: Essays in Honour of Henry G. Schermers*, Dordrecht/Boston/London: Martinus Nijhoff Publishers, 1994.

Bokor-Szego, Hanna, *The Role of the United Nations in International Legislation*, Dr Sándo Simon translator, New York: North Holland Publishing Co., 1978.

Bowett, D.W., *The Law of International Institutions*, London: Sweet & Maxwell, 4th edn, 1982.

Carlsnaes, W., Risse, T. and Simmons, B., eds, *Handbook of International Relations*, Thousand Oaks, CA: Sage, 2002.

Cassese, Antonio, *International Law*, Oxford: Oxford University Press, 2nd edn, 2005.

Cassese, Antonio, *International Law in a Divided World*, Oxford: Clarendon Press, 1986.

Cassese, Antonio, *Modern Constitutions and International Law*, 192 *Recueil des Cours*, Hague Academy of International Law 335 (1985).

Castañeda, Jorge, *Legal Effects of United Nations Resolutions*, Alba Amoia, trans., New York: Columbia University Press, 1969.

Chayes, Abraham and Chayes, Antonia Handler, 'On Compliance', 47 *International Organization* 175 (1993).

Chimini, B.S., 'The Meaning of Words and the Role of UNHCR in Voluntary Repatriation', 5 *International Journal of Refugee Law* 442 (1993).

Chinkin, C.M., 'The Challenge of Soft Law: Development and Change in International Law', 38 *International and Comparative Law Quarterly* 850 (1989).

Coles, Gervase, 'Recent and Future Developments in International Refugee Law', paper submitted to the Seminar on Problems in the International Protection of Refugees, University of New South Wales, 2–3 August 1980 (on file with author).

Dinstein, Yoram, ed., *International Law at a Time of Perplexity: Essays in Honour of Shabtai Rosenne*, Dordrecht: Martinus Nijhoff Publishers, 1989.

Durieux, Jean François and Betts, Alexander, 'Convention Plus as a Norm-Setting Exercise', 20 *Journal of Refugee Studies* 509 (2007).

Feller, E., Türk, V. and Nicholson, F., eds, *Refugee Protection in International Law: UNHCR's Global Consultations on International Protection*, Cambridge: Cambridge University Press, 2003.

Fitzpatrick, Joan, 'Revitalizing the 1951 Refugee Convention', 9 *Harvard Human Rights Journal* 229 (1996).

Garvey, Jack, 'Toward a Reformulation of International Refugee Law', 26 *Harvard International Law Journal* 483 (1985).

Goedhart, Gerrit Jan van Heuven, 'The Problem of Refugees', 82 *Recueil des Cours*, Hague Academy of International Law 261 (1953).

Goodwin-Gill, Guy, 'The Politics of Refugee Protection', 27 *Refugee Survey Quarterly* 8 (2008).

Goodwin-Gill, Guy, 'Refugees and Their Human Rights', Barbara Harrell-Bond Lecture, 12 November 2003, Refugee Studies Centre Working Paper No.17, University of Oxford. Available at http://www.rsc.ox.ac.uk/publications/working-papers/RSCworkingpaper17.pdf (accessed 27 October 2011).

Goodwin-Gill, Guy, 'The International Protection of Refugees: What Future?', 12 *International Journal of Refugee Law* 1 (2000).

Goodwin-Gill, Guy, 'Editorial', 8 *International Journal of Refugee Law* 6 (1996).

Goodwin-Gill, Guy, 'The Language of Protection', 1 *International Journal of Refugee Law* 6 (1989).

Goodwin-Gill, Guy and McAdam, Jane, *The Refugee in International Law*, Oxford: Oxford University Press, 3rd edn, 2007.

Gordenker, Leon, *Refugees in International Politics*, London: Croom Helm Ltd, 1987.

Gorlick, Brian, 'Human Rights and Refugees: Enhancing Protection Through International Human Rights Law', 69 *Nordic Journal of International Law* 117 (2000).

Grahl-Madsen, Atle, *Commentary on the Refugee Convention 1951: Articles 2–11, 13–37*, UNHCR, ed., 1997.

Grahl-Madsen, Atle, *Territorial Asylum*, Stockholm: Almqvist & Wiksell International; London/New York: Oceana Publications, 1980.

Grahl-Madsen, Atle, *The Status of Refugees in International Law: Refugee Character*, Leyden: A.W. Sijthoff, 1966.

Greig, D.W., 'The Protection of Refugees and Customary International Law', 8 *Australian Yearbook of International Law* 108 (1983).

Gruchalla-Wesierski, Tadeusz, 'A Framework for Understanding "Soft Law"' 30 *McGill Law Journal* 37 (1984).

Guinchard, Serge and Debard, Thierry, eds, *Lexique des Termes Juridiques*, Paris: Dalloz, 19th edn, 2012.

Hambro, Edvard, Goodrich, Leland M. and Simons, Anne Patricia, *Charter of the United Nations*, New York/London: Columbia University Press, 3rd edn, 1969.

Hartling, Poul, 'Concept and Definition of "Refugee" – Legal and Humanitarian Aspects', 48 *Nordisk Tidsskrift for International Ret* 125 (1979).

Hathaway, James, *The Rights of Refugees Under International Law,* Cambridge/New York: Cambridge University Press, 2005.

Hathaway, James, 'Who Should Watch Over Refugee Law', 14 *Forced Migration Review* 23 (2002).

Hathaway, James, 'Making International Refugee Law Relevant Again: A Proposal for Collectivized and Solution-Oriented Protection', 10 *Harvard Human Rights Journal* 115 (1997).

Helton, Arthur, 'What is Refugee Protection?', *International Journal of Refugee Law (Special Issue)* 119 (1990).

Higgins, Rosalyn, *Problems and Process: International Law and How We Use It*, Oxford: Oxford University Press, 1994.

Holborn, Louise, *Refugees: A Problem of Our Time: The Work of The United Nations High Commissioner for Refugees, 1951–1972*, Metuchen, NJ: Scarecrow Press, 1975.

Holborn, Louise, *The International Refugee Organization: A Specialized Agency of the United Nations – Its History and Work 1946–1952*, London: Oxford University Press, 1956.

International Council of Voluntary Agencies (ICVA) and the University of Michigan (UM), Overseeing the Refugee Convention, seven working papers prepared for the 11 December 2001 meeting of ICVA and the UM prior to the Ministerial Conference of States Parties to the 1951 Refugee Convention and/or 1967 Protocol Relating to the Status of Refugees (Track 1 of the UNHCR Global Consultations). Available at http://www.icva.ch/doc00000505.html (accessed 27 October 2011).

Jackson, Ivor, *The Refugee Concept in Group Situations*, The Hague: Martinus Nijhoff Publishers, 1999.

Jaeger, Gilbert 'Are Refugees Migrants? The Recent Approach to Refugee Flows as a Particular Aspect of Migration', *Oikoumene (Special Issue, Refugees and Asylum Seekers in a Common European House)* 18, Commission on Inter-Church Aid and World Council of Churches, eds (August 1991) (on file with author).

Johnston, Douglas M. 'Functionalism in the Theory of International Law', 26 *Canadian Yearbook of International Law* 3 (1988).

Joyner, Christopher, ed., *The United Nations And International Law*, Cambridge: Cambridge University Press, 1997.

Keohane, Robert O. 'International Relations and International Law: Two Optics', 38 *Harvard International Law Journal* 487 (1997).

Klabbers, Jan, *An Introduction to International Institutional Law*, Cambridge: Cambridge University Press, 2nd edn, 2009.

Knudson, John, *A History of the League of Nations*, Atlanta, GA: Turner E. Smith, 1938.

Kushner, Tony and Knox, Katherine, *Refugees in an Age of Genocide: Global, National and Local Perspectives During The Twentieth Century*, London: Frank Cass, 1999.

Lewis, Corinne, 'UNHCR's Contribution to the Development of International Refugee Law: Its Foundations and Evolution', 17 *International Journal of Refugee Law* 67 (2005).

Loescher, Gil, *The UNHCR and World Politics: A Perilous Path*, New York: Oxford University Press, 2001.

Loescher, Gil, Betts, Alexander and Milner, James, *The United Nations High Commissioner for Refugees: The Politics and Practice of Refugee Protection into the Twenty-first Century*, Abingdon: Routledge, 2008.

Lucassen, Jan and Lucassen, Leo, *Migration, Migration History, History: Old Paradigms and New Perspectives*, Bern: Lang, 1997.

Macnamara, Dennis and Goodwin-Gill, Guy, 'UNHCR and International Refugee Protection', Refugee Studies Centre Working Paper No. 2, University of Oxford, June 1999. Available at http://www.rsc.ox.ac.uk/publications/working-papers/RSCworkingpaper2.pdf (accessed 27 October 2011).

Marrus, Michael, *The Unwanted: European Refugees in the 20th Century*, New York: Oxford University Press, 1985.

Martin, David, ed., *The New Asylum Seekers: Refugee Law in the 1980s*, Dordrecht: Martinus Nijhoff Publishers, 1988.

Martin, D., Aleinikoff, T., Motomura, H. and Fullerton, M., *Forced Migration: Law and Policy*, St. Paul, MN: Thomson/West (2007).

Maynard, P.D., 'The Legal Competence of the United Nations High Commissioner for Refugees', 31 *International and Comparative Law Quarterly* 415 (1982).

Nicholson, Frances and Twomey, Patrick, eds, *Refugee Rights and Realities*, Cambridge: Cambridge University Press, 1999.

O'Flaherty, Michael, ed., *The Human Rights Field Operation: Law, Theory and Practice*, Farnham: Ashgate Publishing Company, 2007.

The *Oxford English Dictionary*, vols XII and VII and XVII, Oxford: Oxford University Press, 2nd edn, 1989.

Perluss, Deborah and Hartman, Joan, 'Temporary Refuge: Emergence of a Customary Norm', 26 *Virginia Journal of International Law* 551 (1986).

Plender, Richard, 'The Present State of Research Carried Out by the English-Speaking Section of the Centre for Studies and Research', *Right of Asylum*, Hague Academy of International Law 63 (1990).

Ramcharan, B.G., *The Concept and Present Status of the International Protection of Human Rights: Forty Years after the Universal Declaration*, Dordrecht: Martinus Nijhoff Publishers, 1989.

Roberts, A. and Kingsbury, B., eds, *United Nations, Divided World: the UN's Roles in International Relations*, Oxford: Oxford University Press, 2nd edn, 1993.

Robertson, A. H. 'Some Legal Problems of the UNRRA' 23 *British Yearbook of International Law* 142 (1946).

Ruthström-Ruin, Cecilia, *Beyond Europe: The Globalization of Refugee Aid*, Lund: Lund University Press, 1993.

Salomon, Kim, *Refugees in the Cold War: Toward a New International Refugee Regime in the Early Postwar Era*, Lund: Lund University Press, 1991.

Sands, Philippe and Klein, Pierre, eds, *Bowett's Law of International Institutions*, London: Sweet & Maxwell, 6th edn, 2009.

Schachter, Oscar, *International Law in Theory and Practice*, Dordrecht: Martinus Nijhoff Publishers, 1991.

Schachter, Oscar and Joyner, Christopher, eds, *United Nations Legal Order*, Cambridge: Cambridge University Press, 1995.

Schermers, Henry and Blokker, Neils, *International Institutional Law*, Leiden: Martinus Nijhoff Publishers, 5th edn, 2011.

Schnyder, Félix, 'Les Aspects Juridiques Actuels du Problème des Réfugiés', 114 *Recueil des Cours*, Hague Academy of International Law 335 (1965).

Schwarzenberger, Georg, *A Manual of International Law*, London: Stevens, 5th edn, 1967.

Seyersted, Finn, *Common Law of International Organizations*, Leiden/Boston: Martinus Nijhoff Publishers, 2008.

Shaffer, Gregory, 'Can WTO Technical Assistance and Capacity-Building Serve Developing Countries?', 23 *Wisconsin International Law Journal* 643 (2005).

Shaw, Malcolm, *International Law*, Cambridge: Cambridge University Press, 6th edn, 2008.

Shelton, Dinah, ed., *Commitment and Compliance: The Role of Non-Binding Norms in the International Legal System*, Oxford: Oxford University Press, 2003.

Simma, Bruno, ed., *Charter of the United Nations: A Commentary*, Oxford: Oxford University Press, 2nd edn, 2002.

Simpson, John Hope, *The Refugee Problem: Report of a Survey*, London: Oxford University Press, 1939.

Sjöberg, Tommie, *The Powers and the Persecuted: The Refugee Problem and the Intergovernmental Committee On Refugees (IGCR), 1938–1947*, Lund: Lund University Press, 1991.

Slaughter, Anne-Marie, Tulumello, Andrew and Wood, Stepan, 'International Law and International Relations Theory: A New Generation of Interdisciplinary Scholarship', 92 *American Journal of International Law* 367 (1997).

Sloan, Blaine, 'General Assembly Resolutions Revisited (Forty Years Later)', 58 *British Yearbook of International Law* 39 (1987).

Smith, Peter Macalister and Alfredsson, Gudmundur, eds, *The Land Beyond: Collected Essays on Refugee Law and Policy by Atle Grahl-Madsen*, The Hague: Martinus Nijhoff Publishers, 2001.

Stavropolou, Maria, 'Influencing State Behaviour for Refugee Protection: UNHCR and the Design of the Refugee Protection Regime', UNHCR, *New Issues in Refugee Research*, Paper #154, (April 2008). Available at http://www.unhcr.org/481721302. html (accessed 27 October 2011).

Steiner, N., Gibney, M. and Loescher, G., *The UNHCR, Refugees and Human Rights*, New York: Routledge, 2003.

Sztucki, Jerzy, 'The Conclusions on the International Protection of Refugees Adopted by the Executive Committee of the UNHCR Programme', 1 *International Journal of Refugee Law* 285 (1989).

Travis, Alan, 'Shifting a Problem Back to its Source – Would-Be Refugees May be Sent to Protected Zones Near Homeland', *The Guardian*, 5 February 2003.

Travis, Alan, 'Straw Aims to Rewrite Treaty on Refugees', *The Guardian*, 8 June 2000.

Türk, Volker, 'UNHCR's Supervisory Responsibility', 14 *Revue Québécoise de Droit International* 135 (2001).

Van Hoof, G.J.H., *Rethinking the Sources of International Law*, London: Kluwer, 1983.

Verdirame, Guglielmo and Harrell-Bond, Barbara E., *Rights in Exile: Janus-Faced Humanitarianism*, Studies in Forced Migration, vol. 17, Oxford: Berghahn Books, 2005.

Vernant, Jacques, *The Refugee in the Post-War World*, New Haven, CT: Yale University Press, 1953.

Victor, D., Raustiala, K. and Skolnikoff, E., eds, *The Implementation and Effectiveness of International Environmental Commitments: Theory and Practice*, Cambridge, MA: MIT Press, 1998.

Watts, Arthur, *The International Law Commission: 1949–1998*, Oxford: Oxford University Press, 1999.

Weis, Paul, 'The United Nations Declaration on Territorial Asylum', VII *Canadian Yearbook of International Law* 92 (1969).

Weis, Paul, 'The 1967 Protocol Relating to the Status of Refugees and Some Questions of the Law of Treaties', 42 *British Yearbook of International Law* 39 (1967).

Weis, Paul, 'The United Nations Convention on the Reduction of Statelessness 1961', 11 *International and Comparative Law Quarterly* 1073 (1962).

Weis, Paul, 'The Hague Agreement Relating to Refugee Seamen', 7 *International and Comparative Law Quarterly* 334 (1958).

Weis, Paul, 'The international protection of refugees', 48 *American Journal of International Law* 193 (1954).

Zieck, Marjoleine, 'Doomed to Fail From the Outset? UNHCR's Convention Plus Initiative Revisited', 21 *International Journal of Refugee Law* 387 (2009).

Zieck, Marjoleine, 'Voluntary Repatriation: Paradigm, Pitfalls, Progress', 23 *Refugee Survey Quarterly* 33 (2004).

Zieck, Marjoleine, *UNHCR and Voluntary Repatriation of Refugees*, The Hague: Martinus Nijhoff Publishers, 1997.

Zoller, Elisabeth, 'Bilan de Recherches de la Section de Langue Française du Centre d'Étude et de Recherche de l'Académie', in *The Right of Asylum 1989*, Hague Academy of International Law 15 (1990).

UNHCR documents

Agenda for Protection (2003).

Agents of Persecution – UNHCR Position (14 March 1995). Available at http://www.unhcr.org/ refworld/docid/3ae6b31da3.html (accessed 27 October 2011).

Aide Memoire: Directive on Minimum Standards on Procedures for Granting and Withdrawing Refugee Status (18 November 2003). Available at http://www.unhcr.org/ protect/ PROTECTION/43661fd62.pdf (accessed 27 October 2011).

Background Note on the Application of the Exclusion Clauses: Article 1F of the 1951 Convention relating to the Status of Refugees (4 September 2003). Available at http:// www.unhcr.org/refworld/docid/3f5857d24.html (accessed 27 October 2011).

Background Note on the Safe Country Concept and Refugee Status, UNHCR Doc. EC/SCP/68 (26 July 1991).

Background Paper on the Article 1F Exclusion Clauses, (June 1998) (on file with author).

Briefing Notes: UNHCR Welcomes South America/Mercosur Declaration (17 November 2000). Available at http://www.unhcr.org/news/NEWS/3ae6b82358.html (accessed 27 October 2011).

The Cessation Clauses: Guidelines on Their Application (26 April 1999). Available at http://www.unhcr.org/refworld/docid/3c06138c4.html (accessed 27 October 2011).

Collection of International Instruments and Legal Texts Concerning Refugees and Others of Concern to UNHCR (June 2007).

Collection of International Instruments and Other Legal Texts Concerning Refugees and Displaced Persons (December 1995).

Collection of International Instruments Concerning Refugees (1979).

Colloquium on the Development in the Law of Refugees with Particular Reference to the 1951 Convention and the Statute of the Office of the United Nations High Commissioner for Refugees held at Villa Serbelloni Bellagio (Italy) from 21–28 April 1965: Background Paper submitted by the Office of the United Nations High Commissioner for Refugees (1965). Available at http://www.unhcr.org/protect/PROTECTION/3ae68be77.html (accessed 27 October 2011).

Colloquium on the Legal Aspects of Refugee Problems (Note by the High Commissioner), Annex I, U.N. Doc. A/AC.96/INF.40 (5 May 1965).

Comments on Articles 48 and 48 bis of the Draft Council of Europe Convention on Preventing and Combating Violence against Women and Domestic Violence, November 2010. Available at http://www.unhcr.org/4cf4fb2d9.html (accessed 27 October 2011).

Comments to the First Meeting of the Ad Hoc Committee on Preventing and Combating Violence Against Women and Domestic Violence, 6–8 April 2009. Available at http://www.coe.int/t/dghl/standardsetting/violence/UNHCR%20comments%20to%20CAHVIO.pdf (accessed 27 October 2011).

Complementary Forms of Protection (April 2001) (on file with author).

Complementary Forms of Protection: Their Nature and Relationship to the International Refugee Protection Regime, UNHCR Doc. EC/50/SC/CRP.18 (9 June 2000).

Considerations on the 'Safe Third Country' Concept (July 1966). Available at http://www.unhcr.org/refworld/docid/3ae6b3268.html (accessed 27 October 2011).

Convention Plus at a Glance (1 June 2005). Available at http://www.unhcr.org/cgi-bin/texis/vtx/search?page=search&docid=403b30684&query=Convention%20Plus%20at%20a%20Glance (accessed 27 October 2011).

Current Asylum Issues, UNHCR/IOM/28/92; UNHCR/FOM/29/92 (13 March 1992).

Detention of Asylum-Seekers and Refugees: The Framework, The Problem and Recommended Practice, UNHCR Doc. EC/49/SC/CRP.13 (4 June 1999).

Determination of Refugee Status of Persons connected with Organizations or Groups which Advocate and/or Practise Violence, UNHR/IOM/16/78; UNHCR/BOM/16/78 (5 April 1978).

Determination of Refugee Status of Persons connected with Organizations or Groups which Advocate and/or Practise Violence, UNHCR/IOM/78/88; UNHCR/FOM/71/88 (1 June 1988).

The Exclusion Clauses: Guidelines on Their Application (2 December 1996). Available at http://www.unhcr.org/refworld/docid/3ae6b31d9f.html (accessed 27 October 2011).

EXCOM Conclusions (see following list).

Extradition, UNHCR/IOM/23/68; UNHCR/BOM/29/68 (26 June 1968).

Final Report Concerning the Questionnaire on Statelessness Pursuant to the Agenda for Protection: Steps Taken by States to Reduce Statelessness and to Meet the Protection Needs of Stateless Persons (March 2004). Available at http://www.unhcr.org/protect/PROTECTION/4047002e4.pdf (accessed 27 October 2011).

Follow-up on Earlier Conclusions of the Sub-Committee on the Determination of Refugee Status, inter alia, with Reference to the Role of UNHCR in National Refugee

Status Determination Procedure, UNHCR Doc. EC/SCP/22/Rev.1 (3 September 1982).

Gender-related Persecution (January 2000). Available at http://www.unhcr.org/refworld/docid/3bd3f2b04.html (accessed 27 October 2011).

Global Report 2000 (June 2001).

Guidelines on Applicable Criteria and Standards relating to the Detention of Asylum Seekers (February 1999). Available at http://www.unhycr.org/refworld/docid/3c2b3f844.html (accessed 27 October 2011).

Guidelines on International Protection No. 2: 'Membership of a Particular Social Group' Within the Context of Article 1A(2) of the 1951 Convention and/or its 1967 Protocol Relating to the Status of Refugees, UNHCR Doc. HCR/GIP/02/02 (7 May 2002).

Guidelines on International Protection No. 3: Cessation of Refugee Status under Article 1C(5) and (6) of the 1951 Convention Relating to the Status of Refugees (the 'Ceased Circumstances' Clauses) UNHCR Doc. HCR/GIP/03/03 (10 February 2003).

Guidelines on International Protection No. 5, Application of the Exclusion Clauses: Article 1F of the 1951 Convention Relating to the Status of Refugees, UNHCR Doc. HCR/GIP/03/05 (4 September 2003).

Guidelines on International Protection: The Application of Article 1A(2) of the 1951 Convention/1967 Protocol Relating to the Status of Refugees to Victims of Trafficking and Persons at Risk of being Trafficked, UNHCR Doc. HCR/GIP/06/07 (7 April 2006),

Guidelines on International Protection: Gender-Related Persecution within the Context of Article 1A(2) of the 1951 Convention and/or its 1967 Protocol Relating to the Status of Refugees, UNHCR Doc. HCR/GIP/02/01 (7 May 2002).

Guidelines on International Protection: 'Membership of a Particular Social Group' within the Context of Article 1A(2) of the 1951 Convention and/or its 1967 Protocol Relating to the Status of Refugees, UNHCR Doc. HCR/GIP/02/02 (7 May 2002).

Guidelines on Policies and Procedures in Dealing with Unaccompanied Children Seeking Asylum (February 1997). Available at http://www.unhcr.org/refworld/docid/3ae6b3360.html (accessed 27 October 2011).

Handbook on Procedures and Criteria for Determining Refugee Status, UNHCR Doc. HCR/IP/4/Eng./Rev.1 (January 1992).

Handbook on Procedures and Criteria for Determining Refugee Status, UNHCR/BOM/66/80 (31 October 1980).

Handbook for the Protection of Women and Girls (January 2008). Available at http://www.unhcr.org/refworld/docid/47cfc2962.html (accessed 27 October 2011).

Handbook: Voluntary Repatriation: International Protection (1996). Available at http://www.unhcr.org/pub/PUBL/3bfe68d32.pdf (accessed 27 October 2011).

Human Rights and Refugee Protection, Self-Study Module 5, vols 1 and 2 (15 December 2006).

Human Rights and Refugee Protection, Training Module RLD 5 (October 1995).

Implementation of the 1951 Convention and the 1967 Protocol Relating to the Status of Refugees, UNHCR Doc. EC/SCP/54 (7 July 1989).

Implementation of the 1951 Convention and the 1967 Protocol Relating to the Status of Refugees – Some Basic Questions, UNHCR Doc. EC/1992/SC.2/CRP.10 (15 June 1992).

Information Note on Implementation of the 1951 Convention and the 1967 Protocol Relating to the Status of Refugees, UNHCR Doc. EC/SCP/66 (22 July 1991).

Information and Accession Package: The 1954 Convention Relating to the Status of Stateless Persons and the 1961 Convention on the Reduction of Statelessness (2nd edn, 1999). Available at http://www.unhcr.org/protect/PROTECTION/3dc69f1d4.pdf (accessed 27 October 2011).

Interpreting Article 1 of the 1951 Convention Relating to the Status of Refugees (April 2001). Available at http://www.unhcr.org/refworld/docid/3b20a3914.html (accessed 27 October 2011).

Legal Bulletin No. 5, UNHCR/IOM/26/65; UNHCR/BOM/32/65 (15 December 1965).

Letter from High Commissioner Schnyder to Ambassador Baron C.H. von Platen, Permanent Representative of Sweden to the European Office of the United Nations (UNHCR archives and on file with author).

Letter from UNHCR and the Office of the Director-General of the International Refugee Organization (26 April 1951) (UNHCR archives and on file with author).

Membership of a Particular Social Group, UNHCR/IOM/132/89; UNHCR/FOM/110/89 (12 December 1989).

Memorandum from Gilbert Jaeger (Director of Protection) to the UNHCR Regional Representative at UN Headquarters, New York, concerning 'Possible Convention on the Rights of the Child' (16 October 1978) (UNHCR archives and on file with author).

Memorandum from Mr P.M. Moussallli, Director of International Protection, to G.J.L. Coles, Chief, Conference and Treaties Section, concerning Report on the Elaboration of the ILO Convention concerning the Establishment of an International System for the Maintenance of Rights in Social Security (12 July 1982) and attached *Memorandum from N. Cronstedt to G.J.L. Coles, Chief, Conference and Treaties Section, concerning Report on the Elaboration of the ILO Convention concerning the Establishment of an International System for the Maintenance of Rights in Social Security* (25 June 1991) (both documents are available in the UNHCR archives and are on file with author).

Memorandum from the UNHCR, submitted to the United Nations Conference on Consular Relations, U.N. Doc. A/CONF.25/L.6 (4 March 1963).

Ministerial Meeting of States Parties to the 1951 Convention Relating to the Status of Refugees and UNHCR's Global Consultations on International Protection: Background (11 December 2001). Available at http://www.unhcr.org/protect/PROTECTION/3c1622ab4.pdf (accessed 27 October 2011).

Note by the United Nations High Commissioner for Human Rights, International Organization for Migration, United Nations High Commissioner for Refugees, and the United Nations Children's Fund on the Protocols concerning Migrant Smuggling and Trafficking in Persons (21 February–3 March 2000) (on file with author).

Note on Burden and Standard of Proof in Refugee Claims (16 December 1998). Available at http://www.unhcr.org/refworld/docid/3ae6b3338.html (accessed 27 October 2011).

Note on Certain Aspects of Sexual Violence Against Refugee Women, U.N. Doc. A/AC.96/822 (12 October 1993).

Note on Cessation Clauses, UNHCR Doc. EC/47/SC/CRP.30 (30 May 1997).

Note on Determination of Refugee Status under International Instruments, UNHCR Doc. EC/SCP/5 (24 August 1977).

Note on International Protection, U.N. Doc. A/AC.96/377 (6 September 1967).

Note on International Protection, U.N. Doc. A/AC.96/398 (9 September 1968).

Note on International Protection Addendum 2: Implementation of the 1951 Convention and 1967 Protocol on the Status of Refugees – Preliminary Report, U.N. Doc. A/AC.96/508/Add.2 (26 September 1974).

Note on International Protection, U.N. Doc. A/AC.96/527 (20 September 1976).

Note on International Protection, U.N. Doc. A/AC.96/579 (11 August 1980).

Note on International Protection, U.N. Doc. A/AC.96/593 (31 July 1981).

Note on International Protection, U.N. Doc. A/AC.96/609/Rev.1 (26 August 1982).

Note on International Protection, U.N. Doc. A/AC.96/623 (31 July 1983).

Note on International Protection, U.N. Doc. A/AC.96/643 (9 August 1984).

Note on International Protection, U.N. Doc. A/AC.96/660 (23 July 1985).

Note on International Protection, U.N. Doc. A/AC.96/680 (5 July 1986).

Note on International Protection, U.N. Doc. A/AC.96/694 (3 August 1987).

Note on International Protection, U.N. Doc. A/AC.96/713 (15 August 1988).

Note on International Protection, U.N. Doc. A/AC.96/728 (2 August 1989).

Note on International Protection, U.N. Doc. A/AC.96/750 (27 August 1990).

Note on International Protection, U.N. Doc. A/AC.96/830 (7 September 1994).

Note on International Protection, U.N. Doc. A/AC.96/930 (7 July 2000)

Note on International Protection, U.N. Doc. A/AC.96/951, (13 September 2001).

Note on International Protection, U.N. Doc. A/AC.96/989 (7 July 2004).

Note on International Protection, U.N. Doc. A/AC.96/1008 (4 July 2005).

Note on International Protection, U.N. Doc. A/AC.96/1024 (12 July 2006).

Note on International Protection, U.N. Doc. A/AC.96/1038 (29 June 2007).

Note on International Protection, U.N. Doc. A/AC.96/1085 (30 June 2010).

Note on International Protection, U.N. Doc. A/AC.96/1098 (28 June 2011).

Note on Loss of Refugee Status Through Cancellation (4 July 1989). Available at http://www.unhcr.org/refworld/docid/441045d44.html (accessed 27 October 2011).

Note on Refugee Women and International Protection, UNHCR Doc. EC/SCP/59 (28 August 1990).

Note on the Exclusion Clauses, UNHCR Doc. EC/47/SC/CRP.29 (30 May 1997).

A Practical Guide to Capacity Building as a Feature of UNHCR's Humanitarian Programmes (September 1999). Available at http://www.unhcr.org/3bbd64845.pdf (accessed 27 October 2011).

Procedural Standards for Refugee Status Determination under UNHCR's Mandate (1 September 2005). Available at http://www.unhcr.org/pub/PUBL/4317223c9.pdf (accessed 27 October 2011).

Protection Gaps Framework for Analysis: Enhancing Protection of Refugees: Strengthening Protection Capacity Project (SPCP) (2008). Available at http://www.unhcr.org/41fe3ab92.pdf (accessed 27 October 2011).

Protection of Persons of Concern to UNHCR who Fall Outside the 1951 Convention: A Discussion Note, UNHCR Doc. EC/1992/SCP/CRP.5 (2 April 1992).

Protection of Refugees in Mass Influx Situations: Overall Protection Framework, UNHCR Doc. EC/GC/01/4 (19 February 2001).

Question of 'Freedom Fighters' and Liberation Movements in Africa, UNHCR/IOM/22/68; UNHCR/BOM/26/68 (June 1968).

Refugees in Civil War Situations, UNHCR/IOM/138/89; UNHCR/FOM/114/89 (18 December 1989).

Report of the UNHCR, U.N. Doc. A/2011(1951).

Report of the UNHCR and Addendum, U.N. Doc. A/2126 (1952).

Report of the UNHCR, U.N. Doc. A/2394 (1953).

Report of the UNHCR, U.N. Doc. A/2648 (1954).

Report of the UNHCR, U.N. Doc. A/2902 and Add.1 (1955).

Report of the UNHCR, U.N. Doc. A/3123/Rev.1 (1956).

Report of the UNHCR, U.N. Doc. A/3585/Rev.1 (1957).

Report of the UNHCR, U.N. Doc. A/3828/Rev.1 (1958).

Report of the UNHCR, U.N. Doc. A/4104/Rev.1 (1959)

Report of the UNHCR, U.N. Doc. A/5211/Rev.1 (1962).

Report of the UNHCR, U.N. Doc. A/5511/Rev.1 (1964).

Report of the UNHCR, Addendum, U.N. Doc. A/5811/Rev.1/Add.1 (1964).

Report of the UNHCR, U.N. Doc. A/7612 (1969).

Report of the UNHCR, U.N. Doc. A/8012 (1970).

Report of the UNHCR, U.N. Doc. A/34/12 (1979).

Report of the UNHCR, U.N. Doc. A/36/12 (1981).

Report of the UNHCR, U.N. Doc. A/37/12 (1982).

Report of the UNHCR, U.N. Doc. A/47/12 (1992).

Report of the UNHCR, U.N. Doc. A/62/12 (2007).

Report on International Protection, U.N. Doc. A/AC.96/227 (3 March 1964).

The Reunification of Refugee Families, UNHCR/IOM/52/83; UNHCR/FOM/49/83 (18 July 1983).

A Review of Capacity Building in Central and Eastern Europe (August 1996). Available at http://www.unhcr.org/research/RESEARCH/3ae6bcf44.html (accessed 27 October 2011).

Review of Selected Issues for Future Consideration of the Sub-Committee of the Whole on International Protection, UNHCR Doc. EC/SCP/56 (28 July 1989).

Review of the Use of UNHCR Executive Committee Conclusions on International Protection, PDES/2008/03 (UNHCR Policy Development and Evaluation Service, 10 April 2008).

The State of the World's Refugees 2000: Fifty Years of Humanitarian Action (2000).

The State of the World's Refugees: A Humanitarian Agenda (1997).

States Parties to the 1951 Convention Relating to the Status of Refugees and the 1967 Protocol, (as of 1 November 2007). Available at http://www.unhcr.org/protect/ PROTECTION/ 3b73b0d63.pdf (accessed 27 October 2011).

Status of Guineans (Bissau) Abroad, UNHCR/IOM/38/75; UNHCR/BOM/48/75 (1 December 1975).

Status of Mozambicans Abroad after 25 June 1975, UNHCR/IOM/36/75; UNHCR/ BOM/47/75 (14 November 1975).

Strengthening Protection Capacities in Host Countries, UNHCR Doc. EC/GC/01/19 (19 April 2002).

R (Saeedi) v. Secretary of State for the Home Department – Submissions by UNHCR (15 February 2010). Available at http://refworld/docid/4b83fceb2.html (accessed 27 October 2011).

Thematic Compilation of Executive Committee Conclusions (6th edn, June 2011). Available at http://www.unhcr.org/3d4ab3ff2.html (accessed 27 October 2011).

UNHCR Advisory Regarding the Return of Iraqis, September 2005. Available at http:// www.unhcr.org/cgi-bin/texis/vtx/refworld/rwmain?docid=432a89d54.

UNHCR Policy on Refugee Children, UNHCR Doc. EC/SCP/82 (6 August 1993).

UNHCR Position Paper: Relocating Internally as a Reasonable Alternative to Seeking Asylum (The So-Called 'Internal Flight Alternative' or 'Relocation Principle')

(9 February 1999). Available at http://www.unhcr.org/refworld/docid/3ae6b336c.html (accessed 27 October 2011).

UNHCR Position: Visa Requirements and Carrier Sanctions (September 1995). Available at http://www.unhcr.org/refworld/docid/3ae6b33a10.html (accessed 27 October 2011).

Self-Study Module 1: An Introduction to International Protection: Protecting Persons of Concern to UNHCR (1 August 2005). Available at http://www.unhcr.org/refworld/docid/ 4214cb4f2.html (accessed 27 October 2011).

UNHCR Statement on the Right to an Effective Remedy in Relation to Accelerated Asylum Procedures. (Issued in the Context of the Preliminary Ruling Reference to the Court of Justice of the European Union from the Luxembourg Administrative Tribunal Regarding the Interpretation of Article 39, Asylum Procedures Directive (APD); and Articles 6 and 13 ECHR) (21 May 2010). Available at http://www.unhcr.org/refworld/docid/4bf67fa12.html (accessed 27 October 2011).

UNHCR Summary Position on the Protocol against the Smuggling of Migrants by Land, Sea and Air and the Protocol to Prevent, Suppress and Punish Trafficking in Persons, Especially Women and Children, supplementing the UN Convention against Transnational Organized Crime (11 December 2000). Available at http://www.unhcr.org/refworld/docid/ 3ae6b3428.html (accessed 27 October 2011).

UNHCR Tool Boxes on EU Asylum Matters: Tool Box 1: The Fundamentals (November 2003). Available at http:/www.unhcr.org/publ/PUBL/406a8aa11.pdf (accessed 27 October 2011).

UNHCR Tool Boxes on EU Asylum Matters: Tool Box 2: The Instruments (September 2002). Available at http://www.unhcr.org/publ/PUBL/406a8c432.pdf (accessed 27 October 2011).

UNHCR's Position on Certain Types of Draft Evasion (22 January 1991). Available at http://www.unhcr.org/refworld/docid/441025c44.html (accessed 27 October 2011).

UNHCR's Role in National Legal and Judicial Capacity-Building, UNHCR Doc. EC/46/SC/CRP.31 (28 May 1996).

Voluntary Repatriation: Principles and Guidelines for Action, UNHCR/IOM/5/87; UNHCR/FOM/5/87 (10 February 1987).

The Queen on the Application of Al Rawi and Others (Appellants) and (1) the Secretary of State for Foreign and Commonwealth Affairs and (2) the Secretary of State for the Home Department (Respondents) and the Office of the United Nations High Commissioner for Refugees (Intervener). Written Submissions on Behalf of the Intervener (UNHCR), (12 July 2006). Available at http://www.unhcr.org/refworld/docid/45c350974.html (accessed 27 October 2011).

UNHCR and International Criminal Tribunal for Rwanda, *Expert Meeting on Complementarities between International Refugee Law, International Criminal Law and International Humanitarian Law*, Arusha, Tanzania, 11–13 April 2011. Available at http://www.unhcr.org/refworld/docid/4e1729d52.html (accessed 27 October 2011).

UNHCR EXCOM conclusions

EXCOM Conclusion 1 (XXVI) 1975.
EXCOM Conclusion 2 (XXVII) 1976.
EXCOM Conclusion 5 (XXVIII) 1977.

EXCOM Conclusion 7 (XXVIII) 1977.
EXCOM Conclusion 8 (XXVIII) 1977.
EXCOM Conclusion 11 (XXIX) 1978.
EXCOM Conclusion 12 (XXIX) 1978.
EXCOM Conclusion 13 (XXIX) 1978.
EXCOM Conclusion 15 (XXX) 1979.
EXCOM Conclusion 16 (XXXI) 1980.
EXCOM Conclusion 19 (XXXI) 1980.
EXCOM Conclusion 21 (XXXII) 1981.
EXCOM Conclusion 22 (XXXII) 1981.
EXCOM Conclusion 25 (XXXIII) 1982.
EXCOM Conclusion 28 (XXXIII) 1982.
EXCOM Conclusion 29 (XXXIV) 1983.
EXCOM Conclusion 30 (XXXIV) 1983.
EXCOM Conclusion 33 (XXV) 1984.
EXCOM Conclusion 36 (XXXVI) 1985.
EXCOM Conclusion 39 (XXXVI) 1985.
EXCOM Conclusion 40 (XXXVI) 1985.
EXCOM Conclusion 41 (XXXVII) 1986.
EXCOM Conclusion 42 (XXXVII) 1986.
EXCOM Conclusion 43 (XXXVII) 1986.
EXCOM Conclusion 44 (XXXVII) 1986.
EXCOM Conclusion 46 (XXXVIII) 1987.
EXCOM Conclusion 48 (XXXVIII) 1987.
EXCOM Conclusion 51 (XXXIX) 1988.
EXCOM Conclusion 57 (XL) 1989.
EXCOM Conclusion 58 (XL) 1989.
EXCOM Conclusion 59 (XL) 1989.
EXCOM Conclusion 60 (XL) 1989.
EXCOM Conclusion 61 (XLI) 1990.
EXCOM Conclusion 62 (XLI) 1990.
EXCOM Conclusion 64 (XLI) 1990.
EXCOM Conclusion 65 (XLII) 1991.
EXCOM Conclusion 68 (XLIII) 1992.
EXCOM Conclusion 71 (XLIV) 1993.
EXCOM Conclusion 73 (XLIV) 1993.
EXCOM Conclusion 74 (XLV) 1994.
EXCOM Conclusion 77 (XLVI) 1995.
EXCOM Conclusion 78 (XLVI) 1995.
EXCOM Conclusion 79 (XLVII) 1996.
EXCOM Conclusion 81 (XLVIII) 1997.
EXCOM Conclusion 84 (XLVIII) 1997.
EXCOM Conclusion 85 (XLIX) 1998.
EXCOM Conclusion 87 (L) 1999.
EXCOM Conclusion 89 (LI) 2000.
EXCOM Conclusion 90 (LII) 2001.
EXCOM Conclusion 91 (LII) 2001.
EXCOM Conclusion 93 (LIII) 2002.

EXCOM Conclusion 94 (LIII) 2002.
EXCOM Conclusion 95 (LIV) 2003.
EXCOM Conclusion 98 (LIV) 2003.
EXCOM Conclusion 99 (LV) 2004.
EXCOM Conclusion 100 (LV) 2004.
EXCOM Conclusion 101 (LV) 2004.
EXCOM Conclusion 102 (LVI) 2005.
EXCOM Conclusion 104 (LVI) 2005.
EXCOM Conclusion 105 (LVII) 2006.
EXCOM Conclusion 106 (LVII) 2006.
EXCOM Conclusion 107 (LVIII) 2007.
EXCOM Conclusion 108 (LIX) 2008.
EXCOM Conclusion 109 (LX) 2009.

Other documents

Circular Letter by the Secretary-General to All States concerned in the Question of 7 July 1921, 2 O.J.L.N. 485–486 (1921).
Commission on Human Rights Res. 1998/49, U.N. Doc. E/CN.4/RES/1998/49 (17 April 1998).
Commission on Human Rights Res. 2005/48, U.N. Doc. E/CN.4/RES/2005/48 (19 April 2005).
Compilation of General Comments and General Recommendations Adopted by Human Rights Treaty Bodies, U.N. Doc. HRI/GEN/1/Rev.7 (2004).
Constitution of the International Labour Organization. Available at http://www.ilo.org/ilolex/english/constq.html (accessed 27 October 2011).
Constitution of the International Refugee Organization, and Agreement on Interim Measures to be Taken in Respect of Refugees and Displaced Persons, G.A. Res. 62(I), U.N. Doc. A/RES/62(I) (15 December 1946).
Constitution of the United Nations Educational, Scientific and Cultural Organization (UNESCO). Available at http://www.icomos.org/unesco/unesco_constitution.html (accessed 27 October 2011).
Constitution of the World Health Organization. Available at http://www.who.int/governance/eb/ who_constitution_en.pdf (accessed 27 October 2011).
Council of League of Nations, International Assistance to Refugees Report of the Committee appointed by the Council, 17 O.J.L.N. 126–129 (1936).
Council of League of Nations, International Assistance to Refugees, 19 O.J.L.N. 367–368 (1938).
E.S.C. Res. 248 (IX) (1949).
E.S.C. Res. 672 (XXV), U.N. Doc. E/3123 (1958).
Final Act of the 1951 United Nations Conference of Plenipotentiaries on the Status of Refugees and Stateless Persons, 25 July 1951, 189 U.N.T.S. 137.
Final Communique of the 42nd Ordinary Session of The African Commission on Human and Peoples' Rights Held in Brazzaville, Republic of Congo, from 15–28 November 2007. Available at http://www.achpr.org/english/communiques/communique42_en.html (accessed 27 October 2011).
France: *Draft Resolution*, U.N. Doc. A/C.3/L.26 (11 November 1949)
Guiding Principles on Internal Displacement, U.N. Doc. E/CN.4/1998/53/Add2 (22nd July 1998).

High Commissioner of the League, *Report on the Work accomplished up to 15 March 1922*, 3 O.J.L.N. 385–394 (1922).

Inter-Parliamentary Union and UNHCR, *Refugee Protection: A Guide to International Refugee Law* (2001). Available at http://www.unhcr.org/publ/PUBL/3d4aba564.pdf (accessed 27 October 2011).

International Assistance to Refugees: Action Taken on the Initiative of the President of the United States of America, Work of the Intergovernmental Committee, Annex: Resolution Adopted by the Intergovernmental Committee (Evian) on July 14th 1938, League of Nations Doc. C. 244.M.143.1938.XII (1938).

International Law Commission, *Report of the International Law Commission*, 61st Session, 2009, U.N. GAOR, 64th Sess., Supp. No. 10, (A/64/10).

International Law Commission, *Report of the International Law Commission*, 62nd Session (2010) U.N. GAOR, 65th Sess., Supp. No. 10, A/65/10.

Letter from the President of the Comité International de la Croix-Rouge of 20 February 1921, 2 O.J.L.N. 227 (1921).

Memorandum by the Secretary-General of 16 March 1921, 2 O.J.L.N. 225–256 (1921).

Memorandum from the Comité International de la Croix-Rouge at Geneva to the Council of the League of Nations of 20 February 1921, 2 O.J.L.N. 228–229 (1921).

Note by the Secretary General, U.N. Doc. A/C.3/528 (26 October 1949).

Presidency of the European Union, *Austrian Strategy Paper on Immigration and Asylum*, 9809/98 (13 July 1998).

Refugee Rights Network, *APPRN Joint Statement on the Australia–Malaysia Refugee Swap Agreement* (17 May 2001). Available at http://refugeerightsasiapacific.org/2011/05/17/ aprrn-joint-statement-on-the-australia-malaysia-refugee-swap-agreement/ (accessed 27 October 2011).

Report by Mr. Hanotaux, adopted on 27 June 1921, 2 O.J.L.N.755–758 (1921)

Report of the Council Committee Appointed to Draw Up a Plan for International Assistance to Refugees, 19 O.J.L.N. 365–366 (1938).

Report of the Secretary-General, U.N. Doc. A/C.3/527 and Corr.1 (26 October 1949).

S.C. Res. 827, U.N. Doc. S/RES/827 (25 May 1993) Concerning the Establishment of the International Tribunal for the Prosecution of Persons Responsible for Serious Violations of International Humanitarian Law Committed in the Territory of the Former Yugoslavia since 1991.

S.C. Res. 955, U.N. Doc. S/RES/955 (8 November 1994) Concerning the Establishment of an International Criminal Tribunal for Rwanda.

Special Rapporteur on Housing and Property Restitution, The Return of Refugees or Displaced Persons' Property, U.N. Doc. E/CN.4/Sub.2/2002/17 (12 June 2002).

Statute of the Office of the United Nations High Commissioner for Refugees, contained in the Annex to UN General Assembly Resolution 428(V) of 14 December 1950. G.A. Res. 428(V) (14 December 1950).

Statutes of the Nansen International Office for Refugees, 12 O.J.L.N. 309–311 (1931).

Sub-Comm. on Promotion and Protection of Human Rights, 2001/122 (16 August 2001).

The Secretary-General, *A Study of Statelessness, Submitted to ECOSOC*, U.N. Doc. E/1112 (August 1949).

United Kingdom CO/HO Future of Migration Project, *A New Vision for Refugees*, Final Report, January 2003.

United Nations Charter.

U.N. GAOR, 4th Sess., 256th plen. mtg. (4 November 1949).

U.N. GAOR, 4th Sess., 257th plen., 3rd cee mtg. (8 November 1949).

U.N. GAOR, 4th Sess., 258th plen., 3rd cee mtg. (9 November 1949).
U.N. GAOR, 4th Sess., 264th plen. mtg. (2 December 1949).
U.N. GAOR, 4th Sess., 265th plen. mtg. (3 December 1949).
United States of America: *Draft Resolution*, U.N. Doc. A/C.3/L.28 (11 November 1949).
Work of the Inter-Governmental Advisory Commission for Refugees during its Eighth Session, submitted to the Council of the League of Nations on 20 January 1936, 17 O.J.L.N. 140 (1936).

United Nations General Assembly resolutions

G.A. Res. 8 (I) (1946).
G.A. Res. 174 (II) (21 November 1947).
G.A. Res. 319 (IV) (3 December 1949).
G.A. Res. 428 (V) (14 December 1950).
G.A. Res. 1166 (XII) (26 November 1957).
G.A. Res. 1167 (XII) (26 November 1957).
G.A. Res. 1784 (XVII) (7 December 1962).
G.A. Res. 2312 (XXII) (14 December 1967).
G.A. Res. 3274 (XXIX) (10 December 1974).
G.A. Res. 31/36, U.N. Doc. A/RES/31/36 (30 November 1976).
G.A. Res. 35/42, U.N. Doc. A/RES/35/42 (25 November 1980).
G.A. Res. 36/125, U.N. Doc. A/RES/36/125 (14 December 1981).
G.A. Res. 39/139, U.N. Doc. A/RES/ 39/139 (14 December 1984).
G.A. Res. 39/140, U.N. Doc. A/RES/ 39/140 (14 December 1984).
G.A. Res. 40/118, U.N. Doc. A/RES/40/118 (13 December 1985).
G.A. Res. 42/109, U.N. Doc. A/RES/42/109 (7 December 1987).
G.A. Res. 42/144, U.N. Doc. A/RES/42/144 (7 December 1987).
G.A. Res. 43/117, U.N. Doc. A/RES/43/117 (8 December 1988).
G.A. Res. 43/154, U.N. Doc. A/RES/43/154 (8 December 1988).
G.A. Res. 44/137, U.N. Doc. A/RES/44/137 (15 November 1989).
G.A. Res. 44/164, U.N. Doc. A/RES/44/164 (15 November 1989).
G.A. Res. 45/40, U.N. Doc. A/RES/45/40 (28 November 1990).
G.A. Res. 45/140, U.N. Doc. A/RES/45/140 (14 December 1990).
G.A. Res. 45/153, U.N. Doc. A/RES/45/153 (18 December 1990).
G.A. Res. 46/106, U.N. Doc. A/RES/46/106 (16 December 1991).
G.A. Res. 46/127, U.N. Doc. A/RES/46/127 (17 December 1991).
G.A. Res. 47/105, U.N. Doc. A/RES/ 47/105 (16 December 1992).
G.A. Res. 48/116, U.N. Doc. A/RES/48/116 (20 December 1993).
G.A. Res. 49/169, U.N. Doc. A/RES/ 49/169 (23 December 1994).
G.A. Res. 50/149, U.N. Doc. A/RES/50/149 (21 December 1995).
G.A. Res. 50/152, U.N. Doc. A/RES/50/152 (21 December 1995).
G.A. Res. 50/182, U.N. Doc. A/RES/50/182 (22 December 1995).
G.A. Res. 51/75, U.N. Doc. A/RES/51/75 (12 December 1996).
G.A. Res. 52/103, U.N. Doc. A/RES/52/103 (12 December 1997).
G.A. Res. 53/125, U.N. Doc. A/RES/53/125 (9 December 1998).
G.A. Res. 54/146 U.N. Doc. A/RES/54/146 (17 December 1999).
G.A. Res. 54/180, U.N. Doc. A/RES/54/180 (17 December 1999).
G.A. Res. 55/74, U.N. Doc. A/RES/ 55/74 (4 December 2000).
G.A. Res. 56/135, U.N. Doc. A/RES/56/135 (19 December 2001).

G.A. Res. 56/136, U.N. Doc. A/RES/ 56/136 (19 December 2001).
G.A. Res. 56/137, U.N. Doc. A/RES/56/137 (19 December 2001).
G.A. Res. 56/166, U.N. Doc. A/RES/56/166 (19 December 2001).
G.A. Res. 57/183, U.N. Doc. A/RES/ 57/183 (18 December 2002).
G.A. Res. 57/187, U.N. Doc. A/RES/57/187 (18 December 2002).
G.A. Res. 58/150, U.N. Doc. A/RES/58/150 (22 December 2003).
G.A. Res. 58/151, U.N. Doc. A/RES/58/151 (22 December 2003).
G.A. Res. 59/170, U.N. Doc. A/RES/59/170 (20 December 2004).
G.A. Res. 60/129, U.N. Doc. A/RES/60/129 (16 December 2005).
G.A. Res. 61/137, U.N. Doc. A/RES/61/137 (19 December 2006).
G.A. Res. 62/124, U.N. Doc. A/RES/62/124 (18 December 2007).
G.A. Res. 64/127, U.N. Doc. A/RES/64/127 (18 December 2009).
G.A. Res. 65/194, U.N. Doc. A/RES/65/194 (21 December 2010).

Index

academics/academic institutions 61, 68, 75, 76–7, 113, 152, 153, 157
accession *see* ratification/accession
Africa 34, 40, 47–8, 65; African Commission on Human and People's Rights 147–8; African Union (previously Organization of African Unity) 28, 34–5, 68, 87–8, 103, 111; Algerian refugees 27–8; capacity-building activities 140
agents of persecution 71
airports 71, 95
Akehurst, M. 123
Algerian refugees 27–8
aliens, expulsion of 90, 91–2
Allain, J. 124
Allande, D. 61
Alvarez, J.E. 62
amicus curiae briefs 144, 150–1, 155, 168
Annual Protection reports 142–3, 155
appeals 83, 116
application of international law obligations *see* supervisory role
Arboleda, E. 34
Armenian refugees 3, 5, 6–7, 16–17
artistic rights 103
Asia 65, 93
assimilation 87
assistance to refugees 51, 109, 127–8
Assyrian refugees 3, 6–7
Assyro-Chaldean refugees 3, 6–7
asylum seekers 71, 79, 88–9, 98, 100, 130, 157, 164, 167, 169; 1951 Refugee Convention: articles directly applying to 67, 86; 1980s 81–2, 83, 99; capacity-building activities 140, 156; children 31, 72, 107; detention 37, 69, 72, 95, 119–21; end of Cold War 114; European Union 35, 48, 88, 90; extradition 66;

first country of asylum 64, 70, 84, 86, 162; human rights bodies 146–7; human rights instruments 31, 71–2, 106, 107, 108; ICCPR 106; non-embarkation of 83, 86; safe country of origin concept 71, 84, 116; safe third country concept 71, 84, 86, 95; supervisory role of UNHCR 43, 144; temporary protection 36, 67–8, 70, 88, 130, 167; see also *non-refoulement*; status determination
Austria 3, 8, 9, 64
autonomy 23, 85, 100, 108, 129–30, 155, 158, 163
aviation law 109

Baltic States 140
Barnett, L. 80
Belgium 46–7
Bem, K. 27, 65
benefit of the doubt 66
Betts, A. 127, 128
Beyani, C. 83, 168
bilateral agreements 10, 11
Blokker, N. 95
Botswana 94
Bowett, D.W. 90
burden and responsibility sharing 52, 130; Convention Plus initiative 126–8, 130, 164

camps for refugees 84, 109–10, 131, 153–4, 158
cancellation of refugee status 69–70
capacity-building activities 137–42, 153, 156–7, 165, 168
carrier sanctions 71, 83
Cartagena Declaration (1984) 68, 87–8, 111
Cassese, A. 40, 125–6, 143

Castañeda, J. 100, 123
Central America 65
Central European countries 140
cessation clauses to refugee status 68, 71,
    73, 86; *amicus curiae* briefs 150
children 31, 33, 148; accession to 1989
    Convention 134; 'best interests of the
    child' 108; Committee on the Rights
    of the Child 146, 147; detention of
    105; doctrinal positions 71–2, 107,
    122; education 84, 107, 129; EXCOM
    53; General Assembly 52; refugee law
    framework and 1989 Convention 106,
    107–8, 129
Chimini, B.S. 81
Chinese refugees 27
Chinkin, C.M. 62
civil wars 699
co-operation with States 64, 78–81,
    98–100, 152, 162, 166–7, 169;
    capacity-building activities 137–42,
    153, 156–7, 165, 168; divergence 81–5,
    99–100, 142, 162; support for supervi-
    sory role of UNHCR 143–5
Cold War 81, 114
Coles, G. 82
complementary protection 70, 71, 72, 130
compliance 37–8, 48; *see also* effective-
    ness of international refugee law
conflict, people fleeing 51, 68, 88, 109,
    167, 169
consular relations 32
Convention against Torture (1984) 105–7,
    128, 146–7
Convention Plus initiative 126–8, 130, 164
Council of Europe: women and domestic
    violence 31
crime, organized 32–3, 122, 134, 161
crimes against humanity 110, 168
crisis in refugee protection 76, 78, 98–101,
    162–5; changing relationships with
    States 78–85; weaknesses in means to
    ensure effectiveness of law 92–8;
    weaknesses in treaty framework 85–92
cultural, economic and social rights 131
customary international law 61, 98, 115,
    123–5, 164
Cyprus 140

definition of refugee: 1951 Refugee
    Convention 26–7, 34, 64–5; 1967
    Protocol 27–9; crisis in refugee
    protection 83, 86, 87–8, 162;
    doctrinal positions 64–5, 66, 68, 69,

70–1; exclusion clauses 71, 73, 83, 86,
    110, 118–19, 150, 164; gender-related
    persecution 31, 72, 117, 118, 168, 169;
    Handbook on Procedures and Criteria
    for Determining Refugee Status 66, 68,
    70, 74, 104, 147; IRO Constitution 9;
    particular social group 69, 73, 86, 90,
    117, 124; persecution *see separate
    entry*; regional agreements 87–8, 89–90;
    social security rights convention 32
delinquents 67
detention 37, 83, 84, 95; doctrinal
    positions 69, 72, 119–21, 164;
    human rights 104–5, 106
developing countries 141; restrictive
    measures 84
development of international refugee law
    23, 47, 49, 102–3, 109, 160, 166; 1951
    Refugee Convention 20–1, 25, 110–13,
    122, 128; contributions to treaties on
    refugees 25–9, 161; contributions to
    other instruments 29–37, 161; Conven-
    tion Plus initiative 126–8, 130, 164;
    gaps and ambiguities in treaty frame-
    work 37, 85–7, 100, 113–21, 162, 164,
    167; historical foundations 4–6, 7,
    9–11, 22, 161; human rights instruments
    104–9, 110–12, 128–9, 163, 164, 167;
    international criminal law 109, 110,
    111, 163–4; international humanitarian
    law 109–10, 111, 163–4; mandate of
    UNHCR 24; obstacles to completion of
    treaty framework 89–92, 100; regional
    agreements: different standards for
    different states 87–9, 111–12, 162–3;
    UNHCR doctrine influencing 121–6,
    129, 164; *see also* doctrinal positions
development-oriented assistance 51, 127–8
Dialogue on Protection Challenges
    159, 166
diplomatic protection 151
disabilities 146
discrimination 118, 134, 146
doctrinal positions 60–3, 113, 129, 131,
    143, 155, 156, 164; 1950–1966 63–5;
    1967–1981 65–8; 1982–1989 69–70;
    1990s 70–2; 2000 to present 72–3;
    academics 153; *amicus curiae* briefs
    150; authority for issuance of 73–5,
    76; capacity-building activities 141;
    children 71–2, 107, 122; clarifying
    ambiguities 116–21; compilation of
    167; documents prepared for EXCOM
    and General Assembly 66–7, 68, 76;

Torture (1984) 106–7, 128; doctrinal positions 67, 69, 124–5, 164; general principle of law 126
non-State actors 118

Organization of African Unity (now African Union) 28, 34–5, 68, 87–8, 103, 111
Organization of the Islamic Conference 148
organized crime 32–3, 122, 134, 161

Pakistan 93
Papua New Guinea 94
'particular social group' 69, 73, 86, 90, 117, 124
Perluss, D. 124
persecution: agents of 71; gender-related 31, 72, 117, 118, 168, 169; human rights violations 104; International Criminal Tribunals for the Former Yugoslavia and Rwanda 168–9
Pinheiro, P.S. 149
Plender, R. 34, 126
Policy Development and Evaluation Service unit 169
primary functions of UNHCR 14, 22, 160; international protection 14, 18–20, 23, 30, 37, 54–60, 75, 76, 135–6, 152, 163, 170

questionnaires 45, 95

Ramcharan, B.G. 55
rape 118, 168
ratification/accession 38, 39, 48, 49, 76, 132–5, 154, 157, 160, 161, 165; historical foundations 9–10, 11, 17–18, 161; overview of activities 43–4; problems with ensuring 92–4, 101
Raustiala, K. 37
reception procedures/standards 36, 70, 141
refoulement see *non-refoulement*
regional agreements 30, 68, 93, 100, 161; accession 134; capacity-building activities 141; Cartagena Declaration (1984) 68, 87–8, 111; different standards for different states 87–9, 111–12, 162–3; enhanced co-operation with human rights bodies 145, 147–8, 157; European Union *see separate entry*; human rights

31, 105, 109, 145, 147–8; Organization of African Unity (now African Union) 28, 34–5, 68, 87–8, 103, 111; promotional work of UNHCR 135, 137
registration of refugees 54
relationship with States 166–7; capacity-building activities 137–42, 153, 156–7, 165, 168; co-operation 64, 78–81, 98–100, 143–5, 152, 162, 166–7, 169; divergence 81–5, 99–100, 142, 162
research 169
reservations 71, 94, 101, 133, 154, 157, 163, 165; EXCOM conclusions requesting removal of 44; right to work 63
resettlement 54, 113, 114, 127–8
responsibility and burden sharing 52, 130; Convention Plus initiative 126–8, 130, 164
returnees 51, 169
Robertson, A.H. 10
Russian refugees 2–3, 4–5, 6–7, 16–17
Ruthström-Ruin, C. 28
Rwanda, International Criminal Tribunal for 110, 118, 168–9

safe country of origin concept 71, 84, 116
safe third country concept 71, 84, 86, 95
Salomon, K. 8
Schachter, O. 42, 89, 124, 154
Schermers, H. 58, 59, 95
Schnyder, F. 28, 35, 100, 104
Schwarzenberger, G. 153
screening outside country of asylum 83
seamen, refugee 25–6, 44, 161
Second World War 8, 12, 80
September 11 attacks 84, 119
sexual violence/abuse/exploitation 43, 118
Shaffer, G. 156
Shaw, M. 125, 126
Simpson, John Hope 2, 4, 6, 7
Singh, Nagendra 93
Sjöberg, T. 2, 8
Skubiszewski, K. 58
Sloan, B. 123
smuggling 33, 84, 122
social, economic and cultural rights 131
social security rights 32, 35, 161

23059454R00125

Printed in Great Britain
by Amazon